Contending with Hitler is a distillation of recent scholarship on Germany's domestic resistance to the Nazi dictatorship. Comprising twelve original essays by leading German and American scholars, it sets forth the issues that specialists and laymen alike must keep in mind as they try to understand the nature and significance of this complex problem. Unlike most histories of the German resistance, this volume does not restrict its focus to well-known opposition factions such as the Kreisau Circle and the Twentieth of July conspiracy; it also includes investigations of resistance efforts by Jews, women, workers, and young people. The Socialist opposition is illuminated by the personal observations of former West German Chancellor Willy Brandt.

PUBLICATIONS OF THE GERMAN HISTORICAL INSTITUTE
WASHINGTON, D.C.

Edited by Hartmut Lehmann
with the assistance of Kenneth F. Ledford

Contending with Hitler

THE GERMAN HISTORICAL INSTITUTE, WASHINGTON, D.C.

The German Historical Institute is a center for advanced study and research whose purpose is to provide a permanent basis for scholarly cooperation between historians from the Federal Republic of Germany and the United States. The Institute conducts, promotes, and supports research into both American and German political, social, economic, and cultural history, into transatlantic migration, especially in the nineteenth and twentieth centuries, and into the history of international relations, with special emphasis on the roles played by the United States and Germany.

Other books in the series

Hartmut Lehmann and James Sheehan, editors, *An Interrupted Past: German-Speaking Historians in the United States after 1933*

Carol Fink, Axel Frohn, and Jürgen Heideking, editors, *Genoa, Rapallo, and European Reconstruction in 1922*

Larry Eugene Jones and James Retallack, editors, *Elections, Mass Politics, and Social Change in Germany*

Contending with Hitler

VARIETIES OF GERMAN RESISTANCE IN THE THIRD REICH

Edited by

DAVID CLAY LARGE

GERMAN HISTORICAL INSTITUTE
Washington, D.C.
and

CAMBRIDGE
UNIVERSITY PRESS

Published by the Press Syndicate of the University of Cambridge
The Pitt Building, Trumpington Street, Cambridge CB2 1RP
40 West 20th Street, New York, NY 10011-4211, USA
10 Stamford Road, Oakleigh, Melbourne 3166, Australia

First published 1991
First paperback edition 1994

Printed in the United States of America

Library of Congress Cataloging-in-Publication Data

Contending with Hitler: varieties of German resistance in the Third
Reich / edited by David Clay Large.
p.   cm. – (Publications of the German Historical Institute)
Papers originally presented at a conference organized by the
Goethe House New York in April 1988.
Includes bibliographical references and index.
ISBN 0-521-41459-8
1. Anti-Nazi movement – Congresses.   2. Germany –
History – 1993–1945 – Congresses.   I. Large, David Clay.   II. Goethe
House New York.   III. Series.
DD256.3.C66   1992
943.086–dc20   91-24590
                                                  CIP

A catalog record for this book is available from the British Library

ISBN 0-521-41459-8 hardback
ISBN 0-521-46668-7 paperback

Contents

Preface

In April 1988, the Goethe House in New York organized a conference whose goal was to examine various aspects of German resistance against the Nazi regime between 1933 and 1945. One of the aims of this conference was to assemble the leading North American and German specialists on this topic so that they would be able to discuss and compare the results of recent research. Another aim was to raise in America the awareness that a number of Germans had opposed Hitler in various ways and that their destiny had been the continuous focus of scholarly interest and research since 1945. A third aim of this conference was the attempt to analyze the conditions, and the limits, of resistance against a totalitarian regime.

Professor David C. Large of Montana State University kindly prepared for publication the papers given at the conference. The German Historical Institute is indebted to him for his efforts, just as we owe thanks to the Institute's editor, Dr. Kenneth F. Ledford, for his help.

The New York Goethe House, under its director, Dr. Jürgen Ohlau, generously funded the conference; furthermore, they made the papers available for publication in the German Historical Institute's monograph series. It is to them, therefore, that we are especially grateful for this volume of collected essays that shows in a most impressive way how much we have learned in recent years about German resistance against Hitler and how far scholarship has moved beyond Hans Rothfels's *The German Opposition to Hitler* (1948), the first milestone in this long journey.

June 1991   Hartmut Lehmann
Washington, D.C.

Contributors

Willy Brandt is former Chancellor of the Federal Republic of Germany, Honorary Chair of the Social Democratic Party of Germany, and President of the Socialist International.

The late Professor *Martin Broszat* was Director of the Institut für Zeitgeschichte in Munich.

Thomas Childers is Professor of History at the University of Pennsylvania.

Theodore Ellenoff is President of the American Jewish Committee.

Peter Hoffmann is Professor of History at McGill University.

Klemens von Klemperer is Five-College Professor of History at Smith College.

Claudia Koonz is Professor of History at Duke University.

Michael Krüger-Charlé is at the Ruhr University in Bochum.

Konrad Kwiet is at the University of New South Wales, Kensington, Australia.

David Clay Large is Professor of History at Montana State University.

Charles Maier is Professor of History at Harvard University.

Hans Mommsen is Professor of History at the Ruhr University in Bochum.

The late *Detlev J. K. Peukert* was Professor of History at the University of Essen.

Peter Steinbach is Professor of History at the University of Passau.

Fritz Stern is Seth Low Professor of History at Columbia University.

Introduction

DAVID CLAY LARGE

This collection represents a distillation of recent scholarship and commentary on the German resistance problem – on the historical phenomenon itself, its legacy, and the ways it has been interpreted over the past forty years. For those who like their history neat and tidy, who want a unified view of the past that might be serviceable in the present and future, this volume may be a disappointment. In advancing varying approaches to and assessments of the topic at hand, it reflects the extent to which the resistance question is still an open one, still productive of lively (and often quite passionate) debate. This book's chief purpose is to define – or redefine – the issues that academic historians and laymen alike will need to keep in mind as they grapple with the endlessly complicated question of resistance in the Third Reich. But the issues raised here have meaning beyond the history of National Socialism. As Fritz Stern notes in his introductory comments, the German experience in the Third Reich tells us much about how people behave in times of stress – about their self-delusions and petty evasions, as well as their occasional moments of heroism and self-transcendence. And though Hitler may be long gone, the problem of resistance to tyranny "is alive in many battered countries today; it is a subject that, properly understood, can instruct all of us."

Perhaps the most difficult conceptual problem facing students of the German resistance concerns the definition of their subject – the question of which individuals or groups, and what kinds of socio-political behavior, should be included under this rubric. A related question involves the legitimacy of speaking, as many historians continue to do, of a resistance "movement" in Germany. Though the title of the symposium at which the essays in this volume were originally presented, in New York in April 1988, was "The German

1

Resistance Movement, 1933–45," most of the contributors found
too little coherence among the oppositionist factions and circles
to warrant this designation. Their work, and that of many other
students of the subject, suggest that it would be more historically
accurate to speak of "varieties" of German resistance to Nazism.

An appreciation of the complexity and political heterogeneity of
the resistance phenomenon, though particularly pronounced in recent studies, was also evident in some of the pioneering works on the
subject. This fact needs emphasis, for there has been a tendency in
more recent scholarship – reflected indeed in some of the essays in
this volume – to assume that a critical and nuanced investigation
of the German resistance did not begin until the late 1960s. In addition to the well-known pioneering works by Hans Rothfels and
Gerhard Ritter,[1] the Institut für Zeitgeschichte's *Vierteljahrshefte für
Zeitgeschichte* published a number of articles in the 1950s and early
1960s devoted to various dimensions of the resistance problem and
the legacy it left behind. Rothfels's own "Das politische Vermächtnis des deutschen Widerstands,"[2] for example, recognized that the
German opposition to Hitler – even the Twentieth of July conspiracy – was rife with internal political differences, though animated
by a common feeling of moral repugnance for the Nazi tyranny.
Rothfels argued on the occasion of the tenth anniversary of the
failed assassination attempt that an appreciation of the resisters'
moral commitment and self-sacrifice was especially necessary in the
West Germany of the early 1950s, which was so busy with physical
and economic rebuilding that it generally ignored the imperatives
of "spiritual reconstruction." Significantly, Rothfels's concept of
"resistance" extended beyond the military opposition's attempt
to topple the Nazi regime through direct action; it embraced as well
all those less-celebrated efforts by average German citizens to protect or assist the persecuted or to impede the system's functioning
by contravening its myriad rules and regulations. H. G. Adler's
"Selbstvervaltung und Widerstand in den Konzentrationslagern der
SS,"[3] another important early contribution to the resistance literature, explored the varieties of resistance that emerged within the

---

1 Hans Rothfels, *Die deutsche Opposition gegen Hitler. Eine Würdigung* (Krefeld, 1949); Gerhard
  Ritter, *Carl Goerdeler und die deutsche Widerstandsbewegung* (Stuttgart, 1954).
2 Hans Rothfels, "Das politische Vermächtnis des deutschen Widerstands," *Vierteljahrshefte für
  Zeitgeschichte* (hereafter *VfZ*) 2 (1954): 329–43.
3 H. G. Adler, "Selbstvervaltung und Widerstand in den Konzentrationslagern der SS," *VfZ*
  8 (1960): 221–37.

very belly of the beast, the concentration camps. It focused less on open rebellions, such as those at Treblinka and Sobibor in 1943, than on the daily *Kleinkrieg* between the camp inmates and the SS overseers and their minions. In his important early work on the Stauffenberg brothers,[4] Eberhard Zeller highlighted the complexities of Claus von Stauffenberg's political evolution, suggesting that his revulsion over the so-called *Reichskristallnacht* helped place him on the path of opposition. Hermann Graml's "Der Fall Oster"[5] examined the road to resistance traveled by another important Nazi opponent, Abwehr functionary Hans Oster.

These and other early studies of the German resistance, including such notable book-length treatments as Eberhard Zeller's *Geist der Freiheit*, Günther Weisenborn's *Der lautlose Aufstand*, Annedore Leber's two-volume collection of resistance portraits, *Das Gewissen entscheidet* and *Das Gewissen steht auf*,[6] were written under difficult circumstances. Not only were some important primary materials not yet available, but many Germans did not want to hear anything about resistance to Nazism, still considering it an essentially traitorous enterprise. Others tended to dismiss the opposition, especially the Twentieth of July conspiracy, as the work of hopelessly inept reactionaries. Early students of the resistance felt compelled not just to explicate, but also to defend, what their subjects had done.

Given this agenda, it is not surprising that the first works on the German resistance concentrated (though by no means exclusively) on the Twentieth of July conspiracy and the military opposition. While interest in this dimension of the resistance remains strong,

4 Eberhard Zeller, "Claus und Berthold Stauffenberg," *VfZ* 12 (1964): 223–49.
5 Hermann Graml, "Der Fall Oster," *VfZ* 14 (1966): 26–39.
6 Eberhard Zeller, *Geist der Freiheit. Der Zwanzigste Juli*, rev. ed. (Munich, 1963); Günther Weisenborn, *Der lautlose Aufstand. Bericht über die Widerstandsbewegung des deutschen Volkes 1933–1945* (Hamburg, 1953); Annedore Leber, Willy Brandt, and K. D. Bracher, eds., *Das Gewissen steht auf* (Berlin, 1954); Leber et al., *Das Gewissen entscheidet* (Berlin, 1957). It is significant that Zeller's book contains a chapter on leftist resistance, while Leber's collection includes portraits of figures from left-wing parties, unions, and youth groups.
   Other notable early studies on German resistance activities (excluding memoirs and collections of correspondence) include: *Die Vollmacht des Gewissens*, 2 vols. (Frankfurt, 1956, 1965); Karl Heinz Abshagen, *Canaris. Patriot und Weltbürger* (Stuttgart, 1954); James Donohoe, *Hitler's Conservative Opponents in Bavaria, 1930–1945: A Consideration of Catholic, Monarchist, and Separatist Anti-Nazi Activities* (Leiden, 1961); Rudolf Pechel, *Deutscher Widerstand* (Erlenbach, 1947); Erich Kosthorst, *Die deutsche Opposition gegen Hitler zwischen Polen- und Frankreichfeldzug* (Bonn, 1957); Bodo Scheurig, *Freies Deutschland. Das Nationalkomite und der Bund deutscher Offiziere in der Sowjetunion 1943–1945* (Munich, 1960); Max Braubach, *Der Weg zum 20. Juli 1944* (Cologne, 1953); Erika Buchmann, ed., *Die Frauen von Ravensbrück* (Berlin, 1961); Marie Syrkin, *Blessed Is the Match: The Story of Jewish Resistance* (Philadelphia, 1948).

since the mid-1960s scholarly studies of the problem have tended to focus on other practitioners of opposition: Communist and Socialist workers, Jews, youth groups, concentration camp inmates, exiles, women. The present volume substantially reflects this shift in focus. In addition to studies on the conservative opposition and the Kreisau Circle, there are essays here on the varieties of working-class opposition, the Jewish *Widerstand*, and the place of women in resistance activities. The Socialist opposition, both in Germany and later in exile, is represented by the reflections of one of its most noted participants, former chancellor Willy Brandt.

The collection as a whole advances the plea for a conceptual discrimination that preserves basic distinctions between everyday nonconformity, selective opposition to specific policies and practices, and fundamental resistance aimed at overthrowing the Nazi regime. Detlev Peukert calls for a sliding scale of dissident behavior, with *Nonkonformität* at one end and *Widerstand* at the other. More categorically, Klemens von Klemperer insists that historians must not allow the rather plentiful "weeds" of nonconformity or single-issue opposition to overwhelm that rare and "precious plant" in their garden – full-scale resistance to tyranny.

Another issue raised by these essays concerns the broader sociopolitical context or infrastructure in which the resisters operated. If earlier resistance histories often took a biographical approach, more recent studies have examined the "political culture" of resistance and the connections between the opposition phenomenon (or phenomena) and longer-term trends in German society and politics.[7] Following this scholarly direction, several essays in this volume look into the sociopolitical conditions – class, religious, generational, geographical – that helped shape the resistance enterprise. Above all, they make clear that the fragmentation of German society before the advent of the Third Reich militated against effective resistance once Hitler took power. Indeed, they point out how the resistance scene quickly became a kind of microcosm of Germany's splintered social and political order, a welter of separate and often mutually hostile constituencies. Belated efforts by oppositionist coteries like the now-famous Kreisau Circle to overcome class, religious, and ideolo-

---

7 For two useful compendia of recent scholarship on the resistance problem, see Jürgen Schmädeke and Peter Steinbach, eds., *Der Widerstand gegen den Nationalsozialismus. Die deutsche Gesellschaft und der Widerstand gegen Hitler* (Munich, 1986); and Klaus-Jürgen Müller, ed., *Der deutsche Widerstand, 1933–1945* (Paderborn, 1986).

gical differences were hardly sufficient to escape this curse of internal fragmentation. Church-based opponents of Nazism often proved more sectarian than ecumenical in their response to Hitler's challenge. But if the emphasis here is generally on the cultural and sociological determinants of resistance, this volume also contains at least one antithetical approach: Klemens von Klemperer's insistence that the essence of the resistance enterprise remained the willingness of lonely individuals – "solitary witnesses" – to risk their lives in order to end the Nazi regime. Their motives, he argues, were essentially ethical and had little to do with definable political calculations; their desperate acts of resistance constituted "an extraordinary leap into an existential situation that defies historical and social stereotypes."

Connected to this problem of social and political context is the question of the relationship of the various anti-Nazi constituencies to the regime they opposed or (in extreme cases) sought to bring down. In his contribution on working-class resistance, Detlev Peukert points out that even leftist members of the working classes, Hitler's first victims, neither consistently opposed all aspects of Nazi policy nor mounted resistance operations of unvarying intensity. Rather, their opposition, such as it was, responded to the shifting balance of power within the by no means monolithic Nazi regime. The working-class opposition's relationship to National Socialism, in other words, was less dualistic than strangely symbiotic.

If this pattern characterized the working-class opposition's relationship to Nazism, it was even more true of the national-conservative resisters' attitude toward the regime. As a number of these essays show, the conservative and clerical opposition was a deeply ambiguous enterprise, since many of its practitioners tended to share some of the principles, prejudices, and aspirations of the regime they (very belatedly) came to reject. This factor, along with their fixation on the "restoration" of traditional authoritarian values and institutions, made it difficult for most of them to cooperate with the leftist resistance, not to mention that of the German Jews. Indeed, the Christian-conservative resisters' tardy and inadequate response to the persecution of the Jews was the greatest moral failure of the German opposition. As Konrad Kwiet points out in his contribution on the Jewish resistance, the ugly fact is that the Jews were a *minorité fatale* not just for the Nazis but also for the majority of gentile anti-Nazis.

Once some of the conservatives decided during the war to do away with the Nazi regime, their conspiracy faced almost insurmountable obstacles. Unlike resistance groups operating in Nazi-occupied foreign countries (France being a partial exception), the German resisters faced a "homegrown" dictatorship that, until late in the war, enjoyed overwhelming popular support. They realized that their efforts would be rejected as treasonous or antinationalist by many – perhaps the majority – of their countrymen; that, despite numerous foreign contacts, they could expect little substantive help from abroad; that even the successful elimination of Hitler would probably provoke a bloody civil war and ensure the occupation of their country by foreign armies. There were, of course, also myriad technical difficulties, stemming from the conspirators' need simultaneously to penetrate Hitler's elaborate security system and to orchestrate a complicated coup in the midst of war. It should be recalled, moreover, that Stauffenberg, the man who tried unsuccessfully to kill Hitler with a bomb, was handicapped by old injuries, lacking an eye, one hand, and two fingers on the other hand. Quixotic and ill executed as the Twentieth of July coup may have been, however, Peter Hoffmann correctly insists that we should not disparage or dismiss this moment's historic meaning – a meaning rendered all the more significant by the conspirators' realistic assessment of its minimal chance for success. Although Count von Stauffenberg was not quite Camus' Sisyphus, committed to a task he knew could never succeed, Stauffenberg's deed was "existential" in the sense that he understood that the doing of it was more important than the outcome, whatever that might be. And though the July 20 coup attempt was certainly late, Willy Brandt is right to remind us, "Better late than never!"

Consideration of Stauffenberg's sacrificial act introduces a final question raised by the essays in this collection. What legacy – or legacies – did the various forms of resistance bequeath to future generations of Germans? Detlev Peukert notes that the working-class resisters' dreams of a thorough transformation of German society in the post-Nazi era were frustrated by the policies of the Occupation powers, the dictates of the Cold War, and the consuming demands of physical and economic revival. Hans Mommsen and David Large suggest that the various official attempts to exploit the resistance legacy (primarily the Twentieth of July attempt) as a usable "tool" in the democratic reconstruction of West Germany did not succeed in rooting it firmly in the postwar German consciousness. Younger generations in particular, notes Mommsen, were put off by the national-conservative resisters' traditional authoritarianism and military values; youthful radicals sought historical validation for their rebellious politics not so much in the Twentieth of July movement as in less-celebrated acts of anti-Nazi dissent and civil disobedience. The legacy of the conservative opposition, especially Stauffenberg's assassination attempt, also came under fire in the mid-1980s from another quarter: revisionist historians, who argued (as had many Germans in the 1950s) that the elimination of Hitler would have disrupted the German leadership and allowed the Soviets to achieve a more rapid and extensive victory than they did. Noting that the German resistance has always had to struggle for a measure of "historical legitimacy," Charles Maier suggests in his contribution that this struggle will undoubtedly continue into the future.

The present volume is certainly no effort to defend the resistance legacy from its various detractors, past or present. Indeed, it dwells extensively – some may think too extensively – on the inadequacies and failings of the German resistance enterprise as a whole. But in offering their often sharply critical assessments, the contributors to this collection are careful not to impugn the fundamental dignity or honor of the resisters' undertaking on the grounds that their ideals and aspirations were flawed. They are also mindful of Theodore Ellenoff's warning, in his introductory comments, that studies implicating the victims in the crimes of their oppressors "serve to shrink souls and diminish understanding of roles that must be assumed for the future." Nor do they dismiss the various resistance efforts as historically irrelevant because they failed substantially to thwart the Nazis' destructive policies, much less to bring the hateful regime to its knees. As Charles Maier notes, the German resistance deserves commemoration "because its protagonists alone understood that some effort to bring down a monstrous regime must be undertaken by the people whose adulation had facilitated its triumphs." Hitler's Germany may not have been brought down from within, but, as Willy Brandt reminds us, the "other Germany" was a reality, and the moral legitimacy of its cause "retains its validity, irrespective of its limited effectiveness."

The German Resistance Movement
1933–1945

ADDRESS BY WILLY BRANDT

I

We should not, I do not, take it for granted that resistance in Nazi Germany is dealt with completely in this volume. But nobody, in particular our Jewish friends, need fear that I will eclipse one topic by another. Any simple comparison would, of course, be totally out of order. That there were German opponents to, and victims of, Nazism – and, indeed, there were quite a few of them – does not in any way diminish Germany's responsibility for the Holocaust.

Despite all its shortcomings, the "other Germany" was a reality. The moral legacy of resistance retains its validity, irrespective of its limited effectiveness. It did not allow itself to be plowed under – although its impact has not been felt as strongly in the postwar era as I myself, along with quite a few others, would have wished. This legacy deserves to be preserved for future generations in my part of the world.

In saying this, I cannot hide the reservations I have had – and continue to have – with regard to the use of the inflated term *resistance movement*. When I was a young man, we referred to ourselves as the *opposition*. Of course, we knew about the diversity of those opposing the Nazis, and we were aware of their inadequacy. Much of the persecution that took place was not provoked by active opposition; it was based solely on the different nature of some, and the sheer madness for extermination of others. And there was very little resistance deserving of the name that was not soon discovered, with the means available to the totalitarian regime at the time, or even destroyed before it ever got started.

One of the major differences between resistance in Germany and similar movements that emerged in several of the countries occupied after 1939 was that the latter acted mainly in defense of their own national interests. In the case of Germany, those who were against

9

the Nazis constantly ran the risk of being misinterpreted as if they were antinationalists; and this is, in fact, how some foreign observers of contemporary events described them, even after 1945.

I myself had this experience. Equipped with papers that identified me as a Norwegian student, I lived in Berlin during the second half of 1936, looking after a few hundred, predominantly young, Socialists, who – secretly organized in small groups – were trying to get ready for "the day after." In December 1940, I returned by a clandestine route from Stockholm to Norway, which was now occupied by the Wehrmacht and the Gestapo. I did so not only for political but also for personal reasons. What impressed me most at the time was that in Norway – unlike in Germany – one did not have the feeling of being on enemy territory. The number of quislings was too small for that, and yet – although this may not be of much consolation from the point of view of a German democrat – the Nazis never succeeded in rallying all Germans behind them, despite the awesome machinery at their disposal and the vast number of their followers.

All those individuals and groups who risked their lives by refusing to submit to tyranny may not have been able to stop enforced political conformity in Germany, nor were they able to prevent World War II or the Holocaust. But they certainly bore testimony against the notion of collective guilt by an entire nation, and they did so not only at the beginning but also toward the end of Nazi tyranny.

I mentioned Berlin in 1936: Jewish companions who had not been willing or able to emigrate took part in underground activities as if it were a matter of course – although they were at greater risk than the rest of us. It was absurd, but we referred to their and our activities as "illegal," although they were directed against the worst kind of violators of law that ever existed. All of us suffered together, not only from the brutal cowardice and the cowardly brutality that made things easy for the Nazis in their own country but also from the lack of understanding that we were confronted with outside Germany's borders.

In the course of just a few years, the contrast between the fate of Jewish Germans and what was inflicted upon other members of the opposition grew sharply. Even now, I shudder when I think back to how things evolved: from the pogroms – which in the vernacular were trivialized as the *Reichskristallnacht* – to the Wannsee Conference and on to Auschwitz and the other extermination camps, culminating in the murder of many millions of European Jews and thereby putting a bloody end to a rich cultural symbiosis which had made Germany a major civilized nation.

It was not until we were in exile – where our links to the domestic opposition at home became weaker and weaker, until they were almost cut off altogether at the outbreak of the war – it was not until then that some of us realized that the picture we had seen through the glasses of a somewhat forced optimism had been very wrong. The common risks shared by those who were in exile were serious enough as it was, especially after France's capitulation.

II

I do not think that anybody here expects me to wallow in self-castigation. Anyway, I do not propose to trivialize any of the unspeakable horrors that were committed in the name of Germany – and by Germans. By now, two new generations have grown up in my country: But it is still – or maybe once again – advisable to draw attention to the historical burdens and the specific causes that led to the pitiful failure of the Weimar Republic and that drove millions of war victims, unemployed people, small businessmen, and farmers to despair. It is imperative that this horrible experience of how an entire era in European history was turned around in a perverted manner be kept fresh in everybody's mind. It is important to remember: If the "Thousand Year Reich" accomplished nothing else, it was to destroy in twelve years an important chapter of one thousand years of cultural history. But let us not be misled by false simplifications. Of course there was resistance – even if not very strong and not sufficiently concentrated – against the Nazis' quest for power and against their helpers. The long list of murdered victims started long before power was surrendered to them.

In the days following the burning of the Reichstag in late February 1933 (and before the election on March 5, when – despite their intimidation of voters – Hitler's party was able to gain the majority only with the support of ultraconservative nationalists), many thousands of Social Democratic functionaries and nonconforming intellectuals were arrested; all of the more radical groups within the labor movement had already been outlawed. This was followed by the burning of books, the first boycotts of Jewish stores, the banning of parties and independent associations, the *Gleichschaltung* of labor unions, and the establishment of concentration camps; by the end of 1933 there were some fifty of those camps in Germany, if one includes the temporary ones.

When Hitler and his people started World War II in 1939 with the attack on Poland, there were more than one hundred thousand political prisoners in Germany: thirty thousand in prisons and eighty thousand in camps. When foreign prisoners were brought to Germany in the wake of the occupation and during the war, they met fellow sufferers there who had already spent many terrible years in that misery. Not that there were no major manifestations of desperate rebellion in early 1933; not that an important part of parliament did not launch a solemn protest from its platform as late as the spring of 1933, before it was promoted to the highest-paid chorus in the country; but in addition to all the harm that was done to so many families, the true disaster turned out to be the collapse of a whole complex of organizations which had been established as symbols of solidarity but which had offered too little guidance on the individual's personal responsibility in a critical situation, and even less on the individual's duty to protect the constitution. Some of those who tried unsuccessfully to adjust were also subject to persecution. Opposition was building up underground, and – fragmented as it was – people did try to make counterpropaganda, even though the means they had were hopelessly weak, compared to the techniques used by a modern dictatorship, and they were rather disorganized in their refusal to be coopted by the regime and in their willingness to offer inconspicuous help to their neighbors. Shrugging their shoulders, some people nowadays may think little of these groups. To my mind, doing so was – and still would be – a mistake.

The full force of a German-style Fascist regime, with a specific tradition of organization and mentality, was still to come. But this very experience did show that the yardstick for resistance is neither the dogma of a political party nor some kind of group patriotism; it comes to light from a deeper understanding of what human coexistence is all about: an inner obligation never *ever* to remain indifferent in the face of violations of basic human values. If this sort of attitude had been more widespread, the Nazis at least could not have stabilized their regime as quickly as they did. But at any rate, there was a minority which did know what compass to go by, even under very difficult conditions.

Almost all my friends in Berlin and in the Hanseatic cities of northern Germany, with whom I worked at the time, did agree that "safeguarding and consolidating the cadres" – as we called it – had to be a main objective. They, and I together with them, disapproved of mere agitation, as we thought it a pointless sacrifice of human life. Instead, we met in very small groups for orientation and political education. We wanted to prepare ourselves as well as we could for the time when the Nazi regime would falter – whenever that would be. Almost nobody imagined in those days that the regime would last twelve years; we thought it might last four, at most.

This certainly was what one would call opposition, but as resistance it qualified only to a limited extent. After all, what, except for mass arrests, had been accomplished by distributing fliers in the early days? It made much more sense to see to it, on the factory floors, that workers who enjoyed the trust of their colleagues were camouflaged as well as possible. As a cover, many anti-Nazis took shelter in associations that remained fairly nonpolitical or that had changed their names in order to conceal their earlier alignment: choruses, societies of small garden-plot holders, bowling clubs, and others. This may be regarded as a rather modest form of opposition, but in retrospect one should not underestimate the moral support and the organizational potential that these groups were able to offer. Such semilegal associations permitted the exchange of information and were often able to render service to family members of people who were persecuted. Illegal gatherings were also camouflaged as family reunions. Funerals played the role of otherwise forbidden rallies, but often even these were under control.

After the first few years, not many of the small clandestine organizations were able to maintain contacts that extended beyond their local area. Contacts with centers of the German opposition abroad – or with their "border points" – had soon diminished because of the activities of the Gestapo, and they were almost totally disrupted during the war, but they were never cut off completely.

This is again something that I experienced myself. In Stockholm, exiled Socialists and trade unionists from Germany with whom I had very close ties kept up contacts with Bremen, for example, via sailors, until late 1944, so that people in the underground over there were able to discuss postwar programs that had been developed by people like me in Sweden and by like-minded refugees in England. I myself succeeded in establishing conspiratorial contacts with some opponents of the regime working in the administration of occupied

Norway. And on the same day in early May when the Wehrmacht capitulated, a companion from exile got in touch with my mother in Lübeck; he had returned to Germany via Denmark just in time, and he had been able to do so – why not mention it – because of helpful advice from informed American friends.

In the years before the war, there had been quite a few meetings at border points, during which those of us from "outside" were able to exchange information and views with those who lived "inside." In connection with such meetings and on other occasions, written material was smuggled into Germany. Even with our limited possibilities, it was important to us to organize assistance for people who were persecuted or who had been convicted. In the first few years, we even succeeded at times – with the help of pressure from media abroad – in preventing the imposition of death sentences or their execution.

Right now, my thoughts are drifting to a university event that I will attend in early May 1988 at Oldenburg. The reason for this event is the fiftieth anniversary of the death of the German Nobel Peace Prize winner Carl von Ossietzky. As a young man, I was highly involved in a campaign to save this man, who was doomed as a *Moor-Soldat* of Papenburg. Unfortunately, his life was saved for only a very short period of time. Nevertheless, the campaign, which had enjoyed widespread support, marked one of the few defeats that the Nazis suffered in the years before World War II.

III

And what about the churches? Unfortunately, not all of their representatives kept their distance from the regime. However, many of them did. The number of clergymen who ended up in a prison or in a camp was considerable, and many died by the axe or the hangman's noose.

I should note that even receiving a death sentence was not reliable proof that one had belonged to a resistance movement. Some people were executed because they had told a political joke, others because they had made "defeatist remarks" about the likely outcome of the war; others because they had refused to denounce somebody; and yet others because they had, for whatever reason, simply become unpopular with those in power, some of them even coming from their own ranks.

I should not forget to mention that there were certainly also people – acting more as individuals driven by their own conscience than as members of a "movement" – who threw a wrench into the works of arms production; and people who passed on information abroad that helped save human lives and avoid destruction; or people who, at the risk of their own lives, gave shelter to others who were being hunted. Over a long period of time, this type of heroism was obscured instead of being acknowledged. Far too often, doubts were voiced as to the honorableness of the deeds I have just described. And far too small was the number of those who recognized – and said so aloud – that the weakening and the fall of the Hitler regime was also in the best national interest of the Germans.

The late attempt at a rebellion on July 20, 1944, made by military leaders in coordination with various groups of civilian opponents of the Nazis – an attempt which cost many lives – has also given rise to a number of misinterpretations. Abroad, in those countries that were engaged in the war, the question was raised as to whether it was proper to get involved with generals and civil servants who had served Hitler. In postwar Germany, some people asked whether there was any justification for high treason, and yet others asked what good could have come from "reactionary" rebels.

This is no hearsay; these are views that I have been confronted with myself. I never subscribed to the thesis of the reactionary character of this attempted coup. Now that so many decades have gone by, I would find it absolutely incomprehensible if somebody made the same foolish statements. Of course, one can rightly criticize the fact that the attempt was made at a rather late point in time and that it perhaps had not been properly planned; but professional soldiers are usually not trained to make coups.

My view was and is: Better late than never! Even after the summer of 1944, many human lives could have been saved. And as an aside: The group that was involved in the desperate attempt of July 20 is wrongly put into one political corner. In reality, leading Social Democrats, labor unionists, scientists, and theologians were among its members, and not just as passive followers. If they had survived, they probably would have had a major say in Germany's postwar development.

Instead, many of those members of the German opposition who did survive found that they had very little say – or, even worse, that they once again had to turn their backs to the public that they had long wanted to address and to attempts at self-purification. Experience shows that it is not easy to find a common denominator for occupation and revolution.

A message that I would like to convey above and beyond all details is this: The risks of opposition were not a privilege of the labor movement, or of liberal intellectuals who had not been silenced, or of church representatives who did not conform. Opposition – or resistance, if you prefer – was, above all, the language of conscience and the cause of normal conscientious people. May future generations be spared a similar experience.

Willy Brandt's rueful reappraisal of German opposition – he thinks "resistance" is too strong a word – to Hitler's dictatorship summons up from the past the efforts of Social Democrats, trade unionists, and people of conscience to halt National Socialism. The policies of that regime were not specifically directed against them in the same maniacal fashion in which they were leveled against the Jewish population, who became the subjects of officially stated policy mandating their extermination in Germany and wherever the German armed forces conquered.

One should not talk about Jewish resistance as limited solely to Germany Jewry. Resistance, such as it was, has to be seen in broader terms. In the Nazi period, resistance flickered throughout the macabre landscape of death camps and ghettos, from the Atlantic coast to the Russian border. Resistance could be measured in internalized prayer or through unparalleled heroism – battles fought sewer by sewer in Warsaw, recalling the ancient past of the Maccabees and foreshadowing the energetic struggle to establish the future sovereignty of Israel.

For American Jews, and for other Jewish communities, the Warsaw ghetto uprising has become a symbol of pride, expressing the efforts made by so many in other cities and death camps to resist their extermination as a people and as a religion.

Many writers have explored the German people's supine acceptance of the Nazi subversion of their institutions. Especially enigmatic has been the victims' enfeebled resistance to the dismantling of their human rights and their own physical destruction. The analysis drifts darkly from national insanity to ethnic demoralization, then illuminates fitfully a monstrous banality and a complicity that somehow implicates the victims in the crimes of their oppressors. The time will not soon come which will end the investigation of the possibilities for resistance of individual heroism in the context of national horror. Without balance, these exercises serve to shrink souls and diminish understanding of roles that must be assumed for the future.

Jews have had to face another daunting task: resisting the temptation – however understandable – to extirpate Germany from their conscience and cease all communication with Germans. On the other hand, Germans have had to resist the temptation to bury the past in some forgotten recesses of national conscience. Fortunately, both have resisted these temptations.

It is with respect and understanding that we of the American Jewish Committee greet the recollections of Willy Brandt concerning his years in opposition to Nazi Germany. As an organization, for eighty-one years we have been deeply committed to the protection of human rights. Surely it is the spiritual reserve of the individual that buttresses human rights and is essential in providing resistance to the excesses of a frightful regime. It is the same spiritual reserve that recognizes that there has risen from the ashes of that regime a free society, demonstrably committed to the fostering of the values of a free, democratic society.

We are aware that the relationship between Jews and Germans requires constant nurturing so that the past and the present can be recognized in all dimensions of recollection and reconciliation. Both Germans and Jews studied the hideous propensities of totalitarianism. Institutions of communal and academic life were perverted and destroyed. The human spirit was ground out in debasement. We now are engaged in a reciprocal process of under-scoring the worth of rationalism, humanity, unfettered communication, democracy, and pluralism. We both have engaged, and continue to engage, in exchange programs sending young people to explore these concepts in our respective countries. This exploration is needed to understand the depreciation of human rights that is being promoted as a matter of official policy in many regimes around the globe at this very time.

We have, in the broadest sense, undertaken mutual covenants to assert the following principles:

1. We support the international observance of individual human rights and endorse the aspirations of individuals and ethnic groups to move freely and without hindrance across national boundaries. Consistent with this recognition, we support the emigration of ethnic Germans and Jews from the Soviet Union.

2. Together we condemn and forswear violence and terrorism as acceptable techniques of political expression. The use of such means can only erode human dignity and distort the human spirit.

3. Wherever possible we must commit resources to teaching and pursuing pluralism throughout the world. We should encourage the sweeping away of barriers that impose limitations on religious and ethnic groups and allow them to set their own boundaries which shall be observed by others. We should resist the recently emerging forces of fundamentalism, which would impress individuals and groups into rigid standards of conformity.

Finally we must trumpet with pride the sweet and compelling idea of a free society and resist those who would substitute for its values the uncertain promises of efficiency or equal results. To all of the foregoing we are committed, satisfied that the building blocks for this free, democratic society are in place.

On behalf of Columbia University I would like to welcome Willy Brandt, Mrs. Brandt, and Theodore Ellenoff, as well as my distinguished colleagues and friends who have come from far and near to this conference. I want to welcome as well the audience participants. I would also like to thank Dr. Jürgen U. Ohlau, director of Goethe House, who spent nearly two years meticulously preparing for this occasion. To round up so many distinguished speakers, to gain the participation of a great figure in German history, and to coordinate all this can only be called a feat of organization.

But I have another reason for thanking Dr. Ohlau. It occurred to me last night that there is something startlingly appropriate in evoking Goethe for this occasion. Not that we think of the privy councillor in Weimar as a model of resistance, but there was also the young Goethe, who, precisely two hundred years ago this year, published his drama *Egmont*, on which he had worked for twelve years. It is the great, historic drama of a hero caught in a time of tyranny. The brutality of that tyranny is exemplified by the duke of Alba. Egmont is torn between loyalty to his monarch and love of his people and his sense that their ancient rights must be respected. Egmont, the great soldier, is ineffectual: In 1568 the Spanish tyrant has him beheaded, leaving Egmont's people the legacy of a martyr for freedom. Egmont of course brings to mind Beethoven, and Beethoven recalls Fidelio: In short, there was a moral, heroic, deeply apolitical strand of German idealism that tended toward resisting tyranny, toward fighting injustice. It is one of the remarkable absences in the postwar history of the two Germanies that the great drama of the Germany resistance has not found a true artistic interpreter.

But the subject, which many of you know better than I do – some

20

indeed from harsh, firsthand experience – is of incalculable importance. It is important for our discipline of history – the historian
cannot understand National Socialism without understanding the
many strands of opposition and resistance; moreover, the manner
in which the German opposition has been remembered in the Federal
Republic and the German Democratic Republic tells us a great deal
about these two states. We will hear experts on this subject, but let
me venture this perhaps overly simplified view. In their understandable unease about their own past, Germans have developed a dis-
tanced view of the resistance. One would wish that the memory of
the many men and women of the opposition and resistance – in all
their contradictoriness – could be better cherished in Germany. But
the subject of the German resistance is not only a historical or a political issue; it is also a historic moment that tells us a great deal about
human behavior, about the temptations, the compromises, the
evasion, and the heroism of peoples. It is a subject that is alive in
many battered countries today; it is a subject that, properly understood, can instruct all of us.

Let me make one disclaimer at once: I agree with those who have
told us over and over again that no one who has not faced the
torturers himself, who has not lived under the threat of torture and
utter lonely helplessness, has the right to pass judgment on men and
women who did face such horrors. No one has the right to ask for
or expect another to choose martyrdom – and yet the many acts
of courage that did occur in those twelve years ought not to go
unrecorded, acts that ranged from quiet refusal to conform to taking
the final, total risk of actually resisting. One needs to think, as well,
of those Germans who understood the overwhelming danger of
Hitler before 1933, who in countless rallies, speeches, and writings
warned their people against the false redeemer; they were, incidentally, the first to suffer from the wrath of the Nazis, even before the
party's accession to power. Still, to fight Nazism before 1933 did not
require martyrdom, and it is important to remember those who did
try to protect a nation in traumatic crisis and those who willingly
saw their countrymen surrender themselves to a brutal delusion.

We must all be grateful to Willy Brandt for his reflections and
reminiscences. Personal memories are precious, and I found his
matter-of-fact tone, the directness and modesty of his assessment,
deeply moving. He was generous in his restraint: This conference
presumably will have to deal with what Hans Mommsen has called

the failure of the German elites. Perhaps Brandt is too generous in what he says of the churches; their resistance, though real, came late, very late. There were few resisters among churchmen – desperately few men like the twenty-seven-year-old Dietrich Bonhoeffer, who wrote, in May 1933, that of course the church would have to obey the laws of the state but that under some circumstances it would not only be obliged "to bind up the victims who had fallen under the wheel but to put spikes in the wheel itself." As Brandt reminds us, there were many who tried to spike the wheel – but they did so at a time when the overwhelming majority of Germans was joyously or passively pushing the wheel, supporting the regime. One still wonders at the passivity or conformity among the elites of Germany – the professoriat, the civil service, and the military. Again, Brandt's words have a timeless applicability: There was, as he says, "too little guidance on the individual's personal responsibility in a critical situation," and he stresses the "inner obligation never *ever* to remain indifferent in the face of violations of basic human values."

We need to recall the totality of the horror of those years. We need to remember, as well, the fervent enthusiasm for the regime – and the terror which faced those who were known or suspected of resistance; nor should one forget the sheer rage of the Nazis against their earlier opponents. I remember hearing as a child how the great Jewish labor tribune, Ernst Eckstein, leader of the Breslau Socialist Workers Party, was beaten to death by the Nazis and how the Socialist Hermann Lüdemann was dragged through the streets of Breslau on his way to a concentration camp – that same courageous Lüdemann who later voluntarily involved himself in the Twentieth of July rebellion. Again I wish to thank Willy Brandt for his authoritative and just defense of the oft misunderstood acts and thoughts of the Twentieth of July martyrs.

It may be justified (there are special reasons) if I cite one more recollection of a personal kind, a recollection that has particular relevance to today's subject. I can remember my emotions as an eight-year-old, on June 30, 1934, when Hitler liquidated so many of his own worst henchmen. In the process, as you will recall, he killed a former chancellor, Kurt von Schleicher, and his friend and fellow general, Ferdinand von Bredow. The army's acquiescence in that unprecedented act of state murder marked a moment of appalling moral surrender.

The terror of the regime triumphed over the opposition and

resistance of the few; both need to be remembered and will be examined by our colleagues. The memory of the millions of Jews who died in the Holocaust is not violated – indeed it is strengthened – if one recalls as well those men and women who sought to help or to put a spike in the demonic wheel. These are memories to be cultivated, to be forever instructed by – because ours is a dark century; terror as an instrument of government is not dead, and the defense of decency remains an imperative.

1

A Social and Historical Typology
of the German Opposition to Hitler

MARTIN BROSZAT

My purpose in this essay is to develop a historical and social typology derived from an exploration of the broad variety of attitudes toward resistance prevalent in German society under the Nazi regime: attitudes that changed in response to the historical development of the regime and that differed among various sectors of German society.

Formulating this typology requires a definition of resistance that is broader than the one used heretofore. The long-standing, exclusive definition of resistance focusing only upon exceptional cases of fundamental and active opposition has produced an idealized and undifferentiated picture of German resistance. This vision of the resistance was encouraged by the Federal Republic in its early years out of a need to compensate for the past and to legitimize the new republic. As a consequence, scholars have largely ignored the primacy of change within the resistance and the interdependence between it and the Nazi regime, and the relationship between the two has been falsely presented as both static and clearly antagonistic. A revised definition of resistance that includes the less heroic cases of partial, passive, ambivalent, and broken opposition – one that accounts for the fragility of resistance and the inconsistency of human bravery – may in the end inspire a greater intellectual and moral sensitivity toward the subject than a definition that includes only the exceptional greatness of heroic martyrdom.

Furthermore, a discriminating analysis of the broad spectrum of resistance activities cannot ignore the social context within which these activities took place. It must therefore be acknowledged that preconditions allowing for a viable opposition differed greatly among the various sectors of German society. The conditions for opposition were more favorable in agrarian, provincial, proletarian, and aristocratic sectors, where economic hardship had not substantially undermined traditional forms of social behavior. In the urban population and the middle class, long the mainstays of German nationalism and rendered deeply insecure by economic crises, conditions were less favorable. Indeed, within these latter groups, social stress and anxiety engendered a great readiness for opportunistic accommodation to the regime and for denunciation of its opponents.

Finally, we cannot view the history of the German resistance outside of the context of the changes that occurred within the Nazi regime itself. The social history of the German resistance has special significance because Nazism was not a product of foreign rule but of German society itself. The social history of the resistance, therefore, represents the other side of the history of German Nazification. Gradual alterations in the quality and appearance of the Nazi regime occasioned corresponding changes in the modes of resistance: Acts and attitudes of opposition, that is, were often dependent upon the role played by the Nazi authorities at a particular time.

The social and historical typology of resistance that I would like to develop here takes into account the broad spectrum of resistance activities, their social context, and the dependence that changing forms of resistance had upon the transitions occurring within the regime. In advancing this scheme, I shall distinguish three main categories of resistance:

1. The determined, illegal Communist and Socialist opposition that was active during the initial Nazi revolution.
2. The forms of partial resistance emanating from various sectors of the population that were symptomatic of the period of the successful consolidation and expansion of Nazi power between 1935 and 1941.
3. The later, reorganized groups supporting fundamental opposition that had at their center the conservative, military conspiracy whose actions culminated in the plot of July 20, 1944.

This classification of the German resistance into three stages shows that significant and fundamental resistance arose only in the initial and final phases of Nazi rule: that is, either before Nazism had fully developed its magnetic appeal and integrating potential or after this potential had begun to erode. Both of these phases were also characterized by an acceleration of violence and terror. In the long middle phase, however, when the effective consolidation of power by the

Nazis allowed for a comparably moderate form of dictatorship, the fundamental opposition declined to a minimum, and opposition expressed itself mainly in acts of partial or passive resistance.

The oscillation between integration and disintegration within the resistance during these three stages also stemmed from their differing social constellations. During the first years of the Third Reich, the Nazis formed an alliance with the traditional conservative elites and established a cartel of power, at the expense of the suppressed labor movement and the entire leftist and liberal section of German public and political life. The second stage of the regime witnessed the successful extension of control and mobilization of most sections of German society by special Nazi organizations. This phase was marked by the regime's widespread penetration of German society and culture. In the final stage the Nazi system's dissolution was inaugurated by the disenchanted conservative elites, who now formed the core of the fundamental opposition. Let me comment on a few aspects of each of these three prototypes of resistance.

The illegal opposition by Communist and Socialist underground groups – particularly by the stubborn, embittered Communist resistance in the first years – had hundreds of local footholds, especially in the urban and industrial centers of Germany. This branch of the resistance was particularly hard-hit by the Nazi authorities: Tens of thousands of Communists, leftist Socialists, and Social Democrats were arrested, imprisoned, or even murdered. The violent suppression of the Communist and Socialist organizations, which before 1933 represented at least 40 percent of the German electorate, was the most important dimension of the Nazi revolution of 1933–4 and established the main precondition for the subsequent institution of totalitarian rule. Because the Communists were the most tenacious adherents of Marxism, they became the object of the most merciless and radical persecution by the Nazis. Many of the acts of stubborn and desperate resistance committed by the Communists in 1933–4 were reactions to this intense suppression.

Official Communist documents and the records of the Gestapo portray this Communist underground as an ideologically firm and well-organized resistance. A different image of these groups emerges, however, when one focuses instead upon their sociological composition and behavioral and psychological tendencies. This approach reveals a Communist underground whose activism was largely spontaneous and implemented by radical youth groups.

Many of the members were unemployed young men and women who had experienced social degradation and political discrimination. Their rebellion and subsequent persecution had the quality of a vicious circle: Forced unemployment, resulting from low social and educational status led to political radicalization and the formation of rebellious underground groups; the Nazis then arrested these radicals, who, after their release, became the sources of yet more social agitation.

The formation of many of these cells was not necessarily ideologically motivated. Proletarian neighborhoods in suburban industrial districts or in worker neighborhoods provided the communicative structure, and long-standing unemployment yielded the socioeconomic grievances from which the underground movements developed. Moreover, close personal contact between like-minded members of Socialist families, neighborhoods, or working communities and associations within the many-layered Socialist subculture provided the sociological basis for the underground activities. Indeed, these personal connections and shared hardships often turned out to be more important than ideological conviction or party loyalty.

This is not to say that the composition or the politics of the Communist and Socialist opposition were homogeneous. Varying degrees of willingness to commit illegal acts, for example, reflected differences in ideology and class. The Communists tended to support a more radical political creed and the Social Democrats a more pragmatic one. Members of the Communist underground were usually young and often socially disenfranchised – facts that may explain some of their readiness to participate in risky activities. The majority of the Social Democrats, by contrast, were skilled workers or artisans, who generally enjoyed the respect of their non-Socialist, middle-class neighbors in the small towns or urban districts in which they lived. Most of them, firmly bound in their Socialist convictions, proved to be as immune to Nazi ideology and propaganda as the Communists but refrained from dangerous undertakings and illegal forms of opposition. They withdrew instead into an attitude of silent, passive resistance designed to see them through the Nazi era. Although some acts of illegal resistance expressed a youthful adventurousness, the more cautious attitude of the great majority of Social Democrats was in general a testament to this movement's essential commitment to political reason and responsibility. Working within this framework, many Social Democrats engaged in impressive, though largely silent, acts of passive resistance. On the whole their campaign displayed more consistency than that of the Communist underground, which was often erratic and was also undermined by the many members who became traitors.

Only after the Nazi regime had violently suppressed the organizations and activities of the Socialist labor movement could the regime enter its second stage, consisting mainly of its consolidation of power through the extension of Nazi suborganizations into nearly every social, economic, vocational, and cultural field. The pervasive influence exercised through these organizations was an instrument of control and mobilization. But influence was not exerted unilaterally: These organizations formed a vast and pluralistic institutional complex within the regime, a complex of manifold interest groups operating under the cover of what was often only nominal Nazification. Although control and mobilization were the aims of this network, influence was in fact also exerted by the very groups the Nazis sought to control. General adjustments of party affiliations were required to adapt Nazism to the needs of different social, cultural, and professional interest groups. Through this reciprocal influence and adaptation the Nazi regime succeeded in reaching the peak of its integrating strength in the years 1935–41. Other successes further strengthened the regime. It was able to overcome early economic crises, mass unemployment, and initial diplomatic isolation through a series of spectacular national successes – at first politically extorted, then enforced by war – that delivered the basic preconditions for the high degree of popular support that the Nazi regime enjoyed in this period.

During these years, fundamental opposition to the regime dwindled; some tiny resistance groups remained, but their actions were hesitant and inconsistent. Instead, opposition during this stage expressed itself mainly in acts of partial resistance against specific Nazi demands – against, for example, the Nazi attempt to remove or reduce Christian influence on education and public life. In most fields where the Nazis attempted to extend their political, ideological, or organizational claims, they encountered such limited objections. Although this type of resistance by no means amounted to a threat to Nazi rule, it could effectively repudiate, or at least limit, the totalitarian endeavors of the regime. The opportunistic adjustments made by the regime to integrate the traditional elites and various cultural, religious, or special-interest groups constituted a testament to the success of such partial resistance.

At this point we need to discuss a few of the many ways in which this partial or qualified opposition manifested itself in German society during the Third Reich. The majority of former democratic party activists resisted passively by refusing to join the Nazis and by trying to "winter over" the Nazi era in inconspicuous private vocations and activities. Many of them maintained contact with like-minded people, thereby constructing an informal anti-Nazi subculture. Nonconformity was not only expressed privately but also occasionally exhibited in demonstrations. Two prime examples of this were the pilgrimages of thousands of Catholics to local church festivals or holy places (such as occurred in the Rhineland and Westphalia in 1936–7, in reaction to anti-Catholic Nazi policies) and the illegal collective strikes of 1938–9, called in order to prevent the enactment of compulsory measures limiting the social freedom of industrial workers.

Resistance was also carried out in intellectual and cultural forums. In schools and universities, in the sciences and in literature and the theater, many endeavored to maintain and defend established pre- and anti-Nazi traditions, principles, and values.

These forms of resistance, often neglected in traditional histories of *Widerstand*, in fact were types of subversion more capable of undermining the totalitarian dictatorship than efforts at fundamental opposition, which had little chance of success under the watchful and pervasive system of Nazi control.

During the third stage of our typological sketch, beginning in about 1941–2, when the popular trust in a final German victory had begun to fail and the criminal and violent character of the regime had become more fully evident, a growing number of groups and individuals left the shelter of passive nonconformity to engage in conspiratorial and rebellious activities. In addition to illegal coteries of Communists, Socialists, Bavarian monarchists, and Christian trade-unionists, conspiratorial circles were formed within the diplomatic and civil service (for example, the Solf Kreis and the Mittwochsgesellschaft) and within student communities (above all, the Weisse Rose). Most important of these new conspiratorial associations was the famous Kreisauer Kreis (Kreisau Circle), under the intellectual authority of Count Helmuth James von Moltke.

Despite, or perhaps because of, their diverse ideological and political backgrounds, these groups had little contact with one another, and their efforts to coordinate their activities were generally unsuccessful. Even within the more closely associated groups that attempted to kill Hitler on July 20, 1944, there were serious disagreements concerning everything from how to assassinate the Führer and how to divide responsibility for the various tasks connected with the plot to the future domestic and foreign policies of a post-Nazi government.

The inner circle preparing the assault on Hitler consisted of young officers on active duty, as well as older military conservatives, diplomats, and high-ranking civil servants, many of whom had been purged by the Nazis from public life. The plot can therefore be characterized in part as a rebellion of those conservative elites who had initially been incorporated into the Nazi power structure but had subsequently lost influence and office to ardent party members and subservient newcomers.

The conservative elites' disenchantment with the regime was caused not only by their loss of influence but also by their access to information about the progress of the war. Since conservative holders of governmental and military posts had access to independent channels of information, they were less likely to believe Nazi propaganda than the general population (the majority of workers, lacking such channels of information, continued to support Hitler as late as 1944). Indeed, the regime's loss of authority and credibility in the wake of Stalingrad began with the growing disillusionment of well-informed conservative elites.

Despite the accelerating opposition to Hitler within traditionalist circles, ten years of Nazi rule had considerably weakened former strongholds of conservative and aristocratic resistance within German society. There remained small, isolated groups whose bonds were forged by close aristocratic family ties and friendships, along with exclusive enclaves of conservative nonconformers, many of whom were staff officers in the army. These groups nourished an illusory belief in the existence of a firm conservative, even feudal, tradition untouched by Nazi influences. Misguided faith in the existence of this tradition contributed to some serious miscalculations in the planning of the July 20 attempt. Above all, the conspirators overestimated the extent to which they could rely upon old aristocratic loyalties and habits of strict military obedience in the Nazi army. Such false expectations and a certain lackadaisical, aristocratic style may also explain the somewhat haphazard execution of the assault, as well as their underestimation of the energy of the Nazis, who displayed more resolution in suppressing the putsch than did many of the conservative conspirators in mounting it.

The tragic events of July 20, the actions and reactions of both plotters and Nazis, are immensely revealing. The Nazi political ambition and *Wille zur Macht* had overwhelmed the ambitions of the conservatives from the very beginning of their alliance with Hitler. The Führer's conservative partners were overcome, not only because they were less ambitious in their political aims but also because their noble carelessness was not equal to the enraged petit bourgeois ruthlessness that the Nazis mobilized in pursuit of their most destructive aims. The few cases of chivalrous, aggressive courage displayed by young conservatives like Edgar Jung, in 1934, or, ten years later, by Stauffenberg do not substantially revise this picture. Even the dangerously impetuous manner in which the small group of young aristocratic officers around Stauffenberg mounted their attack on Hitler, when older conservatives like Goerdeler hesitated, was essentially a cavalier's brash sally designed to override all objections and scruples. In the end, the martyrlike attitude of the desperate young conservatives was not unlike the rash spirit of self-sacrifice displayed earlier by the Communist youth, who were filled with despair over their political disenfranchisement and anxious to build a social utopia. The young nobles, too, were social outsiders, inspired by self-deception and inflated expectations of their mission's success. Ironically, the resistance efforts of these two groups, whose members did not share the values of modern middle-class society, eventually became the object of posthumous celebration, their acts praised and idealized by bourgeois historians and politicians.

We must include in our revised resistance canon the many instances of everyday civil courage and the steadfast maintenance of democratic convictions during the Third Reich. Many Social Democrats, liberals, and Christian Democrats were able to remain true to their political convictions during the Nazi period through acts of nonconformity and passive resistance. The political and moral responsibility expressed in this behavior should not be omitted in our historical recollection of the German resistance, because it constitutes one of the most valuable traditions inherited by the new democracy of the Federal Republic. It should also be noted that the Nazis' ability to develop, almost with impunity, such murderous, totalitarian fanaticism was probably not so much a result of the weakness and rarity of fundamental or unadulterated resistance as of the scarcity of smaller gestures of civil courage and mere human decency. Had there been more of these, the course of the Nazi regime could certainly have been significantly altered.

2

Working-Class Resistance: Problems and Options

DETLEV J. K. PEUKERT

It is not the purpose of this essay to offer a narrative description of the historical events under discussion. Presuming a knowledge of the central facts connected with the resistance, my concern is to draw attention to key problems in the history of the working-class opposition to Nazism and to provide a critical analysis of the historical achievements of that phenomenon.

I

Any discussion of the historical role of the working-class resistance provokes disputes over concepts and methodology. Too often, indeed, debate on this issue does not get beyond the stage of terminological dispute, since the conceptual presuppositions on which judgments and definitions are based are not made clear. The term "working-class resistance" is especially complex and carries a particularly heavy freight of ideologically charged connotations. It ascribes to a collective entity – the "working class" – a mode of action – namely "resistance" – which is the subject of highly favorable value judgments in the historiography of the Third Reich. The very terms of discussion, in other words, are an invitation to an ideological blurring of individual events and collective conditions, of actual behavior and moral evaluation. In what follows, I will confine myself to using definitions and arguments relating to historical contexts that can be established neutrally and dispassionately; I will look at causes, at people's margin for maneuver, at actions that really took place, at effects that can be specified. Only when the central theses of the argument have been set forth will I proceed to ask how these actions are to be evaluated and whether they belong to a tradition that is desirable from a democratic point of view.

First, a number of preliminary definitions. The term *Arbeiterklasse* (working class) frequently has a dual meaning in the German tradition; it denotes the class *an sich* (in itself), defined in terms of *social features*; and it also denotes the *ideological and organizational* "expression" of this class, or, in Hegelian and Marxist terms, the class *für sich* (literally, for itself). Since the labor movement in Germany before 1933 had evidently mobilized more than one-third of all voters, it became customary to view the *Arbeiterbewegung* (labor movement) and the *Arbeiterklasse* as identical, even though this identification was never entirely justified in empirical terms. In point of fact, it was the "remainder" left by the quotient derived from the political "denominator" and the social "numerator" that was to be of vital historical importance when the German labor movement collapsed in 1933 and groups willing to engage in resistance were formed out of it. It follows that we must always state precisely whether we are speaking about adherence to organizations and traditions of the political labor movement or whether we are referring to collective mentalities, forms of everyday behavior, social status, and structural change in those social groups that may be said to have belonged to the working class. Certainly, political resistance and socially nonconformist behavior may be interrelated, but this must be demonstrated in concrete instances. Indeed, the history of working-class resistance in the Third Reich can be properly understood only if it is recognized that working-class "nonconformist behavior" and "resistance" springing from the political labor tradition did not, as a rule, coincide but tended to take separate courses.

The preceding two sentences contain another terminological distinction relevant to the various forms of conflict with the Nazi regime: that between *Widerstand* (resistance) and *Nonkonformität* (nonconformist behavior). It is my contention that both of these concepts are necessary and that they represent the two end points on a sliding scale of dissident behavior in the Third Reich. We can characterize the range of dissident behavior by using two parameters: the degree to which the behavior was *public*, ranging from "purely private" gestures to highly visible acts; and the degree of *intentional challenge* posed to the regime, ranging from merely isolated instances of grumbling to the intention to undermine the regime as such. Within this framework we can distinguish among types of conflict on a rising scale of complexity and risk, beginning with occasional, private nonconformism, proceeding to wider acts of *refusal*, and then

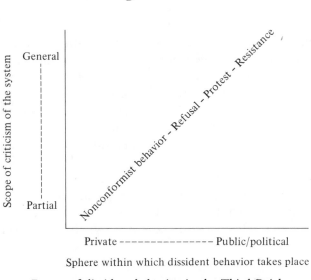

Forms of dissident behavior in the Third Reich

to outright *protest*, in which some intentional effect on public opinion is involved. A form of behavior, finally, may be counted as *resistance* only if it was intended to make a public impact and to pose a basic challenge to the regime (see diagram). The advantage in making these distinctions is plain. On the one hand, we can give a precise, graded analysis of the range of dissident modes of behavior – a flexibility necessary in the study of "totalitarian" regimes. At the same time, we can ensure that the concept of resistance proper does not become diluted or flabby. The result of this approach is that we discover an astonishing variety of types of "nonconformist behavior" in Germany between 1933 and 1945 but little full-scale "resistance."

II

The theme here may be conflict, but one must not neglect conformity. This maxim applies to the study of all forms of noncompliant behavior under totalitarian regimes. Some price is always paid – some form of loyalty accorded to the regime, either in order to disguise implacable opposition or – far more often – because rejection and consent coexist within the same individual. The totalitarian *Gleichschaltung* of public behavior may not bring about the unanimous approval that the regime hopes for, but it is generally sufficient to ensure that diverse complaints about the system do not coalesce, through public discussion, into an integrated attack on the regime as such. And as long as hostile opinion remains fragmented, or indeed survives only as an uncongealed mixture of private opinion and semipublic activity – as was the case in the Third Reich – then it is highly unlikely that the many instances of nonconformist behavior will fuse into coherent political resistance.

But the problem of conformity goes much deeper. It raises the question of whether the working class, or at least significant parts of the working class, had reached a social modus vivendi with the regime, notwithstanding the political resistance carried on by individuals and groups from within the old labor movement. There are several answers to this question, each of which serves to contribute to the total picture.

In its organizational structure and propaganda, the Nazi regime professed to represent the "true interests of the workers," a claim backed up by numerous efforts, by no means ineffective, to translate words into social and economic deeds. Many of the symbolic forms of integration were accepted as genuine by sectors of the working class, though at the same time there was a shrewd perception of conflicting socioeconomic interests and of a disparity between propaganda and performance.

Workers, like other social groups, welcomed full employment (generated by the rearmament boom) and the recovery of pre-Depression living standards as signs of a "return to normalcy." Indeed, they regarded such progress as a kind of IOU, promising future participation in a burgeoning "economic miracle." Yet at the same time, in tandem with the return to full employment, the workers showed an enhanced readiness to engage in social and economic disputes. Owing to their strengthened market position, the workers often came out on the winning end of these disputes.

It should also be noted that National Socialism accelerated, intentionally and unintentionally, certain modernization processes that both imposed new burdens and opened new opportunities. The tensions arising from this modernization process cannot be explained in terms of a simple bipolar model pitting "authority" against "society." They also cut across the traditional division separating "conformists" from "dissidents."

Last but not least, we should bear in mind the enormous number of internecine National Socialist conflicts in which workers became involved on one side or the other. Nazi rule was not a monolithic absolute, and the balance of forces within the system was constantly shifting. Such internal conflict could on occasion strengthen resistance, as the events leading up to the July 20, 1944, assassination attempt demonstrate. We should also remember, however, that in other cases conflict behavior could actually represent conformity – that is, conformity with one of the competing sources of authority.

The purpose of describing this somewhat confusing picture of mixed forms of conflict, overlapping conformity, and nonconformity has been to establish the thesis that the German resistance, including the working-class resistance, was rarely a homogeneous or unambiguous matter. A multiplicity of behavioral styles was the rule. This complexity and opaqueness stemmed from a number of factors: a need for concealment, a wish or need to compromise, or simply a lack of clarity in the perception of one's position.

Fortunately, recent studies on the working class under National Socialism have come to appreciate this complexity, and scholars like Jürgen Falter and Rainer Zitelmann have offered varying points of view regarding the extent to which workers were implicated in the Nazi system. What must be remembered as this work progresses is that the kind of question the historian asks are determined by the degree to which he or she remains open to the complexity of the subject matter at hand. A variety of answers is therefore welcome and proper.

III

My own perspective requires the examination of two general problems: the role of the Nazi dictatorship within the crisis of modern industrial society and the question of whether we can identify any solid attempts – or at least observable traces of attempts – to pursue alternative routes to that laid down by the Nazis. With respect to resistance by the working class, my interest in both continuities and discontinuities raises four subquestions: (1) To what extent did the traditions of the German labor movement, once such an impressive institution, aid political resistance to the Nazi regime? (2) To what degree did the numerous strands of social conflict within the Third Reich become consciously integrated into resistance? (3) What happened to those workers who took part in political resistance and social conflict in the Third Reich, and how did their experience influence the course of events in the postwar period? (4) What role can be ascribed to the history of working-class resistance in the creation of a democratic tradition in Germany? I shall not attempt, in the following discussion, to answer all of these questions, but I shall at least map out the range of information and argument that is needed as the basis for future discussion.

IV

The German labor movement was beaten politically before it offered a fight. That is the crucial fact about the year 1933. The events of 1933 dictated the verdict that was passed on the years that had gone before, and it established the conditions out of which resistance arose in the years that followed.

For all its internal troubles, the German labor movement, counting its Social Democratic and Communist wings, was the largest in the world, with well-tested leaders and members and with many years' experience of struggle behind it. The fact that the Nazi seizure of power in 1933 went virtually unopposed by labor proved how little this image of strength fit the real situation. Political divisions, it seemed, went far deeper in Germany than in most other European countries; the protagonists, after all, had fought a civil war against each other as recently as 1919–23. These divisions were matched by growing polarities within the working class along various lines: skilled versus unskilled workers, old versus young, employed versus unemployed – with the Communist party (KPD) tending to attract the young, unskilled, and unemployed, and the Social Democratic party (SPD) representing the older, skilled people who held jobs. During the extended sociopolitical trauma that gripped Germany after the First World War – which of course was exacerbated by the world economic crisis of the early 1930s – the Social Democrats had displayed immobility and defensiveness as they sought to preserve the remnants of the Weimar Republic, while the Communists retreated into a ghetto of radical rhetoric, according to which destroying the Republic and struggling against "fascism" (and "social fascism") appeared as two sides of the same revolutionary coin. It is questionable whether the German labor movement could have repulsed the Nazis even if it had put up a united front and adopted more effective strategies, but it is nevertheless a tragedy that it failed to rally at the last critical moment and allowed itself to be driven into illegality without committing even a symbolic act of resistance.

From the Nazi point of view, the event in 1933 that crucially determined the future of the labor movement was not the imposing of the ban on workers' organizations, nor even the imprisonment of leading labor officials, but the unbridled "wildcat" terror campaign that the SA (Sturmabteilung) launched in working-class districts. Old scores from the *Kampfzeit* were settled, and numerous temporary concentration camps were set up in which the SA became self-appointed arbiters of life and death. The SA, SS (Schutzstaffel), and police waged a systematic attack on working-class communities that lasted from spring until autumn. By the end of this period, the risks involved in resistance, or even in offering the most passive aid to the resistance, had become so great that the hardy political activists still willing to put their lives on the line had been effectively cut off from the bulk of their former supporters. This split between class and cadre was to remain the central structural feature of the workers' resistance until 1945.

Given the twofold trauma of 1933 – defeat without struggle, and the terror-induced split between the activists and the politically passive proletarian community – the sheer quantity of political opposition, the commitment and self-sacrifice of those involved, and the stubborn determination with which they persisted in secret operations, despite setbacks at the hands of the Gestapo, are certainly remarkable accomplishments. They constitute an immense and historic achievement, quite irrespective of the total impact of the working-class resistance on the Third Reich.

The great years of organized resistance were 1933 to 1935–6. Tens of thousands of people were involved in illegal activities and organizations or distributed anti-Nazi literature. In addition to the traditional labor organizations (the SPD, KPD, and some unions), which survived by establishing leaderships-in-exile and networks of contacts within the Reich, new left-wing organizations sprang up (and older ones became newly active) that responded to the defeat of 1933 by proposing new programs and styles of organization. Those active in resistance and in exile were fired by a complex mixture of motives which can be grouped into three categories: the desire to continue to pursue traditional goals despite the discouragement engendered by 1933; a search for ways of overhauling the labor movement after defeat; and anger at the new Nazi reign of terror so intense that people were prepared to risk their lives to overthrow the regime. (It was a distinctive feature of working-class resistance that those involved in it harbored no illusions, after the spring of 1933, about the nature of the Nazi regime and Nazi terror: Each individual was constantly aware of the ultimate price that might have to be paid.)

By 1935–6, the strength of organized resistance was waning as a result of the Gestapo's efficient bloodletting, the consolidation of the Nazi regime, and a corresponding pessimism on the part of anti-Nazis about the likelihood that the regime could soon be toppled. The insurgent underground organization that had been the norm so far was replaced by loose networks of friends and trusted contacts dedicated to ensuring that the labor movement could go into safe hibernation. There was no alternative to this defensive strategy. At the same time – just as with the middle-class resistance – it was no longer possible to make a clear-cut distinction between prudent restraint and resigned passivity.

Nevertheless, during the second half of the war some elements of these informal networks helped bring about a reorganization of the KPD, the SPD, and the trade unions. People's motives for engaging in resistance during wartime remained highly complex. Until the collapse of the regime seemed imminent – the sole circumstance under which resistance might be successful – the only options were to take comfort in the vague hope that an end could not be too long in coming (an attitude similar to that which had prevailed in 1917–18) or to make the critical decision to act on moral principle, facing the virtual certainty that the act would have limited efficacy. The men of the Twentieth of July conspiracy were by no means the only ones to recognize the moral need to light a beacon of resistance against Nazi crimes, regardless of prospects for success: Leading Social Democrats and Communists shared this fundamental commitment.

In brief, then, one can say that motives for political resistance changed appreciably over time. In broad terms, the initial impulse was the essentially moral one of refusing to give up, despite the defeat of 1933. This gave way to the primarily political calculation that underlay organized resistance between 1934 and 1936, which in turn was replaced by the again more strongly moral aim in wartime of staging a powerful symbolic initiative before the regime's collapse.

V

Unfortunately the main consequence of labor's resistance efforts and of its many internecine disputes was the disintegration of traditional working-class cohesion. And yet, despite severe losses and setbacks, many gains were achieved by the working-class resistance that need to be recognized.

A major loss for the working class was the breakdown of old community relationships, or at any rate of all the political and organizational structures that were bound up with them. Fragments of traditional working-class culture survived but only at the price of depoliticization. This was accompanied by a declining sense of solidarity, or at least of traditional community trust, thanks to fear of terror, the presence of informers, and constant pressure to conform. A crucial factor here was the gap between the older generation, which had been politically socialized before 1933, and the younger people, who had been exposed to Nazi socialization without a compensatory political education from their parents. The intertwining of political organization and social environment that had previously been a hallmark of the German labor movement thus suffered a double destruction after 1933: in the public sphere through the ban on organizations and through various forms of *Gleichschaltung*; in the private sphere by the breach in the younger generation's traditional socialization.

Nevertheless, the changes that took place in the proletarian community could also be seen as beneficial in some ways, creating opportunities for greater vertical and horizontal mobility for working-class youth. Above all, the trend toward disintegration within the traditional community cut across the bipolar conflict between "authority" and "society." That is to say, conflict behavior (and modes of conformity) in the working class were related to two basic parameters: modernization and authority. This will become clear if we make a brief survey of individual fields and forms of conflict.

Between 1933 and 1935, the mood of the workers was depressed and critical. Only as the economy picked up with rearmament and as successes in foreign policy were achieved did the mood alter. Grumbling about the wretchedness of daily life and the misdemeanors of party bigwigs continued, but a certain basic acceptance of the regime, reflected in the pervasiveness of the Führer myth, also developed.

At the same time, the workers' readiness to engage in economic conflict grew, as they exploited the decline in unemployment after 1936 to obtain disguised wage increases. Although political resistance circles tried to politicize these socioeconomic disputes and the Nazi regime warily eyed them as a potential source of trouble, the sharpened conflict posed no real threat to the regime, which quickly granted substantial concessions. The question of what the workers learned in the long run from these disputes is moot: It is better to ask whether they served as a continuation – necessarily informal – of trade-union activism or as training in the dog-eat-dog principles of an individualistic, meritocratic society.

Two competing social patterns emerged in workers' lives. For some, the "economic miracle" of the 1930s marked the return of normality after years of crisis. For others, the same period was one of almost continuous confinement to barracks, as one militarized, all-male environment succeeded another: Labor Service, conscription, frontline duty, and prisoner of war camp. These two life patterns, incidentally, were later to combine in the West German workers' experience of the regimented *Wirtschaftswunder* "normality" in the 1950s.

Virtually no Nazi organization was as effective in mobilizing young people as the Hitler Youth. This was true even of working-class youth, who were socialized after 1933. In addition to its ideological role, the Hitler Youth offered its members opportunities to prove themselves among their peers. These social skills enabled some members of the Hitler Youth generation to make a delayed entry into the reconstituted labor movement after the Nazi defeat in 1945. The League of German Girls and kindred Nazi organizations, despite their anachronistic ideologies, had a similarly dynamic effect on the everyday lives of working-class girls and women. Paradoxically, they fostered certain forms of social emancipation while inhibiting political freedom.

It would be a mistake to see the influence of Nazi organizations on the working class, or even on younger workers, as positive merely in the integrative sense envisaged by the regime. In fact, in the late 1930s and during the war German youth, including working-class youth, showed a growing tendency to distance themselves from the government and its ideals. This process found its clearest expression in the emergence of dissident youth subcultures, like the Edelweiss-Pirates among the working class and "swing fans" among middle-class youth. Alienation from Nazi attempts to achieve total conformity, however, went well beyond these subcultures and gangs. Recent research on young members of Luftwaffe auxiliaries, for example, suggests that the skeptical mind-set of the postwar generation was already established.

The main effect of the Nazi pressure on the public sphere was to provoke a retreat into privacy. This might manifest itself in drawing the line at certain of the regime's demands, and hence contain the germ of resistance. It might, on the other hand, be part and parcel of the straightforward conformism that was fostered by the diet of light entertainment served up, with Goebbels's blessing, well into the war. One writer has accurately spoken of the Germans' "split consciousness," which meant that individual actions – even nonconformist ones – could no longer be concerted, let alone directed toward resistance.

The same was true of the most striking transformation in working-class social history during the Third Reich: the use of millions of foreigners in Germany as forced laborers. The barrier of nationality ruled out a common resistance, solidarity with the foreigners being limited to a few individual gestures. Certainly the widespread refusal by foreign workers to comply with the regime's demands did not spur the German workers to resist in a similar fashion.

The variegated pattern outlined here of limited social conflict, partial conformity, and extensive breakdown of the forms of public behavior and social organization that might have fostered a unified resistance may also help to explain why 1944 was not followed by another 1918. The political and social structures of Nazi Germany, chaotic enough at the outset of the regime and yet more bewildering as they evolved, also served to disorient and fragment resistance. The issues implicit in everyday disputes, which might have served as the social and economic basis of a resistance movement, could not be brought into focus.

German working-class resistance was no different from French *résistance* and Italian *resistenza* in its scope – resistance in these countries was also limited, at least at first – nor did it differ in its willingness to make sacrifices and take risks. The crucial difference was that the social environment and the public sphere, as areas of action, had been fragmented, so that the large number of acts of resistance and instances of conflict that did arise occurred in isolation from one another. The Nazi regime remained in power not simply because of its efficient machinery of terror but because of the disintegration of German society.

VI

What was the legacy of working-class resistance, given that it had repeatedly failed to achieve its self-appointed goals? Those who lost in 1933 by failing to prevent the Nazi seizure of power; those who lost in 1935–6, when the organized underground struggle was wiped out; those who lost in 1939, compelled impotently to watch the outbreak of war; those who lost in the wake of the abortive attempt to kill Hitler on July 20, 1944; those who lost in the spring of 1945, when their attempt to plan a new society through *Antifa* (anti-Fascist) committees was blocked by all four Occupation powers – What did all these men and women carry with them into the postwar period, after twelve years of continually blighted hopes?

To pose the question in these terms is to provide part of the answer. The standing of the working-class resistance was far from high enough to enable many workers' postwar dreams of left-wing hegemony and socialist regeneration to be translated into reality. And there had to be a process of selection before particular labor leaders could be favored with the job of cooperating with the various Occupation authorities. Whatever elements of the resistance spirit managed to survive in postwar German society did so through the efforts of these junior partners of the Occupation forces.

The main results of labor's self-scrutiny during the trials of resistance and exile – commitment to a socialist renewal of social democracy, a move toward unified trade unions, and the Communists' espousal of the anti-Fascist Popular Front line – found expression in the postwar period only after they were filtered through the norms of Allied Occupation policy and then through the dictates of the Cold War. The net postwar effects were accordingly disappointing:

– The rhetoric of change, fired by resistance, faded away. In its place, surviving cadres pursued a pragmatic policy of reconstruction.
– The gulf between new democratic constitutional proclamations and promises of reeducation and de-Nazification, on the one hand, and a 1950s society united in its dedication to reconstruction, hard work, and silence about the past, on the other, was too wide to bridge.
– The depoliticization of working-class communities that had taken place since 1933 could not be reversed. This formed the basis for the emergence of a Social Democratic labor movement in

West Germany and a Stalinist labor movement in East Germany.

– The Hitler Youth generation was democratized and, on the whole, successfully integrated into the organizations of the labor movement. After a period during which the older generation resumed positions of leadership, a new type of official took the helm, for whom skepticism and pragmatism came before ideology.

The seed of the democratic, anti-Fascist ideal did bear fruit, but not until a new generation, born during and after the war, came to challenge the legitimacy of the pragmatism of *Wideraufbau*. The movements of 1968 and the social and liberal reforms of 1969 marked a revival of the legacy of the years 1933–45. This legacy, which had been suppressed both for good and for ill, was now cited as an argument for the possibility, or necessity, of "daring to become more democratic."

VII

The history of postwar perceptions of the years 1933–45 shows that the construction of tradition always proceeds selectively, dividing the unstructured past into elements that are important for the way in which they help make sense of the present. The resistance tradition has become a kind of capital on which anyone who claims to speak for the "other Germany" can draw.

The resistance tradition, as it has evolved in the dominant public version of events in postwar Germany, can be analyzed in terms of the typology proposed by Nietzsche in his "Use and Disadvantage of History for Life" (from *Thoughts out of Season*).

First came the "monumentalist" version of the resistance tradition, inviting public identification with the great heroes of the resistance: in West Germany, the Twentieth of July conspirators; in East Germany, the fighters of the Communist underground. Carl Goerdeler in the first case and Ernst Thälmann in the second symbolized the twin poles of a tradition that was notable for passing over unsuitable parts of the historical record and idealizing and glamorizing the participants.

With the change of outlook in the 1960s came an increasingly critical view, in West Germany, of the history of the resistance. An assault on the hagiography of the Twentieth of July resisters was followed by a search for examples of workers' resistance, though instances of the latter were also soon subjected to the irresistible demystifying pressure of critical historiography.

Despite this, and indeed building on the empirical findings of this newly expanded research into the resistance, there was during the 1970s and 1980s a growing movement toward antiquarian historical work, as researchers investigated the local *Heimat* and everyday life during the Nazi period. A large number of publications and memorials resulted. These have been so effective in establishing a new anti-Fascist, democratic version of the history of the years 1933–45 that the latter-day pro-German apologetics of Ernst Nolte and company are unlikely to make much headway. At the same time, the grass-roots, antiquarian scrutiny of the Nazi era has had the effect of calling into question any neat division of the historical actors into good guys and bad guys. This approach may lead to the relativism of "tout comprendre, c'est tout pardonner"; equally, though, it may lead to better-informed and more finely differentiated judgments as to what kinds of resistance were possible and what were regarded as matters of ethical obligation.

3

Choice and Courage

CLAUDIA KOONZ

The title of this essay reflects two components of resistance to any oppressive state: first, the cognitive choice to discover truth despite public control of the media; and second, the courage to act on that knowledge. As Willy Brandt has commented in his introductory remarks, a resister, by definition, takes serious risks to act illegally in a world where right has become wrong. What is a "risk," and how can historians evaluate what counts as moral action in an immoral world? The answers to these questions have changed in the decades since World War II. Looking at women who opposed Hitler adds a new dimension to an inquiry that has become increasingly complex.

In the decades immediately following the war, many books, published in both Germanies, paid homage to the heroic Resistance, comprised of men who had organized underground cells, planned uprisings against the National Socialists, volunteered in the war against Franco's dictatorship, or opposed Nazism from exile. The Resistance seemed monolithic and masculine. This clean-cut concept of the Resistance mirrored the prevailing vision of Hitler's rule itself as powerful, organized, and centralized. But over the years another view of the Nazi state has emerged in the works of historians as diverse as Uwe Dietrich Adam, Reinhard Bollmuss, Martin Broszat, Hans Mommsen, and Edward Peterson. Similarly the term "resistance" lost its capital letter as research revealed many levels of resistance – perhaps one might even say resistances. As our new paradigms shift, a far more complex vision of both Nazi power and opposition to it emerges.

Yet the English term "resist" remains the same: It comes from the Latin *resistere*, to stand firm. In German, *Widerstand* – "to stand against" – underscores inflexible strength. Although military resistance existed in countries occupied by Germany, it never developed in

49

Germany. Recent research by the contributors to this volume and by many others has revised the myth of the lonely hero. To maintain a heroic stance, one could not stand rigid and alone against evil. One depended on flexibility, a community of trust, and some form of protection to support individual moral or ideological choice. This understanding turns our attention to the context – to infrastructure, community, and ordinary life. Activities that saved lives, rescued victims, and maintained underground anti-Nazi groups inspire our respect and foster new research. As our vision expands beyond the image of the lonely hero, women come into view, because they formed a vital component of subversive subcultures.

The expanding definition of resistance opens up several questions about evidence and evaluation. If we equate resistance with those acts that the National Socialists defined as crimes against the state (for example, actions described as crimes in the laws against "malicious gossip"), we succumb to Gestapo paranoia. If we take at face value the "Deutschland Berichte" of the reports of the executive committee of SOPADE (the Social Democratic Party in Exile), we yield to their authors' wishful optimism. Court records reveal that some Germans were executed for purported "acts against the state" that they did not commit; on the other hand, some protests remained so silent that no one noticed them until after 1945. Still other acts of rebellion may well have been prompted by youthful acting out. Doubts arise when we assess the extent to which particular groups actually damaged National Socialist rule. Some single-issue protests, for example, may well have stabilized the Nazi system by serving as safety valves for dissent.

In short, as our interpretations of the 1933–45 period become more nuanced, judgment becomes more difficult. Detlev Peukert (in Chapter 2 of this volume) suggests two qualities by which we may judge resistance: whether the behavior in question was public, and whether it challenged Nazi power. Both of these tests position the individual in relationship to the community. Fritz Stern, in his introductory remarks, adds a third question that refocuses on the individual by defining resisters as people who believed that only the defeat of Nazi rule could save Germany. All three of these components help us understand women's role in resistance. But first let me make it clear that I have discovered no evidence that Nazi policy toward women motivated anyone (male or female) to oppose the regime. The fact that I was asked to contribute this essay on women and resistance results not from historical reality but from an historical oversight. Until recently, scholars have tended to pass over evidence about women resisters – despite the fact that dozens of women who had been active in the resistance published their memoirs in the years just after 1945. When historians pay equal attention to discovering the record of women's and men's roles in resistance, specialized studies of women will have accomplished their purpose and become superfluous.[1]

The focus on women and resistance has prompted me to refine the term "resister" – a person who openly opposed the Nazis – and to add a separate category for the "opponent" – a person who acted to thwart a particular policy that touched his or her own daily life, while assenting in general to Nazi aims and ideals. Although I could find no women (or men) resisters motivated by specifically feminine issues, thousands of women opposed Nazi eugenics programs (and ultimately euthanasia) because those policies affected them as women and offended their moral beliefs about birth, life, death, and God. Both resisters and opponents acted publicly and undercut Nazi hegemony. But the former worked to defeat National Socialist rule; the latter objected only to single issues that affected them directly.

Whereas resistance in the narrow sense was undoubtedly stronger in the first years of the Third Reich, before state-sponsored terror took its brutal toll, opposition expanded steadily as disillusionment spread. Philipp Jenniger may have been correct in assuming that by 1938 the vast majority of German citizens supported Hitler, but it also seems true that disaffection with one or another Nazi policy had spread among a minority that had initially endorsed Hitler's seizure of power. Opposition to specific aspects of Nazi power grew with each year and became a veritable epidemic after the Battle of Stalingrad. While opponents did not aim at the overthrow of Nazism, they did create a kind of *Sammelopposition* of single-issue dissent that, ironically, resembled the National Socialist mobilization against the Weimar Republic described by Thomas Childers.[2]

In this essay I will illustrate these definitional distinctions as they

1 Of the several excellent studies of women and resistance, the following three provide good starting points for further reading: Hanna Elling, *Frauen im deutschen Widerstand: 1933–1945* (Frankfurt, 1981); Gerda Szepansky, *Frauen leisten Widerstand: 1933–1945. Lebensgeschichten nach Interviews und Dokumenten* (Frankfurt, 1983); Gerda Zorn and Gertrud Meyer, *Frauen gegen Hitler. Berichte aus dem Widerstand 1933–1945* (Frankfurt, 1974).
2 Thomas Childers, *The Nazi Voter: The Social Foundations of Fascism in Germany, 1919–1933* (Chapel Hill, 1983).

relate to the lives of women opponents and resisters. I will begin with two case studies of disaffected women active within Catholic and Protestant organizations and conclude with brief descriptions of women in communities of resisters.

In 1933, the newly appointed *Reichsbischof* Ludwig Müller (renowned for wearing the "cross on his breast and the swastika in his heart") urged all Protestants to rally to the Nazi cause. Paula Müller-Otfried, director of the umbrella Protestant women's organization (Frauenbund), had prayed, in her New Year's address of January 1932, for "a steel-hardened" man powerful enough to save Germany from atheistic Communist revolution. In 1933, she thanked God that this man had arrived. Having welcomed Hitler's power, however, she decided to retire, for reasons that may have included a certain reluctance to comply with *Gleichschaltung*. A much younger, more vigorous advocate of National Socialism succeeded Müller-Otfried. Agnes von Grone joined the National Socialist party and orchestrated "her" organization's *Gleichschaltung* – which meant expelling all members with Jewish ancestors and guaranteeing cooperation with Nazi political goals. Von Grone, as Reichsführerin des Frauenwerkes der Deutschen Evangelischen Kirche, promised to organize energetically (*restlos*) more than two million Protestant women under her leadership. During the winter of 1933–4, it seemed she would succeed. To von Grone, *Gleichschaltung* offered the opportunity to cooperate in exchange for important rewards in the form of budget, influence, and status. Cooperation appeared as empowerment, not surrender.

Many promises from the Ministry of the Interior and from Gertrud Scholtz-Klink, director of the Women's Bureau (Deutsches Frauenwerk), bolstered von Grone's optimism. On several occasions von Grone received assurances that National Socialist organizations allowed, and even sometimes encouraged, their members to belong to women's religious organizations. The right of dual membership (*Doppelmitgliedschaft*), von Grone believed, could facilitate Protestant women's desire to participate in building the new state.[3] By late 1934, however, von Grone faced a crisis. The *Reichsbishof* insisted that she relinquish all autonomy to state and party associations. When she objected, he promoted a rival organization, headed by Rev. Hans Hermenau. Meanwhile the bishop's allies orchestrated

3 Fritz Mybes, *Agnes von Grone und das Frauenwerk der Deutschen Evangelischen Kirche* (Düsseldorf, 1981), and Hans-Jochen Kaiser, *Frauen in der Kirche* (Düsseldorf, 1985).

a gossip campaign, insinuating that she was selfish (*rasender Ehrgeiz*, raging ambition), grasping, and more loyal to church than to party. Her rivals insisted "dass sie zwei Millionen evangelischer Frauen in reaktionärer Weise gegen Staat und Partei führe" (that she indoctrinated two million Protestant women with reactionary diatribes against state and party). During the summer of 1935, von Grone brought these and other allegations to the attention of Walter Buch, Reichsleiter des Obersten Parteigerichts (chief judge of the National Socialist Party High Court).

Among our ranks are the mothers of the SA and SS, who upheld, maintained, and nurtured German popular heritage and the heritage of the evangelical faith as the highest values of the nation throughout the Marxist era. They trust my thoroughly National Socialist leadership.[4]

Shortly thereafter Bishop Müller formally stripped von Grone of her responsibilities, but von Grone continued to fight for reinstatement in the NSDAP into the early 1940s, always insisting on her total devotion to Nationalist Socialist principles. Her "crime" had consisted of independence. Although she wrote to Rudolf Hess and other high party officials, she remained persona non grata. In one sense, until 1945 von Grone did oppose Nazi rule. As her son noted, "My mother never lacked courage" ("An Mut hat es meiner Mutter nie gefehlt"). This quality stood her in good stead after 1945, as well.[5] Although she had insisted for twelve years on her total devotion to National Socialism, she now construed her actions as oppositional. Memory erased her passionate support for National Socialism between 1933 and 1935. Shortly after her death her son insisted that "even during the period from March to May 1935, my mother could never be viewed as a 'true-believer National Socialist'" because he had never seen *Mein Kampf* or any of Rosenberg's writings in the family bookcase. His mother, he said, "stood between two fronts." In a certain sense, he was correct. In National Socialist Germany, divided loyalty was tantamount to treason. But in another way he was wrong. Because the Evangelical Church in Germany collaborated so closely with the Nazi state, von Grone

4 Von Grone to Buch, June 1, 1935, Berlin Document Center.
5 Mybes, *Agnes von Grone*. The caption for a photograph of von Grone reads: "Genügsamkeit und Selbstdiziplin, kämpferische Energie und Kompromisslosigkeit, Aufrichtigkeit und Furchtlosigkeit, aber auch gesellige Unbefangenheit und Lebensfreude Kennzeichnen ihr Leber." (Her life is signified by self-sufficiency and self-discipline, pugnacious energy and uncompromisingness, uprightness and fearlessness, but also by social ease and joy in living.) Ibid., 85.

struggled for her independence against a united church–state front. Agnes von Grone, in short, publicly opposed the National Socialist regime, and she damaged morale among Protestant women who desired to harmonize religious faith with political commitment. She opposed state encroachment on her organizational turf, but she did not resist National Socialism.

Von Grone displayed an acute sensitivity to the arrogance and the contempt for women exhibited by both party and church officials. Hypothetically, a man treated in the same shabby manner might have reacted in the same way. The tone of the correspondence with and about von Grone, however, is so redolent with misogynist insult and innuendo that it is difficult to imagine a masculine equivalent. For that reason I categorize the von Grone saga as distinctively feminine and oppositional – but in no sense resistance.

A case study of opposition in a religious context, however, opens up a more complicated set of moral and political issues. In one of its first major initiatives, the new Nazi government promulgated a series of laws designed to purify the "Aryan" race. Long before the Nuremberg Laws were announced, the cabinet and the Office for Racial Politics (Rassenpolitisches Amt) launched a massive publicity campaign to popularize the policy of forced sterilization of people who suffered from any one of eight handicaps or diseases (severe alcoholism, blindness, and manic depressive psychosis, for example) that racial scientists deemed genetically transmitted. Castration was ordered for men with a record of violent sexual crimes. Women with undesirable genetic makeup could be forced to have abortions. Balancing these "negative" measures, a "positive" propaganda blitz ensued, with crash courses, posters, slogans, radio programs, and new textbooks popularizing the new biological ranking of all citizens.

From the outset, Catholics knew that their faith stood in total opposition to such measures. Not only had *Castii Connubi* stated papal doctrine in 1931, but in early 1934 priests had told their congregations: "According to the guidance of the pope, Catholics are not morally permitted to request sterilization for oneself or others or to aid in carrying out the operation." The leading prelates of Germany, convened at the Fulda Bishops' Conference in late 1933, opposed the legislation and negotiated intensely with state and party officials.

However, as they bargained, the bishops yielded. They asked for (and ultimately obtained) permission for Catholic physicians who opposed sterilization and abortion on moral grounds to refuse to cooperate, unless they were public health officials. Since the 1920s, a small number of Catholics like Bishop Adolf Johannes Bertram, Herbert Muckermann, and Helene Wessel had endorsed "positive" eugenics (measures such as genetic counseling and educational compaigns).[6] Hence when Archbishop Heinrich Gröber of Freiburg ardently defended the aims (although not the methods) of eugenic science, he did not break entirely with precedent. After much discussion, Gröber and other theologians broke the impasse by distinguishing between *Anzeigepflicht* and *Antragspflicht* – the obligation to report people who might be genetically damaged to health officials and the obligation to sign the order for sterilization or abortion.

On the one hand, the archbishop expressly recognized that the obligation to report, imposed upon doctors, institutional directors, and other health care providers by the implementation decree of December 5, 1933, issued under the Reich Law for the Prevention of Hereditary Diseases in no way conflicts with the principles of the Catholic faith and thus may be fulfilled by faithful Catholics without any conflict of conscience. The bishop requested that Catholic nurses in public institutions not be required to participate in the performance of measures necessary to the execution of the law of July 14, 1933. On the other hand, signing the order is impermissible for Catholics.[7]

This tactic of negotiating for exceptions rather than standing fast against state orders that contradicted Catholic doctrine will surprise no one who has read John Conway, Gordon Zahn, or Günther Lewy. Pragmatic considerations counted heavily in the bishops' deliberations. The Catholic church had, in July 1933, signed a Concordat with Hitler that bound all Catholics to obey the law and pledged cooperation. Throughout Germany, Catholics hailed this treaty as the culmination of decades of efforts to overcome their second-class status. Having just achieved equality, they did not welcome the idea of hearing Nazi propaganda cast aspersions on their patriotism because they obeyed Rome before Berlin. Suspicion of disloyalty could have concrete consequences. Directors of schools

---

6 Cornelie Usborne, "The Christian Churches and the Regulation of Sexuality in Weimar Germany," in Jim Obelkevich, Lyndal Roper, and Raphael Samuel, eds., *Disciplines of Faith: Studies in Religion, Politics and Patriarchy* (London, 1988), 99–122; Angelika Ebbinghaus, *Opfer und Täterinnen. Frauenbiographien des Nationalsozialismus* (Nördlingen, 1987), 152–73.
7 Letter dated January 26, 1934. Erzbischöfliches Archiv Freiburg (hereafter EAF), B2/Generalia/19 Sittlichkeit/Sterilisation.

and health-care institutions feared that if they did not comply city officials would stop referring clients and would harass students. "In the case of complete refusal, it is to be feared that the institution will be rejected as 'not standing on the ground of National Socialism' and will receive no more referrals."[8]

My interest here is to pursue the implications of this particular strategy as it related to Catholic women as mothers, nurses, educators, and social workers. The exemption of physicians merely passed difficult moral choices along to the next echelons. Where did the boundary of moral responsibility fall? Letters from worried personnel deluged regional offices. "Our Sisters, through prayer, sacrifice, and atonement, beg for the presence of the Holy Ghost and the gracious (*gnadenvolle*) leadership of God in these difficult times of decision."[9] These staff members and professionals wanted clear guidance about their role in eugenics policies. When they were told that doctrine allowed them to participate in immoral processes, women in health and education institutions were baffled. After having heard their work praised as essential, they suddenly heard their tasks deemed so unimportant that Catholic personnel were ordered to comply with operations declared immoral by the pope. Women knew from personal experience how vital their contact with clients, students, and patients was. Now, when their faith was being tested, they felt abandoned by their prelates.

Their consternation was compounded by the fact that National Socialist policy inadvertently assigned a major role in the eugenics program to religiously affiliated institutions. The state welfare offices (NSV) routinely turned over "hopeless" cases to private religious institutions, so that state resources could be invested only in "hopeful" cases and the "worthy poor." Thus, the greatest percentage of potential targets for eugenic intervention and, later, euthanasia fell under non-Nazi supervision. Further, vague diagnostic categories, combined with abysmal ignorance of genetics, mandated reliance upon the people (usually women) who worked with the individuals in question on a daily basis. Only they could determine, for example, whether a particular child suffered from genetic feeble-mindedness or from a deprived home environment. Catholic person-

---

8 Sr. M. Clementina answers the archbishop's questionnaire. May 25, 1934. EAF. St. Franziskusheim, Schwarzach/Bühl.
9 E. R. Schlattern, Ordenssuperiorat der barmherzigen Schwestern vom hl. Vinzenz von Paul, seven-page letter to Gröber, Freiburg, January 10, 1934. Ibid.

nel fully appreciated their role in the eugenics programs and adapted accordingly.

Insisting that they remained utterly loyal to Nazi aims in general, the personnel in religious institutions displayed deep concern about every facet of the process that took a patient/victim through the stages of identification, testing, hospitalization, surgery, and recovery. What about taking the patient to the hospital for surgery, for example? Did that count as spiritual guidance at a difficult time, or did it constitute delivery of an innocent victim to an immoral operation? What about the impact of the operation on others who lived in the institution? "It is precisely in an institution in which there are many school-aged boys discovering their sexual urges that such a case would come as a sensation and lead to deleterious fantasies and discussions."[10] Such inquiries deluged prelates' offices. Frequently, social workers lamented policies that sterilized prostitutes on the grounds that without fear of pregnancy they would become even more unrestrained in their sexual practices. Separating the questions designed to throw a wrench into the bureaucratic machinery and those motivated by deep spiritual conflict is difficult. Probably many letter writers acted out of a mixture of both impulses. Certainly they knew that obdurate refusal would only mean their dismissal and replacement by someone who would promise total cooperation. They knew, as well, how to use Thomistic inquiry to delay the implementation of every stage of the eugenic legislation.

The thousands of mothers, professionals, volunteers, and nuns who turned to their ecclesiastical superiors for protection and guidance remained permanently disappointed. Not until fairly late in the euthanasia program did prelates take a stand. The objectors (mostly women) acted in public ways and certainly expressed their misgivings about eugenics freely within religious space. Moreover, I suspect that their actions attest to the general unpopularity of the eugenics campaign in the late 1930s; perhaps they even contributed to it. But how can historians judge what compliance rate constitutes "success"? Certainly National Socialist expectations provide no guidelines. Initially, some eugenics "scientists" had predicted that up to 20 percent of the population would be affected by these laws, and moderates guessed seven hundred thousand. In *Kindheitsmuster*, Christa Wolf recalls learning in 1933–4 that "four hundred thousand

10 H. Karsh, Knabenheim Mariadorf, Füfingen, Baden. June 1, 1934, to Gröber. Ibid.

will be sterilized at once."[11] At it turned out, her memory matches the statistics: about three hundred sixty thousand Germans and forty thousand non-Germans were sterilized between 1933 and 1945. Significantly, although enormous fanfare accompanied the introduction of these programs in 1933, after 1936 the annual results went unpublished. This seems to indicate that Nazi officials themselves were disappointed by the compliance rate and feared that more publicity would have a negative effect on morale.[12]

Thus Catholics who interfered with the drive for forced sterilization and abortion did act publicly and, it may be assumed, had an impact on the success of a crucial Nazi program. However, because their opposition sprang from concern about a single issue, I would term them opponents rather than resisters. This does not in any way diminish their courage or effectiveness. But it does suggest that these people (mostly women) did not desire the demise of National Socialism. Gender expectations placed some women in "feminine" occupations that in turn meant they confronted special moral dilemmas associated with those jobs. As long as dissenting personnel could circumvent or undercut the law they hated, they remained model citizens. Indeed, their single-issue objections and fear of reprisal may well have inspired them to scrupulous obedience.

With these examples of a specifically feminine kind of opposition in mind, let us turn to women resisters, to highlight the contrast with opponents. Using Fritz Stern's definition, resisters hated the core of Nazism, not merely its "excesses," and did not hope for a "reformed" or "moderate" version of Hitler's rule. Most histories of the resistance have ignored or underplayed women's participation. Accounts of the Red Orchestra, for example, pass over Mildred Harnack and Libertatus Boysen. Herbert Baum seems more important than Marianne Baum. However, as our notion of the monolithic masculine fragments, historians search out documents related to networks rather than individuals, and women become visible. Although much research remains to be done, it appears that women resisters' motivations did not spring from gender-specific concerns

11 Christa Wolf, *Pattern of Childhood*, trans. Ursule Molinaro and Hedwig Rappolt (New York, 1980), 61.
12 Robert N. Proctor, *Racial Hygiene: Medicine under the Nazis* (Cambridge, Mass., 1988), 95–130. Gisela Bock's study will long remain the classic research on the topic: *Zwangssterilisierung im Nationalsozialismus* (Opladen, 1986). For a criticism of Bock's thesis, see Kurt Nowak, "Coercive Sterilization in Nazi Germany," *Simon Wiesenthal Annual*, 4 (1987): 371–80.

related to their employment or ideology (as in the case of opponents). But the form of their courage did take distinctively feminine shape, because of prevailing notions of appropriate gender behavior.

Social scientists have not yet developed a satisfactory theory as to why individuals decide to comply with or oppose regimes which they despise. Despite attempts by Lawrence Kohlberg and Carol Gilligan to formulate the stages of moral development, we cannot isolate a subgroup of people who we can predict will be brave. We can, by contrast, identify at least two communities that appeared to resist Hitler's propaganda appeals before 1933: voters for Marxist and Catholic parties. At the time of the March 1933 elections, over half of the German population fell roughly into the anti–National Socialist consensus. But with economic recovery, terror, and social control, many of these non-Nazi voters' objections dissolved. And of the millions who hated National Socialism, very few people took risks on the basis of their position. Ample evidence tells us about plans for an uprising, sabotage, assassination, and subversive activities.[13] Records from the Gestapo and the Sondergerichte suggest that perhaps one in five of the Germans arrested for oppositional actions was a woman. But examining the names on the trees dedicated to anti-Nazis on the Avenue of the Just in Berlin – "Recognition of Unsung Heroes" (*Aktion ungesungene Helden*) – a different picture appears. Here women turn up with surprising frequency. Do these general findings mean that fewer women took risks than men, or that more women than men complied? Or does this mean that fewer women were apprehended? Perhaps activities that characterized women's resistance did not occasion as much suspicion as men's, permitting women to evade the police more successfully.

Under the constant threat of police repression, we would hardly expect resisters to experiment with new roles. But reality often forced novel responsibilities on resisters. For example, during the first months of Nazi power, when many Communist and Socialist husbands disappeared or went into exile, wives and daughters assumed the burden of standing fast. Similarly, when political leaders were arrested, the rank and file took up the battle. Pragmatic realities, not notions of reformed roles, produced these reversals. Women and children frequently were taken hostage to help the police gain information about, or from, relatives, employers, or

13 Peter Hoffmann, *The History of the German Resistance*, trans. Richard Berry (Cambridge, Mass., 1977).

comrades. For the most part, however, women and men behaved as they usually had within the family and community. The skills characterized as "feminine" proved useful in underground Germany. Perhaps because of the ubiquitous fear of denunciation or perhaps because Nazism was "homegrown," German resisters did not act like their counterparts in occupied Europe. There was no *maquis*, or partisan force. In fact, the resistance, because it was nonviolent, depended on qualities associated with women: communication skills; insight into the enemy's weaknesses; ability to provide food, shelter, and moral support; and, finally, skill at smuggling. Indeed, it has been observed that pervasive gender stereotyping has rendered women "bicultural" and therefore endowed them with the ability to live between two social realities. Remaining "beneath suspicion," women could accomplish tasks that men could not. Some women, like Ricarda Huch, protested, and yet remained sufficiently circumspect to calm Nazi suspicions even as they participated in resistance networks.

For most resisters, family life played a vital role in their decision making. Unlike Christabel Bieleburg, most wives shared their spouses' commitment and ideals from the outset. In resister couples, the mother who remained at home to care for children while supporting her husband was as brave as a man who went into exile or planned a bomb attack. In short, resistance subcultures depended on women as well as men. Although women did not act against Nazi power from distinctive motivations, their actions within resistance networks were linked to their gender.

Prevailing notions about femininity empowered women resisters in crucial ways to bypass Gestapo surveillance. When messengers, like Susanne Simonis in the Goethe Haus exhibit, crossed frontiers or faced police searches, they took advantage of their adversaries' misogyny to outwit them. Maria von Maltzan – aristocratic, well-educated and idealistic – routinely evaded arrest using bold ruses to divert guards at crucial checkpoints. As Frances Henry pointed out, in her oral history of a small Rhineland town, women tended to perform "human resistance," acts of kindness for neighbors in trouble. Although historians often dismiss such individual acts as apolitical, these brave choices saved lives and helped victims to maintain their morale.[14] H. D. Leuner's book, *When Compassion Was*

14 Frances Henry, *Victims and Neighbors: A Small Town in Nazi Germany Remembered* (South Hadley, Mass., 1984), 67–122.

a Crime, movingly records the courage of ordinary, decent women and men. Similarly, the memoirs of Jews who left Germany almost invariably mention the women and men who aided them and virtually never mention politically or religiously oriented organizations.

Scholars writing about people whom I would call "ordinary" resisters (as opposed to the well-known figures in the Red Orchestra, the Kreisau Circle, or the White Rose) almost invariably structure their studies around biography. Indeed, Hanna Elling listed as one of her chief goals the simple recovery of basic information about women who resisted.[15] The act of historical preservation in itself, she believed, gives meaning to the martyrdom of those who died. Beyond the goal of paying homage to a heritage, what can scholars learn about resisters and opponents? When people who acted bravely describe their actions, they make it sound almost as if they had had no choice. They say they simply acted according to human values; "*Selbstverständlich*," they say. But, of course, the overwhelming majority of the people who shared these "natural," "human" values remained quite deaf to pleas for help or calls to resist Nazi power. No behavioral theory accounts for individual choice.

However, looking at biographical information collected in several recent studies of grass-roots resisters, a few elements seem to form a pattern. In telling their life stories, no resister begins the account of her or his bravery in 1933. On the contrary, their narrative strategies[16] display a consistent self-image characterized by rebelliousness and even defiance in many areas. Like Ingrid Ströbel, author of a study of women's armed resistance to Nazism, whom West German judges in 1988–9 held in "investigative custody" on suspicion of belonging to a terrorist organization, resisters' memoirs emphasize a lifelong attitude of independence.[17] Courageous individuals took risks within their more general idealistic, rebellious vision of the world. Resistance does not emerge suddenly, after the danger is full-blown, but develops out of a life pattern. Sigrid Jacobeit and Lieselotte Thoms-Heinrich present a series of seventeen biographical sketches that highlight unpredictable choices made in

15 Elling, *Frauen im Widerstand*.
16 This term is developed by Luisa Passerini, *Fascism in Popular Memory: The Cultural Experience of the Turin Working Class* (London, 1987), 25–37, 53. "Real experience is subsumed by the symbolic framework, and is selected and interpreted according to its lights" (60).
17 Cf. the article in *Die Zeit*, February 3, 1989, 50.

moments of grave danger.[18] Similarly, Gerda Szepansky characterized her goal in recording oral histories as "an effort to capture each
individual in her deep and unchanging character." In these accounts,
resisters' lives before and after the Third Reich assume great importance. Szepansky's informants repeatedly told her, when she opened
her interviews with questions about 1933, "but that was not my
entire life!"[19]

Scholarship on women resisters suggests that we can discern no set
of socioeconomic categories to explain who was brave. One pattern
emerges, however, and even it must be accepted with caution.
Autobiographical accounts suggest that most resisters were young.
This seems a commonsensical observation, because we think of
idealistic, reckless youth in contrast with older people, whose responsibilities to children, jobs, and community may make risk
taking difficult. But even this generalization may mislead us. De-
mographics, and changing concerns among historians, mean that
grass-roots resisters who were older during National Socialist rule
may well have died during the 1950s and 1960s, when few scholars
worried about collecting information about ordinary resisters, male
or female. After the late 1970s, only the youngest were still alive.

Ultimately, we have not yet developed a theory to explain why
one Socialist joined an underground resistance network and another
became a "beefsteak Nazi" ("red on the inside and brown on the
outside"). Nor can we decide why one Catholic nurse refused to
deliver her charge to an involuntary abortion while another saw the
same operation as preventing further suffering. Individuals, whether
they opposed or supported Hitler and his rule, arrived at the decision
to act based on events that they made meaningful within the context
of their own values and personalities. Even though Samuel P. Oliner
and Pearl M. Oliner have extrapolated a set of traits they believe
comprises the "altruistic personality,"[20] we still remain baffled in
the search for a predictive theory. However, an ideal type might
nonetheless be useful. When we listen to people reflecting on real
risks they took in opposition to state power, their thinking does not
resemble the highest stage of moral development according to

18 Sigrid Jacobeit and Lieselotte Thoms-Heinrich, *Kreuzweg Ravensbrück* (Leipzig, 1987). The
   authors depict women's lives from birth through their imprisonment at Ravensbrück and
   afterward, based on interviews and records.
19 Szepansky, *Frauen Leisten Widerstand*, 9.
20 Samuel P. Oliner and Pearl M. Oliner, *The Altruistic Personality: Rescuers of Jews in Nazi
   Europe* (New York, 1988), 1–12.

Lawrence Kohlberg. They do not operate by a set of abstract rules. Rather, as the Oliner study concludes: "What distinguished rescuers was not their lack of concern with self, external approval, or achievement, but rather their . . . stronger sense of attachment to others and their feelings of responsibility for the welfare of others."[21] Indeed, Carol Gilligan's paradigm of feminine morality may turn out to be the standard for men and women alike: a vision that sees moral dilemmas in terms of "conflicting responsibilities rather than . . . competing rights."[22]

These generalizations serve well as hypotheses about human behavior, but when we evaluate historical behavior we also need a framework that inquires about the degree of risk, the extent of impact, and the nature of motivation. While opponents' and resisters' actions frequently brought heavy reprisals and no doubt damaged morale in the Third Reich, single-issue opponents could make their peace with Nazi power. Resisters, by contrast, did not object to Hitler's state from a partial vantage point. For them, defeat of the putatively legal government alone constituted victory.

21 Ibid., 249.
22 Carol Gilligan, *In a Different Voice: Psychological Theory and Women's Development* (Cambridge, Mass., 1982), 19.

4

Resistance and Opposition: The Example of the German Jews

KONRAD KWIET

German Jews developed various techniques of defense and survival, strategies designed to work against the ideology and policies of the Nazi regime. With these strategies, they deviated from the norms that the National Socialists had prescribed for them. In this essay, I will outline the basic patterns underlying these strategies. These patterns can be divided into two distinct catagories: *resistance* in the narrow sense – defined as politically organized antifascism – and *opposition* in the broader sense, defined as nonconformist behavior.

The opportunities for Jews to resist or oppose the Nazi regime were limited by many external and internal barriers. In 1933, approximately five hundred thousand Jews experienced the termination of the German-Jewish "symbiosis." They found themselves at the mercy of a system that gave them a choice between either accepting degradation in Germany or emigrating. They discussed at length the alternatives of home and exile – whether to stay or to leave. A minority left at once: those in danger for political reasons, Zionists, and those driven out of their professions. But the majority decided to stay. They felt unable to leave the country in which their families had lived for generations and where they felt at home. They were so acculturated and integrated that it was difficult simply to pack their bags and go.

The Reichsvertretung der Juden in Deutschland (National Representative Organization of Jews in Germany) was formed, which, under the leadership of Leo Baeck and Otto Hirsch, made every effort to protect the Jewish community. Nevertheless, differing perspectives, old animosities and tensions, continued to prevail; and the political, social, and religious heterogeneity of German Jewry precluded any unified domestic defense plan. Moreover, the German-Jewish representatives made it perfectly clear from the beginning that their strategies would remain within the bounds of legality.

The possibility of militant resistance was considered – and rejected – as futile. The abdication of liberalism and the rapid destruction of the organized labor movement meant that the two social forces that had once supported Jewish emancipation had disappeared. In addition, there was the fear that any open revolt would lead to harsh reprisals. One other basic assumption determined Jewish strategy: Most Jews believed that the Nazi regime would not remain in power for long, an illusion they shared with many non-Jews. The confident belief that a rapid return to democracy would bring the government-prescribed assault on Jews to an end deterred many from turning their backs on Germany.

Jewish representatives were therefore neither prepared nor able to call for an immediate mass exodus. This would have meant the self-dissolution of the German-Jewish community. "Everyone remain at his post" was the motto of the acculturated and assimilated Jews in 1933. Even later, when some Jews started to leave, Jewish representatives continued to warn against hasty departure and tried to manage the emigration in an orderly fashion. Nor did the Zionist leaders press for immediate mass departure. They were preparing for selective emigration over a long period, in which Palestine would have the highest priority as destination. It rapidly became obvious that both in Germany and abroad there were many obstacles in the path of this escape route, as with all the others.

It took a direct threat to their lives to make most German Jews realize that their ties to Germany could no longer be maintained. This occurred in the form of the *Reichskristallnacht* in November 1938, that bloody pogrom that so deeply seared the Jewish consciousness. After this, most Jews were obliged to give up the notion that they still had any right of domicile in Germany. No longer could they reasonably hope for better times. Their pessimism was justified: In quick succession there followed the measures that destroyed their economic existence through forced labor and ghettoization.

The old debate over whether to leave or stay now ceased. In its place came the imperative: "Get out, at all costs!" A mass panic to flee ensued. Rescue operations began in all the Jewish communities. Priority was given to sending children and young people to the West, particularly to England. Jewish representatives now dared go beyond the bounds of legality. They opened illegal bank accounts to collect donations to finance escapes. The Reichsvertretung paid for the release and emigration of many imprisoned Jews with special funds from an account established by the Robert Bosch firm in Stuttgart. Between 1938 and 1940, Hans Walz, managing director of Bosch, made 1.2 million reichsmarks available for saving Jewish lives. Accepting and disbursing this money represented one of the few violations of the law on the part of the Reichsvertretung. Convinced that the exit doors would soon slam shut, it also addressed increasingly desperate pleas to Jews who had already left and to Jewish organizations abroad to support the emigration of their brethren still in Germany. The Jewish leaders pleaded for donations, sponsorship, and visas. They were understandably embittered by the restrictions placed on Jewish immigration by many Western countries. In any event, the Nazi regime banned emigration in October 1941, and the feverish public efforts to support it had to cease.

In the autumn of 1941 there were still some one hundred sixty-four thousand Jews living in Germany, one-third the Jewish population of 1933. Most of these still intended to leave. The familiar assumption, or the old accusation, that the remaining Jews were unwilling to emigrate belongs to the realm of myth. The opposite was the case.

The Jews were not in a position to stop the destructive course of National Socialist racial policies by themselves. They were dependent on assistance from non-Jews. Persecution and expulsion took place in full view of the German public. With few exceptions, there were no objections among the population at large. The most vehement protest took the form of a single, belated demonstration in February 1943, when a number of women in Berlin appeared outside the prison where their Jewish husbands were held and vociferously demanded their release. They were supported by passers-by, and the men were soon released. The successful outcome of this protest suggests that similar actions – if repeated across the country on a broad scale – might well have altered National Socialist policies toward the Jews.

In November 1938 many Germans watched in shock as the inflamed "wrath of the people" vented itself in the pogroms. Some criticized the destruction of property or complained about "illegal" excesses. But only a few had the courage or inclination to support or

help the persecuted. The Nazis castigated them as "Jew lovers."
Moreover, there were hardly any public protests against the
Jews' ghettoization. Indeed, pressure on the Jews came not only
from above but also from below, making a "solution" to the "Jewish
question" more urgent. A broad anti-Jewish consensus in the population, combined with active support from the ruling elites, made it
possible for the Nazis to drive the Jews into the role of *minorité fatale*.
Certainly at the beginning of October 1941, on the eve of their mass
deportation, they did assume this position. Greatly decimated in
numbers and with a preponderance of old people, separated from
their families and the outside world, stripped of all rights, under-
nourished, impoverished, subjected to forced labor, and denied
freedom of movement, they were herded together into "Jewish
houses" and marked with the fatal yellow star. Clearly the Jews had
become a pariah caste that society saw only as a burden and that the
National Socialists could dispose of as they saw fit. Public silence
reigned virtually undisturbed as one hundred thirty-four thousand
German Jews were taken from their final living quarters and loaded
onto trains that would take them to the extermination sites.

The German Jews could ultimately expect scant solidarity, protection, or assistance from the German resistance movement. At no
time were the various resistance groups able, or willing, to place a
struggle against the persecution of the Jews at the heart of their
activities. At the same time, many obstacles prevented the Jews
themselves from participating in the resistance.

The resistance mounted by the churches had an essentially theolo-
gical basis and was carried out within the framework of a *Kirchen-
kampf* – that is, an internal struggle within the Christian religion.
Clearly there was no place for the Jews here. Nor did the German
Jews have access to the bourgeois-conservative resistance that was in
the hands of dignitaries, bureaucrats, and military officers.

These circles scarcely stirred when Jewish emancipation was re-
voked. On the contrary, the social-conservative and clerical elites
joined forces with the National Socialists in calling for a "traditional
solution" to the "Jewish question." Their resistance to Nazism
in general did not begin until just before the war, when the Jews
had already been effectively excluded from society. There were, of
course, a few exceptions – instances of protest, acts of assistance, and
even some connections between Jewish representatives and resistance
figures in the Goerdeler circle. Nevertheless, it remains a fact that

there was essentially no room for Jews within the conservative-bourgeois resistance. A further indication of the conservative resistance's exclusiveness can be found in its political and ideological program. Carl Goerdeler's famous memoranda are interwoven with traditional political demands, nationalistic strains, and illiberal sentiments. Here and in other plans for a "new order," it becomes only too plain that a critical examination of the "Jewish question" or consternation over the extermination of the Jews had only marginal significance for the resisters.

From the very beginning, members of the suppressed and divided German workers' movement had sought to organize a resistance front against the Nazis. But here too the "Jewish question" played no decisive role. The traditional Marxist model of history prescribed a solution that was to be identical with the dissolution of Judaism. A further barrier that prevented most Jews from participating in the workers' resistance was the Jews' social and political affinity with the bourgeoisie. Unlike the bourgeois opposition, however, the leftist resistance did offer Jewish Socialist and Communist party members and sympathizers the possibility of taking up the struggle against National Socialism.

But here it is important to note that the decision to allow Jewish participation was determined not by any special concern for the Jews but entirely by political conviction. That is, Jews joined the various resistance organizations not as Jews but as convinced Communists, Marxists, Social Democrats, trade unionists, Trotskyites, or anarcho-syndicalists. This state of affairs explains why, in the initial phase of the Nazi regime, no specifically Jewish resistance organizations came into being. Their antifascism was part of the general German resistance and occurred within the framework of specific workers' actions.

Within the realm of this politically organized resistance, approximately two thousand Germans of Jewish origin fought against National Socialism and fascism both in Germany and in exile – first in Spain, and later in the occupied territories and concentration camps. Added to this group were the members of Jewish youth organizations who were involved in the development of a resistance immediately after 1933. Numbering a few hundred, they mostly represented the Left. A special place is occupied by German-Jewish refugees who later fought their way into Allied units campaigning in Europe.

Anti-Fascists of Jewish descent were exposed to the dual danger of being Socialists and Jews. These dangers, which emerged in the mid-1930s, at a time when the organized workers' resistance had reached its peak but under conditions of terror and illegality, brought a change in some Jews' own sense of their Jewishness. They found themselves isolated – classified as Jews not only by the Nazi regime but also by their non-Jewish comrades in the resistance movement.

Under the impact of massive waves of arrests and trials, the exiled leftist leaders made decisions that deprived the Jewish anti-Fascists of an organizational base. The Socialists decided against the reconstitution of illegal groups in Germany. The Communists continued the struggle but with a changed concept and mode of operation. The exiled Communist leadership's order to remove Jewish Communists from the depleted resistance ranks in Germany, "in the interest of our own safety," was one such modification. In 1936–7, in Germany and some other countries, Jews faced the alternative of either emigrating or forming purely Jewish groups. These alternatives cleared the way for the formation of a resistance organization that is regarded as the example par excellence of German-Jewish resistance: the Herbert Baum group. This Jewish Communist group did not, however, take up the anti-Fascist struggle until after Germany had attacked the Soviet Union, and its program was designed largely on the Communist model, not on a specifically Jewish basis. Furthermore, the Baum group was almost totally isolated. An invisible ghetto wall separated it from the German population. Even within the Communist underground, it functioned as an outsider organization. In addition, it operated outside the Jewish community, whose leadership disapproved of its activities, if only for reasons of security.

In 1941, the inner core of the Baum group consisted of thirty-two members, the youngest eighteen, the oldest thirty-two. Nearly all of them were of lower-middle-class background and had been forced to work in Berlin factories, primarily in the huge Siemens plant. The climax of their anti-Fascist activities was a spectacular act of sabotage. In May 1942, members of the group attempted to destroy the Nazi propaganda exhibit called "The Soviet Paradise" in the Berlin Lustgarten. The coup failed, with disastrous results for the group and for Berlin Jews in general. The Gestapo took rapid revenge: Five hundred Jewish hostages were murdered. In July 1942, the minister of justice was able to report to Hitler that the Baum ringleader had been condemned to death by a special court. Further arrests and trials ensued, and in a few weeks the group had been virtually liquidated: Only four members survived.

We must now turn to the second category of anti-Nazi activity – opposition in the broader sense, including active nonconformity and passive noncompliance with the Nazi system. Nonconformist behavior was initially expressed in open protest. This took many forms. Individual Jews and Jewish organizations in Germany protested against defamation and discrimination in telegrams, letters, and memoranda addressed to Nazi authorities. Jewish representatives proclaimed their indignation in speeches, sermons, publications, and cultural events. Jews circulated anonymous pamphlets, broadsheets, letters, and slogans. They plastered their protests on the sides of mail-boxes, telephone booths, bus and subway cars and stations, private houses, and public buildings. Many Jews refused to obey Nazi directives. Some, for example, would not call themselves "Sara" or "Israel," the identification code the Nazis insisted they employ starting in 1938. Others, from 1941 on, declined to sew the large yellow star on their clothing. Jews expressed their rebellious sentiments toward their non-Jewish countrymen and the Nazi authorities through curses, insults, and even acts of violence.

The German public seemed to take no notice of these protests and cries of alarm. The Nazi authorities, however, reacted vigorously to the Jews' efforts at self-defense, defaming them as *üble Judenhetze* (evil Jewish agitation), *staatsfeindliches Verhalten* (behavior hostile to the state), *Heimtücke* (seditious attitudes), or even *Hochverrat* (high treason). The punishment varied accordingly from a warning, to "protective custody," to execution.

These open protests virtually ceased after the *Kristallnacht* pogrom of November 1938. As a *minorité fatale*, Jews were now leading a highly precarious life that seemed (and indeed proved to be) provisional. Rebellion and indignation had to assume different forms, find new outlets. With the beginning of the deportations, there were only two ways of avoiding the persecutors: suicide or escape into the underground.

There are no reliable statistics on the number of Jewish suicides or attempted suicides during the Third Reich; probably they numbered close to ten thousand. Even in its initial phases, the Nazi terror drove hundreds of Jews to suicide. There was a rash of suicides during the boycott of Jewish businesses in April 1933 and in response to the *Anschluss* (annexation of Austria) in March 1938 and to the pogrom of November 1938. The number of Jewish suicides reached its peak during the period of deportations, when more than three thousand individuals, or roughly 2 percent of those called up for "evacuation," decided to end their lives. (In Berlin, in fact, the proportion of suicides was as high as 4 percent.) Those choosing this way out were generally of advanced age (average age sixty-five) and a high degree of assimilation. Nearly all of them waited until the last moment, the arrival of the deportation notice. Clearly, the official order to vacate their homes and prepare for "relocation" made it manifest to them that they had now been cast out from society once and for all. Desperation broke their will to live. In the last hours before death, memories of childhood and families preoccupied them. They thought of their children who had emigrated, and they left behind loving and painful farewell letters. They thought of the nation in which they had grown up as good and productive citizens, the place they had always considered their home. With their suicide, they took their leave of the shattered German-Jewish symbiosis.

Whether such acts of desperation should be classified as a form of resistance is a question that we cannot answer here. Rabbis might include them within the category of *kiddush hashem* – acts of heroism that reflect the ultimate commitment to Judaism. In this vein, the Israeli historian Uri Tal has recently argued that the mass suicide of secularized German Jews during the Holocaust falls within the Jewish tradition of religious martyrdom.

Between 10,000 and 12,000 German Jews preferred the hazards of living underground to compliance with the Nazi deportation orders. Most of these tried to find hiding places in Berlin. In 1943 there were probably about 5,000 Jews living in hiding – roughly 7 percent of the Jews registered in Berlin in 1941. When the city was liberated at the end of the war, 1,402 Jews surfaced. In other words, three of every ten Jews who went underground in Berlin survived. In occupied Western Europe, the chances of survival were somewhat better; in Eastern Europe even worse.

Jews living underground had to overcome many barriers and dangers. First and foremost were the surveillance and persecution nets that the National Socialists had thrown over the *minorité fatale*. Anyone who attempted to evade registration faced draconian punishment. Paradoxically, disappearing into the underground meant that one first had to overcome Jewish representational institutions. The Reichsvertretung sent out the registration forms and was responsible for ensuring that the transportation of deportees took its "proper course." This meant, among other things, that the Jewish officials strongly advised against any refusal to comply with deportation orders.

Added to this was an understandable fear of taking up a radically new and dangerous mode of existence. Disappearing meant giving up a legal way of life for a subterranean existence that promised no long-term security or escape – just a chance of survival. It also entailed finding non-Jews who were prepared to risk their own lives by taking in fugitives for days, months, or perhaps even years. During the war and deportation period, there were still gentile Germans – particularly in Berlin – who did what they could to save Jews. Relations, old friends, and former servants often offered the first refuge. Some Jewish forced laborers met fellow workers who advised them to disappear and then helped them to cover their illegal life in the underground. The fugitives were constantly looking for safe addresses. Inevitably, however, many hiding places were exposed by informers or destroyed by Allied air attacks.

Life in the underground required courage, endurance, social adaptability, and financial resources. Ration cards and counterfeit papers were essential. Demand for these was so great that they commanded high prices on the black market. As the war dragged on, more and more non-Jews – resistance fighters, forced laborers, and prisoners of war – also went underground, adding an element of competition for scarce resources. When the Jews' financial reserves gave out, they became entirely dependent upon the generosity of their rescuers and protectors for rent money, clothing, food, and papers. (Unfortunately, as far as we know the small German Jewish-aid organizations never gained access to the escape funds collected in Western Europe and distributed through central assistance organizations.)

There were few opportunities for Jews to revolt against the destruction of life once they had reached the extermination camps and other killing centers. They had had a long and tortuous journey behind them. Those survivors who climbed out of the railway boxcars were starved, exhausted, broken people who had passed through all the phases of moral defamation, social discrimination, rigid ostracism – who had, in short, come to know all too well the full hopelessness of their situation.

Old people were herded together with women and children on the railway platforms. Selection occurred immediately and ensured that a high proportion of old people and children were driven to the gas chambers without delay. Those who were ordered into the barracks as able to work had no real chance to defend themselves; their murder had simply been postponed. Their remaining days were governed by strict isolation, even from other camp inmates, who often shared their jailers' brutal anti-Semitism. Thus most Jews were excluded from the resistance groups that sprang up in the camps. The Jews understood, too, that any individual acts of defiance or resistance on their part would mean instant death – the end even of the slim hope that postponement might somehow ultimately turn into salvation. Of course their sense of futility was fully justified: Of the one hundred thirty-four thousand Jews deported from Germany, only eight thousand returned.

In conclusion: Prior to and during World War II there were many opportunities to save Jewish lives, but few were taken. Non-Jews in Germany and abroad offered little solidarity or assistance. It is easy today, with hindsight, to criticize the passivity of the Jewish victims and the failure of their leaders – a historiographical trend that has gained increasing popularity. However justified this criticism may be in some respects, it all too frequently overlooks one decisive factor: Even if the Jews had overcome their own misgivings and shortcomings, their internal disputes and diverging attitudes, this would by no means have cleared the way for an effective response to Nazi persecution. With few exceptions, the Jews in Germany, like the Jews in the countries the Germans invaded, stood alone. And alone, they were not in a position to divert or halt the escalating course of Nazi destruction. Their strategies for defense and survival encountered treacherous obstacles thrown up by the broader society in which they lived, the society most of them had believed was their own. The limits of Jewish resistance and opposition, the ineffectiveness of Jewish protests and rescue efforts, should therefore be attributed less to those who initiated them than to those who ignored or sought to abort them.

5

From Reform to Resistance:
Carl Goerdeler's 1938 Memorandum

MICHAEL KRÜGER-CHARLÉ

I

Carl Goerdeler's attitude toward the National Socialist regime became increasingly critical after he resigned as mayor of Leipzig in April 1937. He recognized that his hopes for reforming the Nazi system from within were illusory, given the realities of that system. Especially when abroad, he did not hide his growing fears about the situation at home. Nevertheless, in the first year or so after his resignation he did not carry his criticism much beyond what he had repeatedly expressed in memoranda to Hitler since 1933. Goerdeler's critical comments abroad should not be mistaken for an attitude of fundamental opposition; rather, they echoed the spirit of those national-conservative circles who feared that a shift of power in favor of Nazi radicals like Himmler, Goebbels, and Heydrich was imminent – a development that might well mean the final defeat of Hitler's conservative critics.

The events of 1938 seemed to justify those fears. A wave of changes in personnel and organization within the government swept away the remnants of the regime's conservative and moderate facade and initiated a vigorous policy of foreign expansion. As a result, Goerdeler became even more disillusioned about the regime he had once hoped to channel onto a safely conservative path. So disenchanted was he that just before and during his second visit to England, in the spring of 1938, he even considered emigrating. Instead, he increased his efforts to secure foreign support for the opposition within the Wehrmacht command, a course of action upon which he and former chancellor Heinrich Brüning had agreed after a long talk in Brussels.[1]

---

1 See Heinrich Brüning, *Briefe und Gespräche 1934–1945*, ed. Claire Nix (Stuttgart, 1974), 167.

Goerdeler spent the last four months of 1938 in Switzerland, making two trips from there to Italy and southeastern Europe. During his absence, two events took place in Germany that further soured his view of National Socialism: the Munich Four-Power Agreement and the so-called *Reichskristallnacht* (Night of the Broken Glass). Truly horrified by these events, Goerdeler used his time abroad to write a memorandum (hitherto unknown) that sheds significant new light on the thinking of a conservative politician finally prepared to cross that crucial borderline between reformist criticism and fundamental resistance. In a 320-page manuscript, Goedeler set forth the economic, social, legal, constitutional, and foreign policy changes that he believed were essential for a thorough recasting of the German state. Long passages read like the political legacy of a man who, having been deprived of the means of political action after his resignation from his Leipzig position, was obliged to deny his naturally pragmatic disposition.

I will limit my comments here to a brief analysis of those parts of the memorandum concerned with constitutional questions and foreign policy, leaving out Goerdeler's social and economic ideals. But it should be understood that this memorandum, taken as a whole, illustrates a fundamental – albeit belated – opposition to National Socialism. Not only does it formulate a rejection of the Nazi state on moral grounds; it also sets forth the political structure of a post-Hitler Germany.

The Munich Agreement had deeply disappointed Goerdeler's expectations regarding the possibility of achieving basic change within the Reich. As his British friend, industrialist A. P. Young, remarked in October 1938, Goerdeler's usually optimistic attitude gave way to a mood of increasing resignation in the face of Hitler's successful foreign policy. In order not to remain entirely inactive, Goerdeler set forth his hostile views on the National Socialist regime in his memorandum. Unlike the sections on foreign policy, the sections concerning economic, domestic, legal, and educational policy are handwritten and were probably composed between September and November 1938. It is not clear why this document remained unknown for so long, but there is no question as to its authenticity.[2]

---

2 That memorandum was given to me by the Goerdeler family. Unless a different reference is given, the following quotations are from that memorandum, which will shortly be published as part of an edition of Goerdeler's writings.

Goerdeler's memorandum, which he saw as an "indivisible entity," directly attacked the radical core of the National Socialist dictatorship. It advocated the dissolution, even the prohibition, of Nazi organizations like the DAF (German Labor Front), replacing them with a system of corporate interests. The Nationalsozialistische Deutsche Arbeiterpartei (NSDAP) itself was to be deprived of its monopoly status, permitted to exist henceforth only "in honest, open competition with other political convictions, since no state has yet been ruined by such diversity." Indeed, said Goerdeler, prohibiting diversity of political expression was sheer "nonsense," since prohibited parties would simply "go underground and then become truly dangerous."

Political life as a whole was to be reorganized according to a system of corporate interests and bodies from the local to the national level. In this arrangement, self-government was to play a key role – a characteristic feature of Goerdeler's political thought. The *Deutsche Gemeindeordnung* (German Municipal Code) of 1935, to which Goerdeler had contributed substantially,[3] was to be maintained, but elections of municipal representatives were to be added. For the national legislative framework, he proposed a dualistic representative body (Volksvertretung) consisting of a corporate section (Reichsrat) and a sort of chamberlike body (Reichstag), whose members were to be elected indirectly by an electoral assembly. A majority vote in the Reichstag, however, would be required only for passing the budget or an amendment to the constitution. Aside from these powers, the Reichstag would be granted the right to interpellate the government. The power to formulate legislation was to be vested in the executive branch – the office of chancellor – and the holder of this office could be removed only through an extremely complicated "no confidence" vote, requiring a majority in both houses of parliament. Believing that "Germany historically needs the monarchy," Goerdeler would accept nothing but a monarch as the formal head of state, representative of the Reich, and commander in chief. The sovereign would also appoint the chancellor and the state secretaries. One can easily see that in essence this plan bears a striking resemblance to the Bismarckian constitution.

According to Goerdeler, these policies would be put into practice

---

3 See Michael Krüger-Charlé, "Carl Goerdelers Versuche der Durchsetzung einer alternativen Politik 1933–1937," in Jürgen Schmädeke and Peter Steinbach, eds., *Der Widerstand gegen den Nationalsozialismus* (Munich, 1985), 383–404.

three months after the "restitution of law and individual freedom" –
a code phrase for the domestic upheaval he envisaged. Though he
never explicitly said who would be in charge during these transitional months, it seems likely that the Wehrmacht would have constituted the executive power, since Goerdeler wanted high-ranking
officers to act as trustees of many former Nazi organizations and
also proposed that all concentration camps be placed under military
administration "to ensure humane treatment of inmates." All this
shows that Goerdeler – while demanding fundamental change – was
certainly no revolutionary or violent *frondiste*. Even in his despair he
foresaw only the forced resignation – not the annihilation – of the
Nazi government. He continued to reject the idea of assassination –
just as he would after his arrest six years later, when he imagined that
he might still talk Hitler out of his disastrous policy.

Goerdeler's constitutional ideas clearly show that his main concern
was strengthening the executive power. Once elections were completed, the Reichstag would retain only an advisory function, whereas the executive, despite the proposed no confidence provision,
would be able to enact legislation without any real responsibility
to parliament. Goerdeler preferred self-government over centralized
democracy because he believed that the latter left too much room for
demagogical elements. Generally speaking, his 1938 constitutional
outline showed how much he was still under the influence of his
political experiences during the Brüning administration. His views
were not yet so authoritarian as they would become in *Das Ziel*,
an opposition tract that he and others wrote some time later (1941),
but they pointed in that direction. (Incidentally, this interpretation
minimizes the importance of pinpointing the exact date of *Das Ziel's*
composition or Goerdeler's precise role in it.)[4]

In light of the 1938 memorandum, the problem of the different
constitutional positions within the conservative resistance gains new
importance. The memorandum permits a more accurate character-
ization of the movement's programmatic discussions and a clearer
sense of the various participants' attitudes and contributions. Other
members of the conservative resistance vehemently disagreed with
Goerdeler's plan for a post-Hitler regime. In the fall of 1939, Ulrich

---

4 In Wilhelm Ritter von Schramm, *Beck und Goerdeler. Gemeinschaftsdokumente für den Frieden
  1941–1944* (Munich, 1965), 81. For a different opinion as to the date, see Hans Mommsen,
  "Gesellschaftsbild und Verfassungspläne des deutschen Widerstandes," in Walter Schmitthenner and Hans Buchheim, eds., *Widerstand im Dritten Reich* (Cologne, 1966), 14, esp. note
  109.

von Hassell and Johannes Popitz rejected Goerdeler's project as "plebiscitarian," which suggests that the latter must have unsuccessfully presented his 1938 memorandum during discussions of the conservatives' so-called *Programm*.[5] Von Hassell and Goerdeler agreed only on the need to restore the monarchy; Popitz, on the other hand, preferred to leave this question open. Von Hassell projected the retention of many National Socialist organizations, thereby showing a willingness to accept the Nazi principle of *Gleichschaltung*, through which independent organizations had been subsumed or "coordinated" into Nazi groups. At the same time, von Hassell decisively ruled out a return to free elections and multiple parties. He allowed only for a vague "cooperation of the people," to be achieved through local self-administration. In essence, as Hans Mommsen noted, this program constituted little more than a "military dictatorship along the lines of the illusions of 1934."[6] Popitz's "provisional constitution"[7] closely resembled von Hassell's *Programm*, but it contained no checks on executive power whatsoever and would therefore have turned the authoritarian "state of emergency" into a state of constitutional normalcy for the indefinite future. Since it gave virtually unlimited power to a "Reich administrator" (*Reichsverweser*), Popitz's proposal can only be seen as a dictatorship modified by vague promises for adherence to "the rule of law." In short, the constitutional drafts put forth by von Hassell and Popitz suggested less a return to Bismarck's conservative constitutional monarchy than to the authoritarian system of "presidential dictatorship" that subordinated all social entities to the primacy of the state.

Goerdeler, on the other hand, clearly stood in the tradition of the *Präsidialkabinett*, which provoked von Hassell and some of the Kreisau Circle to call him a "reactionary."[8] As von Hassell saw it, Goerdeler wished to return to "parliamentary forms," which was true enough in comparison with the authoritarian command system advanced by Popitz. The constitutional plans that Goerdeler drafted in 1938 and took up again in *Das Ziel* affiliate him more clearly with the moderate-conservative wing of the Kreisau Circle than with

5 In Friedrich Freiherr Hiller von Gaertringen, ed., *Die Hassell-Tagebücher 1938–1944* (Berlin, 1988), 449. This is a revised and enlarged edition of the diaries first published in 1946.
6 Mommsen, "Gesellschaftsbild und Verfassungpläne," 60.
7 In Hiller von Gaertringen, *Hassell-Tagebücher*, 462.
8 Ibid., 347.

the group around von Hassell and Popitz. Elements of his 1938 memorandum seem somewhat more authoritarian when they reappear in *Das Ziel*, reflecting, no doubt, a certain degree of compromise with the other two. This compromise notwithstanding, *Das Ziel* also makes evident Goerdeler's unwillingness to support policies that might give rise to another dictatorship. He must, therefore, be credited with more independence, and the Goerdeler–von Hassell–Popitz "group" should no longer be seen as a homogeneous entity within the national–conservative resistance.

Goerdeler would have had to repress his pragmatic and activist bent totally had he limited himself in late 1938 to "reckoning" with National Socialism through pen and paper. His memorandum closes with the words "When this advice will be put into practice, I cannot say. It is in God's hands. But I need not emphasize that I will do everything to hasten that hour." Since, in his opinion, the Munich Agreement had prevented the resisters from sweeping away the Nazi regime, he said he was now willing to rely entirely "on the dormant potential of the German people to save their own country." Instead of relying primarily on pressure from abroad to influence the Reich's political decisions, he now felt the need "to jump on the ship of state and take the wheel, so that the vessel might be steered through the Scylla of complete political repression and the Charybdis of the destruction of Christian culture."[9] At this moment – October 1938 – he went so far as to ask Fritz Wiedemann, Hitler's aide, whether he might not again be needed in the Reich administration.[10]

Indeed, in the second half of November all traces of his earlier feelings of resignation seem to have disappeared. Now in his letters he again urged his British friends toward new initiatives against Hitler: "The latest events must have made things clear," he urged. "One must see that nihilism is coming."[11] Clearly, Goerdeler's new activism was closely related to the recent pogroms. Beside heightening his moral indignation, this radical escalation of violence made him realize that the radicals were clearly in control and that the conservatives, his own political friends, had indisputably lost their

---

9 Quotations from a letter from Goerdeler to Schairer of October 19, 1938, in Goerdeler's papers in the possession of Mrs. Meyer-Krahmer.

10 Letter from Goerdeler to Wiedemann of October 19, 1938, in Bundesarchiv Koblenz, NS 10, vol. 335, p. 153.

11 Quotations from a letter from Goerdeler to Schairer of November 17, 1938, in Goerdeler Papers, Bundesarchiv Koblenz, vol. 9; cf. also Public Record Office, FO 371/21665 C 14809.

struggle to influence the course of Reich politics. The events of November 9 also added urgency to his conviction that the call for radical internal change expressed in his memorandum needed to be answered immediately. Just as before Munich, he hoped to convince the Western powers – especially Great Britain – to pressure Hitler into a settlement of all outstanding questions, but now he wanted as a condition for negotiations the immediate cessation of all Nazi-inspired violence at home and abroad. Should Hitler refuse to negotiate on these terms, Goerdeler promised appropriate action from within Germany to bring about a new government willing to settle with the West. This combination of foreign intervention with domestic change was an important ingredient in the foreign policy section of Goerdeler's 1938 memorandum, and it is to that section of the document that I must now turn my attention.

II

Goerdeler saw his role with foreign contacts as that of an unofficial mediator with semiofficial and secret connections – a position from which he believed he could steer Anglo-German relations toward a mutually acceptable agreement.[12] He would cling to this conviction throughout most of the war.

Except for an addendum written on October 3, 1938, Goerdeler had probably drafted the foreign relations section of his memorandum as early as June or July 1938. His major concern was to avert the war that he believed German foreign policy was likely to provoke. He believed that a "peaceful agreement" with the other European powers, particularly Great Britain, might bring about a satisfactory accommodation of "vital German interests." These included gaining colonial concessions, strengthening the mark, resolving the Sudetenland question, and eliminating the Polish Corridor, which, for the West Prussian Goerdeler, amounted to a "thorn in the flesh of German honor."[13] (Poland, was a bête noire for Goerdeler – not a country with which Germany should try to negotiate. On other occasions he proposed that a "small war" against an internationally isolated Poland

12 On Goerdeler's relations with Great Britain, see A. P. Young, *The "X"-Documents: The Secret History of Foreign Office Contacts with the German Resistance, 1937/39*, ed. Sidney Astor (London, 1974). A German edition, edited by Helmut Krausnick, was published in 1989 in Munich.
13 Quoted from the memorandum for Hitler of summer 1934, in Goerdeler Papers, Bundesarchiv Koblenz, vol. 12, p. 22.

would be the most effective way to retrieve the former German lands in the Corridor.)[14] Aside from the Polish question, on which Goerdeler was rabid, his foreign policy ideas, particularly his linkage of diplomatic settlements with a restoration of international trade, reflected the tradition of Manchester liberalism that he had adopted. This way of thinking made him strongly oppose both forced rearmament and autarkic schemes like the Four-Year Plan as viable approaches to foreign and economic policy.

Goerdeler's foreign political aspirations centered on an agreement with Britain (which he believed France would have to accept) that would secure the Reich's "vital interests" – even if these interests were achievable only at the expense of Czechoslovakia and Poland. Britain, he believed, would be amenable to this necessary revision of the Versailles Treaty if Germany supported England in the Mediterranean and the Far East. He knew that this concession to England would deprive the alliances with Italy and Japan of much of their strategic rationale, but apparent "common interests of the white race in Asia," along with the "more reliable British authority in the Mediterranean," made this compromise advisable. It would, after all, ensure that Germany's role in Europe equaled Britain's.

Today one can only guess why Goerdeler set down these ideas. After the weekend crisis of May 1938, when Czechoslovakia mobilized against Germany, he tried repeatedly to talk to Hitler, only to be put off by Wiedemann. It seems that rumors accusing Goerdeler of plotting a putsch with the English had been circulating among Hitler's entourage. These rumors occasioned an investigation by the justice ministry, initiated by General Brauchitsch with Goerdeler's consent.[15] This episode showed that Goerdeler's position in the Reich was becoming increasingly precarious, though he still had a few influential friends who protected him from the Gestapo. On the other hand, the very fact that such information could reach Berlin also revealed the degree to which Goerdeler's foreign contacts were entangled in a confused web of dubious mediators, special interests, amateur and genuine secret-service agents.

Toward the end of July, Goerdeler finally let Wiedemann know that he would now submit to Hitler (via Chancellery Secretary

---

14 Cf. Goerdeler's memorandum "Die Idee," written in prison in November 1944, among Goerdeler's papers in the possession of Mrs. Meyer-Krahmer, 9.
15 Cf. letter from Goerdeler to Wiedemann of April 29, 1938, in Bundesarchiv Koblenz, NS 10, vol. 335, p. 161.

Lammers) a detailed, written version of his thoughts on foreign policy.[16] It seems likely that this draft later became the foreign policy section of his 1938 memorandum. The report in the files of the Foreign Office on Goerdeler's talks with A. P. Young in Rauschen (East Prussia) in August show that Goerdeler still believed that peace with Britain was desirable and possible, even if Germany annexed Czechoslovakia, which he believed was inevitable. However, the warning he is said to have given Young – "that Hitler want[s] the Sudetenland even at the price of war with Britain, while the army command believe[s] war to be disastrous" – is missing in the written version of the memorandum.[17]

A few weeks later, Goerdeler and Young met in Switzerland to discuss a possible coup d'état. Although he still believed a German annexation of territory to be the only solution to the Czechoslovakian crisis, Goerdeler predicated the coup on Britain's and France's public declaration of their unwillingness to tolerate any longer the German dictator's insatiable lust for expansion. Goerdeler's hope for a German Sudetenland receded as he increased his efforts to prevent a new world war and to orchestrate a coup with London's assistance. His plans were similar to those that had been pursued since May 1938 by Generals Beck and Halder, State Secretary Weizsäcker, and Admiral Canaris and those employed by Oster and Gisevius in preparing the overthrow of Hitler's regime. The first indication of the existence of a joint political–military opposition aiming at a fundamental change in the system occurred when the military and Foreign Office antiwar party joined forces with the Oster/Gisevius conspiracy in September 1938.[18]

How long and to what degree Goerdeler was involved in the opposition's plans is difficult to say. Undeniably he knew members of both groups. Moreover, the description he gave Young of the situation inside the Reich indicates that he was not only fairly well informed about these plans but that his contacts with the British had given him some role in them. It is not clear, however, whether his contact with the British Foreign Office had been authorized by the opposition. Nevertheless, the information transmitted and the proposals made to the British government through Young fit perfectly

16 Letter from Goerdeler to Wiedemann of July 20, 1938, ibid., 159.
17 Young, *"X"-Documents*, 50.
18 Cf. Klaus-Jürgen Müller, "Struktur und Entwicklung der national-konservativen Opposition," in Militärgeschichtliches Forschungsamt, ed., *Aufstand des Gewissens. Der militärische Widerstand gegen Hitler und das NS-Regime 1933–1945* (Herford, 1985), 263–310, esp. 277.

into the pattern of the antiwar party's numerous attempts to influence London's attitude.

"Chamberlain saved Hitler" was Goerdeler's very disappointed response to the Munich Agreement.[19] Yet when the results of the conference were promulgated on September 30, they could not shake Goerdeler's conviction that a peaceful settlement of Europe's problems was possible, and indeed imperative. In the supplement to the foreign policy section of his memorandum, he demanded that Germany "forego, in the future, attempts to reach by war what could be achieved by peaceful means." He urgently warned against "any adventurous policy of expansion." After Munich, he believed that France had been reduced to the level of a "secondary power" and that Britain had suffered a "severe loss of prestige." Nevertheless, he continued to maintain that an alliance with England would secure once and for all Germany's position in Central Europe.

After Munich, Goerdeler also reassessed the value of the Soviet Union within his strategic framework, thus anticipating the Nazi-Soviet pact of August 1939. An agreement with Russia seemed to offer Germany "supremacy and independence in naval operations," a "guaranteed supply of raw materials," and, if cleverly exploited, "a supreme role in the political and economic reconstruction of Russia." Of course this presumed a penetration of Eastern Europe far beyond a mere revision of the eastern borders of the Reich. In this respect, the Munich Agreement had created a new set of circumstances for Goerdeler to take into account; it widened the range of strategic options he had to consider in his campaign to revise the Treaty of Versailles. The crucial ingredient in his plan to gain the Polish Corridor was to isolate Poland internationally, which might be achieved in one of two ways: either through an agreement with Britain that left Germany free to act as it pleased in the East, or through an alliance with the Soviet Union that restored the Eastern and Central European power structure to its pre-1914 status. Poland would then be left with the choice of either voluntarily giving up the Corridor or engaging in an armed conflict it was bound to lose.

In a tract entitled "Principles of Agreement between Britain and Germany," which he wrote in Switzerland in December 1938, Goerdeler set forth similar considerations.[20] These principles, he

---

19 From a letter from Goerdeler to American friends of October 11, 1938, quoted in F. Krause, *Goerdelers politisches Testament* (New York, 1945), 57–64.
20 Cf. Young, *"X"-Documents*, 150, and Public Record Office, FO 371/21665 C 14809.

said, spelled out the foreign claims of the anti-Nazi opposition at that moment. In essence, they were identical to the views that he advanced in his larger memorandum regarding the Corridor and German interests in the East. He saw the "nonviolent restoration of a reasonable order in Russia" as an instrument for stabilizing the precarious balance of power in Europe – a development that would be in the interest of both powers.

London's negative evaluation of these proposals, however, threw cold water on this scheme, as well as on Goerdeler's "offers" to inaugurate new bilateral disarmament talks or to revive the moribund League of Nations. In light of the Franco-German Declaration of Nonaggression that was published on December 6, 1938, this reception was not surprising. That declaration increased London's suspicion that Germany meant to push Britain out of Europe and to limit France's European sphere of interest to the area west of the Rhine. London was convinced that this guarantee of the Franco-German boundary left Germany free to pursue her revisionist objectives in the East. It looked as if a reordering of the European continent with the Reich in a position of uncontested hegemony was beginning to take shape. Indeed, a new edition of Kaiser William II's infamous September Program of 1914, which posited a German-dominated *Mitteleuropa*, seemed to be in the offing. To London, Goerdeler's project differed from Hitler's only in method, not in aim. And even the difference in method now seemed insignificant: Had not Hitler just proved his willingness to renounce violence, at Munich?

Though Germany's annexation of the rest of Czechoslovakia in March 1939 seemed to confirm Goerdeler's warnings about Hitler's aggressive intentions, London did not respond as Goerdeler had hoped it would. Instead, the pre-Munich situation repeated itself. Goerdeler expected the Western powers to issue a statement demanding Germany's withdrawal from Czechoslovakia. Anticipating Hitler's refusal to do so, he again hinted at the possibility of a military coup that would create the conditions for fruitful negotiation. But since Goerdeler also held fast to his ambitious foreign policy claims of December 1938, it is not surprising that London reacted negatively. Britain was understandably more concerned with its own national interests than with the apparent needs of an internal German opposition. To reproach the British government with shortsightedness or an inability to distinguish Hitler's racial imperialism from the deeply patriotic revisionism of the resistance misses the point, in two respects. On the one hand, it rashly elevates an ex post facto interpretation of Whitehall's policy between 1937 and 1939 to the rank of historical truth. On the other hand, it expects foreign nations to view the opposition's promotion of traditional Prussian-German hegemonial policy as an acceptable alternative to Hitler's ambitions – and in so doing to forget their historical experiences with Germany and possibly neglect their own national interests. The conduct and claims of Goerdeler and other national-conservative resistance figures who importuned the British contributed significantly to London's difficulty in distinguishing the swastika from the Black-White-Red banner of the nationalist opposition.

The concept of foreign policy that Goerdeler developed in 1938 did not change essentially during the war years. As he had in 1938 and 1939, he continued to expect England to guarantee the future of Germany so that the anti-Hitler generals might take action. Von Hassell, on the other hand, disapproved strongly of this strategy, insisting that it was fatal to make internal resistance contingent on external intervention.[21] Not until just before the July 20, 1944, assassination attempt did Goerdeler become convinced that before one could count on help from abroad decisive action must be taken within the Reich.

As for foreign policy goals, Goerdeler held on to his revisionist ambitions to the end, though they began to recede somewhat under the influence of a new Europeanism. Germany's victories in the West and the first successful months of the Russian campaign left him just as cold as Hitler's racial imperialism, and yet he did not doubt – even when the Reich's eventual defeat seemed inevitable – that Germany had a right to hegemony in Central Europe. As late as April 1943, in a comment on an *Economist* article describing strains in the anti-German alliance, he could write:

The antagonism between England and Russia . . . now allows us to use the chance missed in 1938/39 to bring about an agreement with England that might secure the European East and permit us to find allies among those nations whose population today hostilely opposes us, such as Norway, Denmark, the southeastern countries, and even Poland and Czechoslovakia. Like the compass needle toward the magnet, they will turn toward a Germany which respects their independence and their vital interests, since

21 Cf. Hiller v. Gaertringen, *Hassell-Tagebücher*, 128.

their political existence depends on whether the influence of Bolshevist Russia can be successfully contained.[22]

Germany a bulwark against bolshevism, and the Wehrmacht a controlling authority in Central Europe – such proposals evoked no sympathetic reaction from the Allies, except from some agents of the U.S. Office of Strategic Services in Switzerland. London saw the German army as a constant source of danger, rather than as an instrument of benevolent political control. Yet if Goerdeler and other conservative resisters still clung to such notions, this was not simply out of a lack of realism. There were deeper reasons, particularly the complete inability of the resistance and the Western powers to communicate with each other and the painful disparity of their respective interests and perceptions.[23] The resistance thought of itself as part of a frontline attack against Hitler that shared a common enemy and common strategic aspirations with the West. The Allies, however, did not recognize the resistance as a viable partner in their struggle against Hitler; they saw themselves united in a common crusade against a Nazi regime which seemed to them to be an emanation of Prussian-German militarism. For them, the distinction between Hitler's Germany and "the other Germany" was hard to fathom – especially since the foreign policy of the national-conservative resistance offered not so much a reformed Germany as another Reich.

---

22 Goerdeler papers in possession of Dr. Reinhard Goerdeler, April 16, 1943, 8.
23 Cf. Klemens von Klemperer, "Nationale und internationale Aussenpolitik des Widerstandes," in Schmädeke and Steinbach, eds., *Widerstand gegen den Nationalsozialismus*, 639–51.

6

The Conservative Resistance

PETER STEINBACH

If one wishes to discuss the resistance of the German conservatives to National Socialism, one must first consider the central terms "resistance"[1] and "conservatism."[2] Neither term has a fixed meaning, because both reflect the development of German history since the 1920s.

Historically, resistance must be understood as a phenomenon that varied according to the time of its occurrence and the intensity of the political pressures to which it responded. In this essay, resistance to Nazism is defined as any form of opposition to a regime that attempted to control every aspect of political, cultural, religious, and social life. The Nazi government sought to construct an order that made far-reaching demands on every German citizen and thereby conflicted with other comprehensive visions of social organization – for example, the ideals of the churches.

The extensive demands of the Nazis not only evoked the opposition of their traditional and most outspoken adversaries – the working-class movement – but also challenged a number of conservative parties, interest groups, and institutions that initially had accepted parts of the Nazi program. This held especially true for the groups that were the declared enemies of the Social Democrats, the Communists, and the free trade unions. The Catholic church, for example, which had strongly opposed political and cultural liberalism, did not hesitate to cooperate with the Nazis in the summer of 1933, the critical period when the party consolidated its power.[3]

---

1 See Peter Steinbach, "Der Widerstand als Thema der politischen Zeitgeschichte. Ordnungs-versuche vergangener Wirklichkeit und politischer Reflexionen," in Gerhard Besier et al., eds., *Bekenntnis, Widerstand, Martyrtum* (Göttingen, 1986), 11ff.
2 See Hans Gerd Schumann, ed., *Konservatismus* (Cologne, 1974).
3 Ernst-Wolfgang Böckenförde, "Der deutsche Katholizismus im Jahre 1933. Eine kritische Betrachtung," in Gotthart Jasper, ed., *Von Weimar zu Hitler* (Cologne, 1968), 317ff.

Even those Catholics who early on disapproved of the *Reichskonkordat* – the fateful alliance between the Vatican and the Nazi regime – did not initially see the need for opposition. Not until the Catholic youth organizations came into conflict with the Hitlerjugend and the Nazis threatened religious education did these Catholics resort to public protest. Bishop Galen, later called the "Lion of Münster," launched one of the most important early protests of this sort. The Ketteler House in Cologne, a center for Catholic workers, also opposed the church hierarchy's cooperation with Hitler and eventually emerged as an important source of conservative resistance.[4]

Germany's Protestant community constituted another repository of conservative opposition to the Nazi regime. Organized in several regional churches and divided by different confessional traditions, the Protestant resisters never formed a homogeneous movement. Most of them, especially the clergy, remained unreconciled to the disappearance of the German monarchy. They and the majority of their congregations did not accept the Weimar Republic because they were still attached to the traditions of the *Obrigkeitsstaat* – that is, the political culture of the monarchy. Many of them welcomed the Nazis' seizure of power because they mistook it for a reestablishment of "order" and traditional state authority. The choice between Christianity and National Socialism did not become an issue for them until the autumn of 1933, when the Bekennende Kirche (the Confessing Church) was constituted. Up to that point they had tried to reconcile cross and swastika – "Kreuz und verhakenkreuztes Kreuz."[5] This attempt at reconciliation implies that at the beginning the conflict was not a clash between church and state but an internal debate within the Protestant community.

Political conservatism was also highly fragmented – a fact that makes this phenomenon hard to pin down. It was represented not only by the conservative political parties but also by small rightist groups and circles like the *Tatkreis* (action circle) that formed around Hans Zehrer. The German nationalists associated with Alfred Hugenberg hoped to constrain and "domesticate" Hitler by surrounding him with a conservative coalition in 1933. Yet their efforts to do so were quickly thwarted by Hitler's stunning *Gleichschaltung*

---

4 See the excellent collection of essays by Ludwig Volk, *Katholische Kirche und Nationalsozialismus* (Mainz, 1987).
5 Klaus Scholder, *Die Kirchen und das Dritte Reich*: vol. 1, *Vorgeschichte und Zeit der Illusionen 1918–1934* (Frankfurt, 1977); Scholder, *Die Kirchen und das Dritte Reich*: vol. 2, *Das Jahr der Ernüchterung 1934 – Barmen und Rom* (Berlin, 1985).

(coordination) of all potential rivals for power, including conservative parties, newspapers, and organizations. Hitler's foreign political successes, which seemed somewhat to compensate for his domestic hard line, also helped to paralyze the conservatives. After all, they favored not only his *Reichskonkordat* with the Vatican but also his attack on the Versailles system and his rearmament program. With these accomplishments, the Führer was well on the way to realizing the Old Right's dream of social harmony combined with the reassertion of German power.

Given this situation, it is not surprising that conservatives did not play a significant role in the anti-Nazi opposition that emerged in the first phase of the Third Reich. Opposition was largely the prerogative of working classes and leftist organizations. Only a few members of the Young German Order[6] and the National Bolshevist movement – left-leaning conservatives who had no access to the centers of political power – took an active part in the early resistance efforts. Most of these, moreover, eventually joined Communist resistance groups, as did, for example, Harro Schulze-Boysen and Beppo Römer. Not before the summer of 1934 did Edgar Jung[7] and Gero von Boese try to establish a conservative nucleus of opposition within the Hitler government. Both of them were murdered by the Nazis in the so-called Röhm putsch of June 1934.

By this time many of the anti-Nazi German conservatives undoubtedly sensed their dilemma: They had supported a system that they continued partly to admire but also had begun to despise. They tried to clarify their position by talking over their views privately in groups composed primarily of professional colleagues. It soon emerged that most of them disapproved of Hitler's apparent determination to gain political hegemony in Europe through war, a goal they found too risky, given what they saw as the inadequate rearmament of the Wehrmacht. Their opposition to Hitler's war plans peaked in 1938, at the time of the Czechoslovakian crisis and the Munich Conference.

Significantly, the conservative resistance that began to crystallize in the late thirties around foreign policy considerations did not systematically address such important domestic injustices as the suppression of the working-class movement and the persecution of the Jews. A domestic issue that did command the conservatives'

6 Robert Werner, *Der Jungdeutsche Orden im Widerstand 1933–1945* (Munich, 1980).
7 Edmund Forschback, *Edgar J. Jung – ein konservativer Revolutionär* (Pfullingen, 1984).

attention was a conflict between the Confessing Church and the Nazi regime over the admissibility of baptized Jews into the church. The Nazis' rejection of this practice was an article of racist faith, while for Protestants it was a question of "spiritual" freedom and thus a starting point for more open opposition to the regime on the part of some conservatives. Initial qualified support gave way to partial opposition, then committed resistance. Martin Niemöller, a former nationalist submarine captain who became a leading figure in the Confessing Church, personified this transition especially clearly.

Another branch of the conservative opposition materialized in the late thirties in response to what its adherents perceived as the growing incompetence of the Nazi regime. Carl Goerdeler and General Ludwig Beck,[8] for example, objected more to Hitler's methods than to his goals. They were not – unlike the working-class resistance – driven to their position by Nazi terror and oppression; rather, they experienced personal persecution as a result of their action.

Many of these belated conservative resisters had originally occupied important positions within the system and had tried to change policy from within. In 1938 General Beck resigned his commission because his criticism had failed to have any effect. Later he became the head of the military opposition, an opposition that was strongly influenced by conservative ideals. Goerdeler, former mayor of Leipzig and Reich commissioner for price control, also became frustrated with his inability to change the Nazi system from within. He organized oppositionist circles and made contacts with other anti-Nazi groups in order to coordinate the resistance in a kind of countercabinet or countergovernment.

This operation was necessarily small and selective, a network of intimate clubs or circles designed to prevent penetration by informers or Gestapo agents. Here, in these groups, anti-Nazis who were still part of the Reich administration came into contact with resisters who had already cut their connection to the regime. These former officials and officers, who became the driving force behind the conservative opposition during the war, profited greatly from the information they gleaned from the insiders stationed in the Military Headquarters or the Abwehr (Admiral Canaris' counterintelligence office). Through such excellent contacts, the resisters were almost as

8 See Klaus-Jürgen Müller, *General Ludwig Beck* (Boppard, 1980).

well informed about state policy as the inner circle of top Nazis. They knew of Hitler's plans for military aggression, of the genocide program, of the Reich's critical supply problems. They were also well aware of Hitler's shortcomings as commander in chief of the Wehrmacht.

The last phase of conservative resistance, beginning in 1941, was essentially a military affair, involving active-duty officers associated with General Friedrich Olbricht, Major-General Henning von Tresckow, Colonel Hans Oster, and former Generals Erwin von Witzleben and Erich Hoepner. Limitations of space prevent a detailed discussion of the connections between this military opposition and the ongoing civilian resistance. Suffice it to offer here a list of reasons that will summarize why conservative officials, military and civilian, moved from insider criticism to active resistance.

1. Some of the resisters had been demoted by the Nazis and then tried to rationalize their personal dissatisfaction by criticizing the system. Figures like Hoepner, Witzleben, and ambassador (to Italy) Ulrich von Hassell more or less belonged to this group.

2. Others found reason for their opposition in their experience as Nazi administrators. They began by objecting to specific decisions or policies, then came to see the Nazi regime as a monolith that had to be resisted *in toto*.

3. Still others were shocked by the regime's cruel suppression of the peoples in the occupied countries and its plan to establish a brutal empire in the East. Belatedly recalling the moral values of the conservative tradition, they came to see Hitler's rule as the empire of the devil. Looking back, they identified the regime's handling of the Röhm putsch as an important turning point in their own political development. Escalating feelings of moral repugnance for the Nazis, enhanced also by the *Kristallnacht* pogrom of 1938, ultimately yielded fundamental opposition and active conspiracy. This trend was most clearly exemplified by Hans Oster and his circle.

4. A number of civil servants explained their opposition by referring to the principles of the *Berufsbeamtentum*, the professional civil service. They felt bound to the abstract state and to traditions of competence and responsible administration. They recalled the philosophical ideals of the *Rechtsstaat* and natural law. Taking advantage of the internal chaos of the Nazi bureaucracy, they did what they could to thwart the system. They saw their conspiratorial activities within the bureaucracy as an attempt to "prevent the worst."

5. At the very top of the government were some anti-Nazis like Johannes Popitz, who envisioned the establishment of a restoration-ist regime after the fall of Hitler. Representing the most reactionary wing of the resistance, Popitz and his circle should not be lumped together with the Goerdeler faction, which stood for rather more liberal (though still nationalist and conservative) principles.

6. Yet another conservative opposition group – the circle that formed in Freiburg around the historian Gerhard Ritter and econo-mists Adolf Lampe and Constantin von Dietze, later joined by Erwin von Beckerath – was animated primarily by intellectual and theore-tical considerations. They wrote an important memorandum on the place of Christians in political and social organization. In another tract, they foresaw the reorganization of the market economy after the fall of the Third Reich. Some of them also turned to social questions, where they often displayed highly authoritarian perspec-tives. Dietze's memorandum on the Jewish issue, for example, agreed with many of the Nazi prejudices and policies, though it did not advocate genocide. Here, indeed, one starkly encounters the tragic limits of the conservative opposition.

7. A generally neglected conservative resistance group was the Association of German Officers, comprised of military men who had come together in Russian prisoner of war camps during the war. German Communists living in the Soviet Union initiated this asso-ciation as a branch of the *Nationalkomitee Freies Deutschland*.[9] The officers associated with General Seydlitz, and later General Paulus, who were connected to this group wanted to conserve the German national state within the borders of 1937 or 1938. In this respect their ambitions were perfectly compatible with those of the conservative political and military resisters in Berlin. These two factions could never work together, however, because the Berlin conservatives regarded the Moscow-based association as an instrument of Stalin's foreign policy. As late as 1944, Adam von Trott studied the program of the National Committee as a key to Soviet intentions toward postwar Germany.

8. Finally, there was a small conservative resistance group that emerged out of the tradition of German geopolitics. Taking as their primary reference point Germany's central location in Europe, this

9 Bodo Scheurig, *Freies Deutschland. Das Nationalkomitee und der Bund Deutscher Offiziere in der Sowjetunion 1943–1945* (Cologne, 1984).

faction's adherents defended the Reich's search for continental hegemony and for world power through colonies. Quixotically enough,
these men put their faith for a time in Rudolf Hess, a student of
geopolitics. Their only adherent of lasting note was Hess's political
adviser, Albrecht Haushofer, who wrote (just before his murder by
the Nazis in 1945) the moving *Moabiter Sonette*.

9. All the factions, small groups, and circles just discussed faded
into insignificance after early 1944, when members of the so-called
Kreisau Circle like Count Peter Yorck von Wartenburg finally found
ways of broadening the base, the principles, and the appeal of conservative anti-Nazism. Yorck threw off the restrictive ideals of the
corporate state and (under the influence of fellow conspirator Count
Helmuth James von Moltke) put forth more liberal principles of
state organization and self-government. This enabled him to establish connections with members of the working–class resistance like
Julius Leber and Wilhelm Leuschner. Together the men of the
Kreisau Circle set about designing a new European order that
aimed at overcoming the divisive traditions and claims of the old
nation-state.

Having examined the various conservative resistance factions and
their motivations, it is now necessary to try to place conservative
anti-Nazism within the framework of the German resistance movement as a whole. Though they played an important role in resistance
activities between 1938 and 1942, the conservatives gradually lost
their influence during the last years of the war. Horrified by the
conflict's escalating destruction, individual resisters like Tresckow,
Stauffenberg, and Hofacker finally broke out of their isolation and
launched a desperate joint effort to overthrow the hated regime.
Their moral commitment prompted them to act without regard for
personal consequences or even for their chances of success. They
were out to destroy the regime, not to reform it according to conservative values. Deep reservations within the resistance movement
regarding the restorationist program of Goerdeler and von Hassell
make clear that in 1944 Stauffenberg and the other dedicated conspirators, especially those of the Kreisau Circle, were not willing to
accept the leadership of the traditional conservatives. They knew that
the conservatives would never succeed in gaining broad support in
German society, that their ties to nonconservative elements of the
German middle class were too tenuous, that their connections to
the working classes, still represented by the Social Democrats and

the Communists, were virtually nonexistent. The conservatives could not compete with representatives of the Catholic workers' movement like Bernhard Letterhaus or Catholic social reformers like Jakob Kaiser, not to mention those anti-Nazis who had their roots in the socialist trade-union movement or the Center party. In addition to such questions of social policy, foreign policy considerations also helped to isolate the conservative resisters. They were unwilling to come to terms with the Allies' demands for an unconditional surrender or with the probability that postwar Germany would be divided into occupation zones. Debates within the resistance over whether Germany should commit itself to the West or the East anticipated controversies over alignment during the occupation period and Cold War.

Preoccupied with questions of national restoration, the conservative resisters remained relatively indifferent to the human crimes committed by Nazis. Though they were not in agreement with the Nazis' solution to the "Jewish Question," the "Final Solution" was by no means a prime factor in motivating their resistance. In this respect they differed from the Kreisau Circle, which drew up a plan for the eventual punishment of the Nazi *Rechtsschänder* – the abusers of moral law.

Of course most members of the conservative resistance did not live to see the final collapse of the regime they had come – albeit belatedly – to oppose. Some of them – like Berlin police chief Count Wolf Heinrich Helldorf and deputy chief Count Fritz von der Schulenberg – were still in the service of the regime when they were executed. Conservative military officers, members of the Goerdeler group, aristocrats belonging to such anti-Nazi societies as the Sperr circle and the Mittwochsgesellschaft were killed for having engaged in "high treason."

What was the broader significance of the cause for which these men died? Certainly we should respect the conservative resistance's display of moral and political steadfastness in confronting a regime that had abandoned all principles of human dignity. Their tragedy, however, was that their cause was doomed from the outset, for the conservatives sought refuge in the political values of the nineteenth century, rather than turning to modern conceptions of democratic pluralism. That German conservatism was able to move with the times after 1945 was due partly to the Nazis' decimation of the chief carriers of the old authoritarian traditions. The adaptability of postwar conservatism was also a function of new developments in political Catholicism, in the Catholic working-class and trade-union movements, and in what remained of German liberalism. In postwar Germany it was largely these groups who took over the heritage of German conservatism – a heritage that had been severely discredited by the Nazis' abuse of traditional conservative values.

7

The Kreisau Circle and the Twentieth of July

THOMAS CHILDERS

For Arthur G. Haas

I

Since the publication of Hans Rothfels's pioneering work on the German resistance to National Socialism some thirty years ago, the conceptualization of "resistance" has undergone a profound transformation, a transformation strikingly illustrated by the contributions to this volume. In addition to essays focusing on those well-known groups and individuals whose actions culminated in the attempted coup of July 20, 1944, we have essays on women in the resistance, the Jewish resistance, working-class resistance, as well as forms of resistance or opposition in everyday life. This broadened conceptualization of resistance, or opposition, or dissent, in the Third Reich is a vivid reflection of major departures in the historiography of the Nazi regime that began in the last decade. The heightened attention to social history, most successfully realized in the Institut für Zeitgeschichte's ambitious Bavaria project, with its thematic emphasis on "resistance and persecution," and in the growing body of research in *Alltagsgeschichte* associated with Detlev Peukert, Ian Kershaw, and others, has most certainly provided a fresh and revealing perspective from which to examine the relations between state and society, conformity and nonconformity, collaboration and dissent in the Third Reich.[1]

---

1 See the six volumes of the Bavaria project published under the editorship and direction of Martin Broszat, *Bayern in der NS-Zeit* (Munich, 1979–83); the works of Detlev Peukert, especially *Volksgenossen and Gemeinschaftsfremde. Anpassung, Ausmerze and Aufbegehren unter dem Nationalsozialismus* (Cologne, 1982); and *Die Reihen fast geschlossen. Beiträge zur Geschichte des Alltags unterm Nationalsozialismus*, ed. Detlev Peukert and Jürgen Reulecke (Wuppertal, 1981); Ian Kershaw, *Popular Opinion and Political Dissent in the Third Reich: Bavaria, 1933–1945* (Oxford, 1983).

This essay, however, will focus on one group whose resistance, *Widerstand*, was unambiguous, a group that would emerge as one of the major civilian actors in the organized resistance: the Kreisau Circle. Of the various German groups that engaged in resistance activities against the National Socialist regime, the Kreisau Circle, with its heterogeneous membership of East-Elbian aristocrats, socialists, Jesuits, Protestant clergymen, and Foreign Office officials, is in many respects the most intriguing. With its unique blend of Christianity and socialism, its stress on the value of the individual, its preference for a decentralized, organically structured state, its distrust of mass democracy, political parties, and labor unions, its demand for the breakup of Prussia and the creation of a larger European community, the Kreisau Circle's call for the nationalization of basic industries as well as a form of *Mitbestimmung* represented a self-conscious attempt to build on the failures of the Weimar Republic and to forge a new political and social order. It is not, however, the Kreisau program for a post-Nazi state, about which Hans Mommsen has written so persuasively,[2] that is at issue here but rather the circle's role in the unsuccessful coup d'état of July 20, 1944.

Until the publication of Ger van Roon's basic study in 1967,[3] no comprehensive treatment of the circle existed. The standard surveys of the German resistance had, of course, dealt with the Kreisau Circle, often in substantial detail, but the extent of the circle's involvement in the July 20 plot remained undetermined. Although the few surviving members of the circle offered their reflections on the question, a consensus of opinion on the group's activities in 1944 was not forthcoming. While Theodor Steltzer maintained that the circle had dispersed months before July 20 and, moreover, had consistently rejected political assassination on moral grounds,[4] Eugen Gerstenmaier retorted that far from collapsing in early 1944, the circle had actively participated in the political planning for the coup.[5] The lines of debate were, thus, clearly drawn when Roon's

---

2 Hans Mommsen, "Gesellschaftsbild und Verfassungspläne des deutschen Widerstandes," in Walter Schmitthenner and Hans Buchheim, eds., *Der deutsche Widerstand gegen Hitler* (Cologne, 1966), 73–167.

3 Ger van Roon, *Neuordnung im Widerstand. Der Kreisauer Kreis innerhalb der deutschen Widerstandsbewegung* (Munich, 1967).

4 Theodor Steltzer, *Von deutscher Politik* (Frankfurt, 1949), especially 77–8.

5 Eugen Gerstenmaier, "Der Kreisauer Kreis," in Erich Zimmermann and Hans-Adolf Jacobsen, eds., *20. Juli 1944* (Bonn, 1960), 33–4.

impressive *Neuordnung im Widerstand* appeared. With its imposing wealth of documentation, Roon's study quickly established itself as the standard work on the Kreisau Circle. It did not, however, end the debate over the circle's participation in the putsch.

Elaborating Steltzer's interpretation, Roon contended that the group's activities came to a halt in January 1944 when Helmuth James von Moltke, the circle's co-leader, was arrested. Without Moltke, Roon argued, the circle lacked a cohesive center and therefore gradually dissolved. Those Kreisauers who did contribute to the plot did so as individuals, not as members of the circle.[6] Roon's conclusions were subsequently adopted by Karl Dietrich Bracher and by Christian Müller in his biography of Claus von Stauffenberg.[7] They were, however, vigorously challenged by Gerstenmaier and questioned by Peter Hoffmann in his mammoth *Widerstand, Staatsstreich, Attentat*.[8]

Did the circle dissolve in January 1944, as Steltzer and Roon maintain? Were the Kreisauers really the "conscientious objectors of the resistance,"[9] or did the circle become an active participant in the political preparations which culminated in the July 20 plot? Only by examining the nature of the circle's organization, its operating procedures, and its development in the final months of 1943 and into 1944 can one gain the proper perspective from which to assess the activities of the individual Kreisauers after Moltke's arrest and the extent of their participation as a group in the unsuccessful coup d'état.

The circle was first organized in 1940 by Moltke and Peter Yorck von Wartenburg, young East-Elbian aristocrats with a keen interest

---

6 Roon, *Neuordnung*, 287–8. The brief chapter dealing with the Kreisau Circle and the Twentieth of July attempt added to the English edition of Roon's work adds little to his previous treatment of the circle for the period after Moltke's arrest. See Ger van Roon, *German Resistance to Hitler: Count von Moltke and the Kreisau Circle* (London, 1971), 269–74.

7 See Karl Dietrich Bracher, *The German Dictatorship: The Origins, Structure, and Effects of National Socialism* (New York, 1970), 449; and Christian Müller, *Oberst i.G. Stauffenberg. Eine Biographie* (Düsseldorf, 1970), 366–9.

8 Eugen Gerstenmaier, "Der Kreisauer Kreis," *Vierteljahrshefte für Zeitgeschichte* (henceforth *VfZ*) 15 (1967): 232, and Peter Hoffmann, *Widerstand, Staatsstreich, Attentat. Der Kampf der Opposition gegen Hitler* (Munich, 1969), 428–9. Similarly, Michael Balfour and Julian Frisby, in their biography, *Helmuth von Moltke: A Leader against Hitler* (London, 1972), conclude that the circle did survive Moltke's arrest, its time and energies being devoted largely "to the question of cooperation with Claus Stauffenberg" (300). Pursuit of this point, however, was beyond the scope of their work.

9 John Wheeler-Bennett, *The Nemesis of Power: The German Army in Politics, 1918–1945* (New York, 1967), 545.

in social questions and a profound faith in the revivifying potential of Christianity. By 1943 it had expanded to include representatives of the socialist resistance, the Christian churches, and the government service. The formidable socialist influence within the circle was contributed by Carlo Mierendorff, Theodor Haubach, Adolf Reichwein, and, in the final phase of the circle's work, Julius Leber. Mierendorff and Leber had been Social Democratic Reichstag deputies during the last years of the Weimar Republic, while Haubach had played a prominent role in the Reichsbanner Schwarz Rot Gold. Reichwein, a widely respected pedagogical theorist, had been a frequent contributor to the leading socialist journals of the Weimar period. The Catholic church was represented by Fathers Alfred Delp and Augustin Rösch, Bavarian Jesuits deeply concerned with problems of social reform, while Harald Poelchau, a Berlin prison chaplain, and Gerstenmaier, an official of the German Evangelical Church's foreign office, presented the Protestant position. Experience in local, state, and national government was brought to the circle by a number of men with careers in various phases of public administration. These included Horst von Einsiedel, Carl Dietrich von Trotha, Paulus van Husen, Hans Lukaschek, Hans Peters, and Steltzer. Finally, Adam von Trott zu Solz and Hans von Haeften, officials in the Foreign Office, contributed significantly to the circle's deliberations on foreign affairs.[10]

Between 1940 and August 1943, Moltke, Yorck, and their friends concentrated their efforts on drafting a political program for a post–National Socialist German government. As a security precaution, much of the circle's work was done in small groups which met in Berlin and sometimes in Munich, each concentrating on relevant questions within particular areas of social, economic, cultural, and foreign policy. As a rule, the work of these groups was so independent that their participants knew only those who were directly involved in their own small group.[11] Only Moltke and Yorck, who served as coordinators, commanded an overall view of the circle's activities. Thus, although the circle's political program was formally drafted during three large conferences held at Kreisau, Moltke's Silesian estate, during 1942 and 1943, the foundations for these

10 Biographical sketches of the circle's members are found in Roon, *Neuordnung*, 56–209.
11 Interview with Harald Poelchau.

gatherings had been painstakingly laid in the smaller meetings, primarily in Berlin.[12]

By the winter of 1943–4, the work of the Kreisau Circle had reached the end of its programmatic phase. Aside from several papers dealing with foreign policy, the final Kreisau documents were composed in August 1943, and with the drafting of these documents the circle's political preparatory work was essentially completed.[13] Although differences remained, the basic outline for a new German state had been sketched, which they believed would serve as a point of departure for a new post-Nazi government on "X-Day," the day of Hitler's fall.

Work on the drafts certainly did not cease entirely after the autumn of 1943, nor did the circle consider its documents as composing an unamendable and sealed political program, for discussions of the documents continued well into the summer of the following year.[14] This programmatic polishing, however, was the work of Moltke, Yorck, and their friends in Berlin. "First Instructions to the *Land* [State] Commissioners" and "Basic Principles for the New Order," the final Kreisau documents, were in fact products of this editing and reworking by the inner circle in Berlin.[15]

Although the formulation of a social and political program for the post-Hitler era was the primary concern of the Kreisau Circle, its resistance activities by no means came to an end with the completion of the programmatic stage of its work. Having drawn the blueprint for a new Germany, the Kreisauers were able to turn their attention to concrete organizational measures in preparation for X-Day. This change in objectives was to have significant implications for the general working arrangements within the circle. From its inception, a basic tenet of the circle's organizational procedures had been to

---

12 The appellation "Kreisau Circle" was never actually used by Moltke, Yorck, and their friends. They referred to the group simply as "the friends," as I learned from my interviews with Barbara von Haeften and Rosemarie Reichwein. According to Roger Manvell and Heinrich Fraenkel, the term *Kreisauer Kreis* was coined by Roland Freisler, the infamous Nazi judge who tried the July 20 conspirators. Manvell and Fraenkel, *The Men Who Tried to Kill Hitler* (New York, 1966), 206.

13 Steltzer, *Von deutscher Politik*, 77.

14 Interview with Paulus van Husen.

15 The actual drafting of "First Instructions to the *Land* Commissioners" was done by Moltke, Yorck, Trott, and Gerstenmaier. See the unpublished collection of letters, notes, and other materials in the possession of Clarita von Trott zu Solz, cited hereafter as "Materialsammlung."

consult or involve only those persons who were specially qualified to deal with the topic currently under consideration. As long as the circle's energies were primarily concentrated on formulating a program which could be supported by both Christian churches and the German working class, repeated consultation with all or most of the circle's members was of great importance. The large conferences at Kreisau were therefore indispensable in providing an expanded forum for debate and discussion and in fixing the circle's plans in written form. With the circle's program basically complete, large conferences at the Moltke estate were no longer necessary, and after the conference in May 1943 no further meetings at Kreisau were held.[16]

Finding trustworthy and qualified men to assume political responsibility in the different regions of the Reich on X-Day became the circle's primary task in the summer of 1943.[17] Selecting and contacting these *Land* commissioners, who were to act as governors in the initial period of transition, did not require consultation with the circle as a whole and could be carried out on a more individual level. In the same way, revision of the drafts could be handled by Moltke, Yorck, and the Berlin Kreisauers without necessarily involving the entire circle. The active base of operations for the *Freundeskreis* had always been Berlin, but after May 1943 the circle's activities began to center more and more on Yorck's small house in Berlin at Hortensienstrasse 50.[18] It was the beginning of a trend which was to characterize the work and structure of the circle for the remainder of its existence.

The circle's efforts to find men willing to assume political leadership in the respective *Länder* on X-Day were not undertaken in a political vacuum, and these activities brought the circle into increasing contact with the group around Carl Goerdeler, perhaps the most active civilian figure of the German resistance since 1938, and ultimately with the military conspirators. Although the technical preparations for the overthrow of the regime were to be made by the military, the task of providing qualified and reliable men to assume

16 Freya von Moltke, "Helmuth James Graf von Moltke, Lebensbericht," unpublished composition, September 15, 1948.
17 Roon, *Neuordnung*, 257. Selection of the *Landesverweser* had actually begun in late 1942.
18 After both their apartments were destroyed during the same air raid early in the winter, Moltke and Gerstenmaier resided with Peter and Marion Yorck in the house at Hortensienstrasse 50. According to Clarita von Trott, the Yorcks' house was "a sort of headquarters." Clarita von Trott, "Materialsammlung."

political leadership throughout Germany fell to the various civilian groups within the resistance. Though the line between the military and civilian sectors was certainly fluid, the resistance leaders felt that this arrangement allowed them to meet the necessities of military planning while at the same time ensuring the essentially civilian character of the overall undertaking. This arrangement also presumed at least a minimum of cooperation between the two leading civilian groups, and the attempt to establish this vital degree of unity was a major motif within the resistance during late 1943.[19]

It was in this context that the Berlin Kreisauers became involved in discussions concerning the composition of the future cabinet. They were, of course, very interested in the membership of that cabinet, but they were careful never to compose lists which might be discovered by the Gestapo. Neither Moltke nor Yorck sought official positions in the new cabinet, and many Kreisauers believed themselves too young to be considered for top ministerial posts. Though they did not wish to be associated with Goerdeler's conservative social and political concepts, they were reluctantly willing to accept him as chancellor of an interim, transitional government.[20] Their real hopes were placed on a "second wave," which they believed would sweep Julius Leber to the head of the government.[21]

Leber, however, had not contributed to the programmatic work of the circle. He had not played a role in the preliminary discussions or the actual formulation of the Kreisau program.[22] Although Leber remained aloof from the circle's meetings, he was kept informed of its work by his friends Mierendorff and Haubach. While favorably inclined toward the Kreisau drafts, he was convinced that one could not foresee what situation X-Day would bring, and he therefore refused to commit himself to particulars. For Leber, the first goal

---

19 See Hoffmann, *Widerstand, Staatsstreich, Attentat*, 410–40. See also Paulus van Husen's unpublished composition "Report on my participation in the enterprise of the 20th July 1944." Husen indicates that ties between the Goerdeler group and the Kreisau Circle grew more intimate during 1943. According to Husen's report, when General Beck decided "to join with Goerdeler," communication between the groups increased, and the Kreisauers made available information gained through their studies to the Beck-Goerdeler group. Furthermore, Hans Bohnenkamp discloses that in early January 1944 (before Moltke's arrest), his friend Adolf Reichwein was concerned about the recently increased contact with the Goerdeler group. Hans Bohnenkamp, *Gedanken an Adolf Reichwein* (Braunschweig, 1949), 19–20.
20 Interviews with Freya von Moltke and Eugen Gerstenmaier.
21 Roon, *Neuordnung*, 259.
22 Interviews with Freya von Moltke, Eugen Gerstenmaier, and Harald Poelchau.

was the overthrow of the regime. Yet, like the Kreisauers, he considered Goerdeler's political concepts and socioeconomic objectives "insufficiently constructive."[23]

The gap between Leber and the circle began to diminish only after the death of Carlo Mierendorff, the circle's leading socialist member, in an Allied bombing raid in December 1943. Moltke was determined to draw Leber closer to the circle and had therefore begun discussions with him. Those contacts were just warming up, however, when Moltke was arrested in January 1944.[24] The death of Mierendorff had been a severe blow to the Kreisauers, but the arrest of Moltke imperiled the very existence of the circle.

II

Despite the loss of Helmuth von Moltke, the Kreisau Circle did not dissolve in January 1944. Moltke's arrest was not in any way connected with the work of the Kreisau Circle,[25] and after an initial period of anxiety his friends resumed their activities. In fact, the frequency of the circle's meetings in Berlin increased, rather than diminished, in the early months of the new year. In Yorck's small house, the active Berlin Kreisauers continued to meet, and it was to Yorck that those Kreisauers removed geographically from the capital turned periodically for the latest information.[26] Roon's contention that the circle's highly diverse membership found itself deprived of

23 Julius Leber, *Ein Mann geht seinen Weg. Schriften, Reden, und Briefe von Julius Leber*, ed. Gustav Dahrendorff (Berlin, 1952), 284–5. For Leber's views on Goerdeler and the Kreisau Circle, see also Dorothea Beck, *Julius Leber. Sozialdemokrat zwischen Reform und Widerstand* (Berlin, 1983), 173–82.

24 "He is a decidedly good man," Moltke wrote of Leber in early January 1944, "especially now with Carlo gone. Yet he is very one-sided in practical things and places much less value on intellectual considerations than I do." Moltke's letter to his wife, January 2, 1944, in Roon, *Neuordnung*, 234. The letter was written after a six-hour discussion between Moltke, Yorck, Trott, and Leber at Hortensienstrasse 50. Balfour and Frisby, *Helmuth von Moltke*, 293–4.

25 Moltke, who was attached as an international lawyer to Admiral Canaris's counterintelligence agency (the Abwehr), had discovered that the Gestapo intended to arrest his friend Otto Kiep. Moltke warned him; the warning was discovered; and Moltke was arrested. For a detailed account of Moltke's service as an adviser to the Oberkommando der Wehrmacht (OKW), see Ger van Roon, "Graf von Moltke als Völkerrechtler im OKW," *VfZ*, 9 (1970): 12–61. Roon suspects that Moltke's arrest may have been part of a larger Gestapo action directed against Canaris's Abwehr organization.

26 Interviews with Eugen Gerstenmaier and Paulus van Husen. That Yorck continued to serve as a source of information for those Kreisauers not in Berlin is also evident from comments in Hans Lukaschek, "Was war und wollte der Kreisauer Kreis?", unpublished speech, and Theodor Steltzer, *Sechzig Jahre Zeitgenosse* (Munich, 1966), 159, and *Von deutscher Politik*, 78.

its common center after January 19, 1944, is an assertion that cannot be sustained.[27]

With Moltke gone, the role of *Geschäftsführer* was assumed by Peter Yorck, and until July 20 he remained at the center of the circle's activities.[28] Reichwein and Haubach maintained close contact with Yorck after January 19, as did Trott, Haeften, Gerstenmaier, Husen, and Leber. Heinrich Gleissner, who had close ties with Haubach and Reichwein, reports that his two socialist friends met very often with Yorck, "especially after the arrest of Count von Moltke."[29] Trott's letters to his wife from this period also attest to a close relationship with Yorck,[30] as do those of Hans von Haeften.[31] Gerstenmaier lived at Hortensienstrasse 50, and Husen was in almost daily contact with Yorck until shortly before July 20.[32] Leber's role within the circle, despite his rather infrequent attendance at meetings in Hortensienstrasse, also grew considerably after January.[33]

Furthermore, Yorck's increasingly close relationship with his cousin Claus von Stauffenberg, who by early 1944 was clearly emerging as the driving force of the resistance, made him an important link between the military conspirators and his Kreisau friends and contributed greatly to his central role in the circle's development after January 1944. Stauffenberg's efforts to convince Yorck of the necessity of action against the regime proved successful, and Yorck's conversion in early 1944 heralded a new course for the Kreisau Circle.[34]

27 Roon, *Neuordnung*, 287.
28 Interviews with Eugen Gerstenmaier and Paulus van Husen.
29 Letter to the author from Heinrich Gleissner. Haubach moved into Gleissner's apartment after his own had been destroyed in an air raid. Gleissner's apartment was the scene of numerous meetings of the socialist members of the circle.
30 Between January and July 1944, Trott's letters to his wife indicate, as Clarita von Trott comments, that Yorck and her husband "were continuously together." Trott's letters from February 3, 5, and 14, 1944, and March 12 and April 30, 1944, for example, all allude to discussions with Yorck.
31 Haeften's letters, throughout the first months of 1944, make repeated reference to visits and meals with "Peter and Marion," and several letters mention bicycling to Hortensienstrasse 50. Barbara von Haeften states that Yorck, Trott, her husband, and the other Berlin Kreisauers were in closer contact after Moltke's arrest because of the changing political situation. Interview with Barbara von Haeften.
32 Interview with Paulus van Husen. Confirmed by Marion Yorck von Wartenburg.
33 Lukaschek, "Was war und wollte der Kreisauer Kreis?" and interview with Marion Yorck von Wartenburg.
34 Stauffenberg visited Yorck on January 19, 1944. Coming on the day of Moltke's arrest, Yorck's meeting with his cousin, who was to exert a crucial influence on the development of the circle in 1944, was indeed symbolic. Moltke mentioned a visit by Stauffenberg to Yorck on the evening of January 19. Marion Yorck, who was at home with her husband that evening, does not recall such a visit. Stauffenberg usually met Yorck during the day,

As before, the meetings in this period were not conducted on a regular basis. When an important issue arose or an event occurred which required consultation, the word was passed, and a meeting was held.[35] Although the circle's meetings were held at different sites, including the apartments of Trott, Husen, and Haeften, Hortensienstrasse 50 was most frequently the scene of the circle's deliberations.[36] Attendance also varied slightly from meeting to meeting, as indeed it always had. The participants, however, were drawn almost exclusively from the active core of Berlin Kreisauers: Yorck, Trott, Gerstenmaier, Haeften, Husen, Reichwein, Haubach, and increasingly Leber. Only during their rare visits to Berlin could Steltzer, Lukaschek, or Father König, the usual representative of the Bavarian Jesuits, participate in the circle's activities, and thus their contribution to and knowledge of day-to-day developments diminished as the year progressed. Steltzer's contention that the circle's work came to a halt in January 1944 is perhaps understandable but certainly misleading.[37] Only when viewed against the backdrop of the continuing meetings and mutual consultation between the Berlin Kreisauers from January through July 20 do the actions of the individual Kreisauers, which might otherwise seem disconnected or isolated, appear in their proper perspective.

The increased frequency of the circle's meetings in 1944 was a

---

ostensibly in an official military capacity, and the meeting on January 19 probably took place in Yorck's office. Yorck had held a position on a Wehrmacht economics staff since 1941, but he was not inclined toward things military and was in no position to evaluate purely military plans for X-Day. Their conversations therefore dealt almost exclusively with political questions. Interview with Marion Yorck von Wartenburg. See also Helmuth James von Moltke, *A German of the Resistance: The Last Letters of Count Helmuth James von Moltke*, ed. Lionel Curtis (London, 1946), 48.

35 Interviews with Eugen Gerstenmaier and Paulus van Husen. The best example of these operating procedures can be found in the circle's discussion of Reichwein's plans to contact the Communist resistance. That discussion is treated later in this essay.

36 Eugen Gerstenmaier, "Der Kreisauer Kreis," *VfZ* 15 (1967): 227, and interview with Marion Yorck von Wartenburg.

37 Steltzer, *Von deutscher Politik*, 77–8. Steltzer's lack of firsthand knowledge of the continued and intensified meetings of the circle in Berlin is reflected in his appraisal of the effects of Moltke's arrest: "With his arrest, our political work ceased. What happened later was the responsibility of different individuals and cannot be evaluated as favorable or detrimental to the Kreisau Circle." Steltzer, who except for brief and infrequent trips to Germany remained in Norway throughout this period, gives as support for this assertion a conversation with Freya von Moltke during a visit to Kreisau in early 1944. From her he "discovered that our political work rested." For Helmuth and Freya von Moltke, this was undoubtedly correct, but as the latter has explained, after January Peter Yorck did not inform her of the circle's continued activities and she did not inquire about them, because to do so would have been both dangerous and unnecessary. Interview with Freya von Moltke.

reflection of changing political currents within the resistance and renewed activity within the military sector. By early 1944 Stauffenberg had clearly replaced Goerdeler as the driving force of the resistance, and between January and July 20 his political influence with the civilian groups grew rapidly.[38] With the emergence of Stauffenberg and his increasingly close ties with Yorck and Trott, the Kreisau Circle found itself drawn into the very heart of the active conspiracy against Hitler.

The Kreisauers, it should be emphasized, were never merely passive observers or lofty idealists disdaining action while planning for a post-Nazi era, as they are so often portrayed. Although the Kreisauers were divided on the issue of assassination, the years 1942–3 were witness to numerous attempts on their part to persuade influential military leaders to overthrow the regime. Moltke and Yorck were particularly active in this regard, despite their disavowal of political murder.[39] Trott's discussions with British and American diplomatic contacts in Sweden and Switzerland were also intended to contribute to foreign acceptance of a new German government after a successful putsch.[40] Religious and ethical considerations held Moltke, Yorck, Steltzer, and Haeften back from endorsing assassination, and fear of a new stab-in-the-back legend also created misgivings in the circle.[41] Moreover, the continued procrastination of the generals eventually drove Moltke to the conclusion that no action could be expected from them at all, and his disgust with their indecision mounted with each passing month.[42]

Moltke, however, was arrested just as Stauffenberg was emerging as the central figure of the conspiracy, and the question of what role Moltke might have played in the months before July 20 is now

38 Müller, *Oberst i.G. Stauffenberg*, 408 and 402. Müller emphasizes, however, that Stauffenberg had by no means assumed a position of political dominance within the resistance.
39 Countess von Moltke and Countess Yorck von Wartenburg, unpublished composition, 1945. "Since 1942 attempts had repeatedly been made to establish contact, usually through persons like Friedrich von der Schulenburg and Ulrich Wilhelm von Schwerin, with officers who were ready to execute a *Staatsstreich*." In his unpublished report, Husen also adds that "the *Kreisauer Kreis* had always been in close connection with the military circles, especially through Yorck.... When General Beck decided to join with Goerdeler – he regarded our ideas as a bit too newfangled – we put ourselves at their disposal, with regard to our persons and the results of our studies."
40 Hoffmann, *Widerstand, Staatsstreich, Attentat*, 428. Hoffmann is correct in observing that Moltke's trips to Sweden and Turkey should also be viewed in this light. See also Roon, *Neuordnung*, 278–86.
41 Ibid., 285.
42 Countess von Moltke, "Helmuth James Graf von Moltke, Lebensbericht," unpublished.

of course merely a matter for speculation. But the activities of his Kreisau friends in Berlin, even those who harbored reservations about the *Attentat*, give overwhelming evidence of their acceptance, if not unreserved support, of assassination.[43]

Yorck, who was in increasingly close contact with his cousin in early 1944, became one of Stauffenberg's best friends and one of his most trusted political advisers in matters of administrative, social, and cultural reform.[44] Stauffenberg agreed with Yorck and the Kreisauers on the crucial role of Christianity in a revived German society, and their discussions of internal reform continued into June.[45] Along with Fritz von der Schulenburg and Ulrich Schwerin von Schwanenfeld, Yorck concentrated on plans to assure communications and cooperation between the military and civilian political appointees on X-Day. Yorck and Schulenburg helped to select persons to fill administrative posts in the new government,[46] further demonstrating the Kreisau influence on the important selection of personnel for X-Day.

Trott was also included in that small group of friends to whom Stauffenberg turned for advice and consultation on political affairs. Trott's trips to Sweden and Switzerland, where he had cultivated contacts with Allied diplomatic circles, made him an invaluable source of information, and he quickly became Stauffenberg's closest adviser in foreign affairs.[47] During 1944 Trott made his final visits to both neutral countries, where his discussions with British and American diplomats revolved around the question which had dominated his discussions with them since 1942: What policy would the Allies adopt in regard to a new German government following the overthrow of the Nazi regime? The disappointing results of those

---

43 Basing his conclusions on Roon, *Neuordnung*, Müller claims that the Kreisau Circle "as such" played a small role in Stauffenberg's calculations because Moltke's arrest meant the end of the circle's work and because of the circle's "basic conviction" that they should act only after Hitler was dead. Like Roon's, Müller's treatment of the Kreisau Circle suffers from an overemphasis on the role of Moltke and the concomitant assumption that Moltke's personal convictions were those of the entire circle. Müller, *Oberst i.G. Stauffenberg*, 366–9.

44 Eberhard Zeller, *Geist der Freiheit. Der 20. Juli* (Munich, 1965), 293, and Joachim Kramarz, *Stauffenberg, 15. November 1907–20. Juli 1944. Das Leben eines Offiziers* (Frankfurt, 1965), 137.

45 Karl Heinrich Peter, ed., *Spiegelbild einer Verschwörung. Die Kaltenbrunner-Berichte an Bormann und Hitler über das Attentat vom 20. Juli 1944. Geheime Dokumente aus dem ehemaligen Reichssicherheitshauptamt* (Stuttgart, 1961), 167.

46 Ibid., 110. Also see Yorck's testimony before the Volksgerichtshof, in E. Büdde und P. Lütschess, *Die Wahrheit über den 20. Juli* (Dusseldorf, 1953), 86.

47 Müller, *Oberst i.G. Stauffenberg*, 379.

discussions were reported not only to his Kreisau friends but to Stauffenberg as well.[48]

While Trott was absorbed in questions of foreign policy, another Kreisauer, Hans von Haeften, also accepted a more active role in the unfolding conspiracy. Although still troubled by deep religious misgivings about assassination, Haeften in 1944 accepted responsibility for the reorganization of the Foreign Office and was to secure its control on X-Day. This meant selecting reliable officials to function in the Foreign Office during the transitional phase. He was also to assume the position of state secretary in the new government. Since he shared an apartment with his brother Werner, who was Stauffenberg's aide, Haeften remained well informed of Stauffenberg's activities.[49]

Paulus van Husen and Eugen Gerstenmaier, close friends of Yorck, also remained active members of the circle after January 19. Husen was in regular contact with Yorck, and in early July, at Yorck's request, agreed to assume the post of state secretary in the interior ministry after the coup. Although Gerstenmaier was not tapped to take an official position in the new government, he also remained a regular participant in the circle's discussions at Hortensienstrasse 50 and joined Yorck and the other conspirators at the coup headquarters in the Bendlerstrasse on July 20.[50]

While the role of those Kreisauers who did not live near Berlin diminished during 1944, Julius Leber was drawn ever closer to the circle. Though he had always remained in close contact with Reichwein and Haubach, he became more intimately acquainted with Yorck and Trott during this period. In April, when Hans Lukaschek visited Yorck at the latter's estate in Silesia, Yorck reported that "in our circle Leber is stepping very much into the foreground."[51] Moreover, along with Yorck and Trott, Leber became one of

---

48 Trott's negotiations with Allied agents in Sweden and Switzerland, which dealt primarily with the issue of unconditional surrender, have been investigated at great length by a number of scholars. Although questionable in interpretation, Christopher Sykes's *Troubled Loyalty: A Biography of Adam von Trott zu Solz* (London, 1968), offers the most comprehensive treatment of Trott's foreign contacts. See also Henrik Lindgren, "Adam von Trotts Reisen nach Schweden 1942–1944. Ein Beitrag zur Frage der Auslandsverbindungen des deutschen Widerstandes," *VfZ* 18 (1970): 274–91, and Klemens von Klemperer's forthcoming work on the foreign policy concepts and foreign contacts of the various resistance groups.
49 Barbara von Haeften, interview with the author and letter to the author.
50 Husen, "Report on my participation in the enterprise of the 20. July 1944."
51 Lukaschek, "Was war und wollte der Kreisauer Kreis?"

Stauffenberg's closest civilian collaborators and, eventually, his choice for chancellor of the new government.[52]

Leber's socialist friends Theo Haubach and Adolf Reichwein also played significant roles in the last phase of the circle's work. Both were among the Kreisauers who participated regularly in the meetings at Hortensienstrasse 50 after the arrest of Moltke. Along with Gerstenmaier, Haubach continued to take an interest in refining and editing the Kreisau documents in an effort to keep them relevant to the current situation, although as the months passed work on the documents dwindled.[53] Through Leber and Yorck, Haubach was aware of Stauffenberg's plans, and after July 5 he saw Stauffenberg more often.[54] Haubach was to assume the direction of the information agency in the new government.[55]

Adolf Reichwein was not to hold a position in the new government, but he was active on another front of considerable importance. Throughout 1944 Reichwein had pressed relentlessly for the establishment of contacts with the underground Communist party, and in late June his efforts proved successful. This issue had been debated with increasing frequency since January, with Leber and Reichwein consistently emphasizing the desirability of Communist representation within a broadly based *Volksfront*. They were convinced that the viability of a new German government in the crucial period following its assumption of power depended on the solidarity of the political forces of the resistance. Only a broad people's movement, Leber argued, would be strong enough to challenge the Nazis, and without the cooperation of the Communists such a unified popular front would be impossible. Moreover, both Leber and Reichwein hoped that Communist participation would create an effective counterweight to the conservative influences within the conspiracy.[56]

Through friends in Jena, Reichwein had made contact with the Communist organization led by Theodor Neubauer and Magnus Poser, and he also sought to begin talks with members of the Berlin Communist party Central Committee.[57] By late June, after much debate, the stage was set for a meeting between Leber, Reichwein,

---

52 Müller, *Oberst i.G. Stauffenberg*, 375; Kramarz, *Stauffenberg*, 173.
53 Interview with Eugen Gerstenmaier.
54 Letter to the author from Heinrich Gleissner.
55 Hoffmann, *Widerstand, Staatsstreich, Attentat*, 436.
56 Interview with Rosemarie Reichwein. See also Annadore Leber, "Dr. Leber und Stauffenberg," *Telegraf*, June 16, 1946; Franz Josef Furtwängler, *Männer, die ich sah und kannte* (Hamburg, 1951), 215; and Roon, *Neuordnung*, 275.
57 Kurt Finker, *Stauffenberg und der 20. Juli 1944* (Berlin, 1967), 175–6, and interview with Rosemarie Reichwein.

and members of the committee. The question of whether they would meet their Communist counterparts as individuals or with the support of the circle was settled at a meeting in the Hortensienstrasse house on June 21. The meeting, which was attended by Yorck, Reichwein, Leber, Haubach, Husen, and Lukaschek, ended with the circle's somewhat reluctant support for the move. The uneasiness of the Kreisauers about the alliance with the Communists, which the circle endorsed in principle, sprang from a well-founded fear of Gestapo infiltration of the Communist underground, not from a political reluctance to integrate the Communists into the gathering conspiracy.[58]

The meeting took place on the following evening, and although a second discussion was arranged for July 4, Leber became suspicious and decided not to attend. Reichwein, however, was intent on continuing the talks. Despite the obvious risks involved, the rudimentary foundations for further discussion seemed to have been laid, and he was hesitant to let the talks lapse.[59] Thus, on the evening of July 3, Reichwein visited Yorck in the Hortensienstrasse for a final discussion before meeting with the Communists.[60] Once again, before an important step was to be taken, Yorck was consulted.

On the following day, Gottfried von Nostitz, having just arrived in Berlin from his post at the German consulate in Geneva, was invited to dine with his friends Trott and Haeften at the latter's apartment. On his last visit to Switzerland Trott had indicated to Nostitz that a putsch was in the making and had spoken enthusiastically about Stauffenberg. Trott had assured him that at the appropriate time some pretext would be found to have him summoned to Berlin. Trott, Haeften, and Nostitz were joined that evening by Yorck, and during and after dinner the imminence of X-Day was discussed. Yorck seemed particularly well informed and led the

58 Hans Lukaschek, "Widerstand im Dritten Reich," *Erziehung und Beruf* 9 (1959): 95. Interview with Paulus van Husen. Husen insists that the anxiety which Reichwein's plans evoked stemmed more from a fear of Gestapo penetration of Communist circles than from ideological considerations.

59 Gerhard Nitzsche, *Die Saekow-Jacob-Bästlein Gruppe* (Berlin, 1957). It is scandalous that there is no major examination of the Communist resistance in Germany available in English. Allan Merson's *Communist Resistance in Nazi Germany* (London, 1985) is a welcome beginning, though it is unfortunately marred by a highly ideological and polemical perspective. See also Tim Mason, "Workers' Opposition in Nazi Germany," *History Workshop Journal* 11 (1981): 120–37. The best treatment remains Detlev Peukert, *Die KPD im Widerstand. Verfolgung und Untergrundarbeit an Rhein und Ruhr, 1933–1945* (Wuppertal, 1980).

60 Interview with Rosemarie Reichwein.

conversation. Nostitz, who had long known Yorck and was familiar with his previous reservations concerning the *Attentat*, was astounded by the transformation in Yorck's attitude. He seemed to have an air of "mission" (*Sendung*) about him. Haeften, too, had undergone a change but still seemed to harbor doubts about the undertaking.

Late in the evening a message was received that indicated that Reichwein had not returned from his meeting with the Communists. There was reason to believe that he had been arrested. An animated discussion followed in which Haeften, who only hours before had expressed misgivings about the operation, was moved to utter: "If nothing is done from our side now, they will pick us off one by one, and our work will have been in vain." The Kreisauer who had most tenaciously challenged the *Attentat* had at last been swayed into acceptance of the action.[61]

Stauffenberg was informed of Reichwein's disappearance that same night by Trott,[62] and on the following morning he learned from Haubach that Leber too had been arrested.[63] The situation was desperate. Not only was Leber considered indispensable in Stauffenberg's political calculations, but the possibility loomed large that under Gestapo torture information might be extorted from the pair which would endanger the entire conspiracy. The situation demanded immediate action, and on the evening of July 5, Trott, Haeften, Yorck, and other members of the conspiracy who had gathered at the home of Schwerin von Schwanenfeld were informed by Berthold von Stauffenberg that some form of action was imminent.[64]

During the next ten days Stauffenberg was ordered to Hitler's headquarters three times but, for a variety of reasons, failed to detonate the bomb he carried with him.[65] On each of these occasions the small group of conspirators with specific duties to perform on X-Day was alerted. Included in this select group were Yorck, Trott, and Haeften.[66] On July 10, Husen and Lukaschek learned that

61 Interview with Gottfried von Nostitz.
62 Ibid.
63 Zeller, *Geist der Freiheit*, 366. The circle's worst fears had been realized. A Gestapo agent had attended the meeting with Leber, Reichwein, and the Communists. See Hoffmann, *Widerstand, Staatsstreich, Attentat*, 429–30.
64 Interview with Gottfried von Nostitz. Nostitz also attended this meeting.
65 For details, see Hoffmann, *Widerstand, Staatsstreich, Attentat*, 450–6.
66 See Yorck's testimony before the Volksgericthof, quoted in Büdde and Lütchess, *Die Wahrheit über den 20. Juli*, 86–7; Hans von Haeften, letter to his wife, July 13, 1944; and Clarita von Trott zu Solz, "Materialsammlung."

Stauffenberg intended to carry out the assassination himself, but since they were not slated for specific duty on X-Day they were not informed of the date.[67]

On the evening of July 16, Yorck and Trott attended another meeting with Stauffenberg and several officers who were to figure in the implementation of Operation *Walküre*, as the coup was code-named. After a review of the military situation in the West, a discussion of foreign policy ensued, during which Trott, supported by Yorck, advocated an assassination followed by simultaneous negotiations with both the Allies and the Soviet Union. From his contacts with Allied diplomats, Trott realized that a separate peace with the West, excluding the Soviet Union, would never be accepted in London or Washington, and he suffered no illusions about the possible peace terms Germany would be handed. Like Yorck and Leber, Trott considered a total military occupation of Germany unavoidable. After considerable debate, this "central solution" seems to have been agreed upon as the proper course of action, and Trott was to be included in the German delegation chosen to negotiate with the West.[68]

Two days later, on July 18, Stauffenberg seems to have become fairly certain that he would be summoned to another conference in Hitler's Wolfschanze headquarters on July 20. Once again, the inner circle of conspirators was informed. That group included Yorck, Trott, and Haeften.[69]

The dramatic events of July 20, 1944, have been described often and in considerable detail and need not be recounted here. Stauffenberg's attempt on Hitler's life failed, and by midnight the putsch had collapsed. As for the Kreisauers, Gerştenmaier (who had returned to Berlin on July 20, found a message from Yorck and rushed to the Bendlerstrasse) and Yorck were arrested in the headquarters of the coup. Trott and Haeften, who had stood ready to assume control of the Foreign Office, were arrested shortly thereafter. Within days, all the major figures of the circle were arrested. On August 8, Yorck was tried and executed; Trott and Haeften met the same fate later in August; Reichwein in October; Leber, Moltke, and Haubach in

---

67 Lukaschek, "Was war und wollte der Kreisauer Kreis?" Lukaschek was to hold the position of *Landesverweser* for Upper Silesia, but, as Yorck explained at his trial, political appointees were not notified because of the need for the greatest possible secrecy. Büdde and Lütschess, *Die Wahrheit über den 20. Juli*, 86–7.

68 Peter, *Spiegelbild einer Verschwörung*, 497, 101, and 175.

69 Ibid., 110. Also see Yorck's testimony before the Volksgerichthof, quoted in Büdde and Lütschess, *Die Wahrheit über den 20. Juli*, 85–6.

January 1945; and Father Delp in February. Gerstenmaier, Steltzer, and Husen escaped with prison sentences, while Lukaschek, who was tried after Judge Roland Freisler's death in an air raid, was acquitted.[70]

In the months that led to the Twentieth of July attempt, the loose structure of the Kreisau Circle had been maintained and the meetings in Berlin had continued, despite the loss of Helmuth von Moltke. Peter Yorck, assuming the role of *Geschäftsführer*, had not only continued to provide the circle's members with a common center and meeting place but also, under the influence of Stauffenberg, had given the circle a new direction. During this period, as the circle gradually became involved in the active preparations for X-Day, Julius Leber's relationship with the Kreisauers grew more intimate. Although Stauffenberg by no means dominated the politics of the resistance, his inclination toward the political attitudes of Leber and his Kreisau friends contributed significantly to the emergence of Leber as the civilian resistance's most dynamic political figure in the last months before July 20.

The political tensions within the resistance had not eased by July 20, and the Kreisau Circle was only one of several groups that figured prominently in the political composition of the resistance. The assertion that Stauffenberg hoped to install a "Kreisau government," with Leber as chancellor and Trott as foreign minister,[71] is therefore mere speculation. Certainly Goerdeler and the Leuschner-Kaiser group had both played important roles in the developments leading to the coup, and their influence in the formation of a post-Nazi German government would have been considerable. While they, like Leber and the Kreisauers, were dependent on Stauffenberg for the execution of the *Staatsstreich*, they had not surrendered political control of the resistance to him.

Still, primarily due to the rise of Stauffenberg and his close relationship with Yorck, Trott, and Leber, the Kreisau Circle was

70 Roon, *Neuordnung*, 291–3.
71 Gert Buchheit, *Ludwig Beck. Ein preussischer General* (Munich, 1964), 207. Despite the close rapport between Yorck and Stauffenberg, Kramarz goes too far when he maintains that Stauffenberg, "if not in the proper sense a 'member of the Kreisau Circle,' . . . belonged, nonetheless, to its intellectual domain." Kramarz, *Stauffenberg*, 139. Müller quite correctly views this as an exaggeration. Müller, *Oberst i.G. Stauffenberg*, 367 and 575. Müller's skepticism is shared by Hans Mommsen, who contends that although Stauffenberg shared the Kreisauers' political views in a number of ways, he was pursuing his own, somewhat nebulous, ideas. Mommsen, "Gesellschaftsbild und Verfassungs-pläne," 157.

drawn into the mainstream of the active conspiracy. The circle did not play a crucial role in the events of July 20. Its primary duties in the operation were political and administrative and were to have followed the successful coup. Yet the actions of Yorck, Trott, and Haeften on July 20 clearly indicate the extent of the circle's involvement in Stauffenberg's plans. Moreover, the circle's participation in the political preparations for X-Day had been considerable. Since the completion of the Kreisau program in May 1943, the circle had moved slowly from the fringes of the resistance toward its active center. Instead of dissolving in January, the Kreisau Circle had become an integral part of the conspiracy which culminated in the Bendlerstrasse on that sultry Thursday in July 1944.

8

The Second World War, German Society, and Internal Resistance to Hitler

PETER HOFFMANN

I

The Second World War was, like the First World War, long regarded as in a class of its own in terms of death, destruction, and cruelty. It was accompanied by genocidal measures on a vast scale against the political infrastructure and population of the Soviet Union, against the 5.7 million Soviet prisoners of war (of whom 3.3 million lost their lives in captivity), and against the Jews in Europe, of whom over 5 million were murdered. The commanders of *Einsatzgruppen* and *Einsatzkommandos* (mobile killing squads) encountered little difficulty with German military authorities; frequently they may have been surprised at the amount of cooperation they received.[1]

Since the Second World War, the world has become more accustomed to mass killing on a comparable scale in countries in Africa and Southeast Asia and in the Persian Gulf region. From time to time one hears mentioned the mass murder of the Armenians in 1915, and the Stalinist mass murder of (some 14 million) Ukrainian farmers is beginning to be acknowledged even by the Soviet government. It becomes increasingly difficult to brush off these events as irrelevant to Western civilization; we can no longer try to isolate them by chronological encapsulation or by assigning responsibility to "national character" or to impersonal "forces." It is necessary to confront the

---

1 Eberhard Jäckel and Jürgen Rohwer, eds., *Der Mord an den Juden im Zweiten Weltkrieg: Entschlussbildung und Verwirklichung* (Stuttgart, 1985); Raul Hilberg, *The Destruction of the European Jews*, rev. ed. (New York, 1985); Christian Streit, *Keine Kameraden: Die Wehrmacht und die sowjetischen Kriegsgefangenen 1941–1945* (Stuttgart, 1978), 9–10; Helmut Krausnick and Hans-Heinrich Wilhelm, *Die Truppe des Weltanschauungskrieges: Die Einsatzgruppen der Sicherheitspolizei und des SD 1938–1942* (Stuttgart, 1981); Ino Arndt, Wolfgang Scheffler, "Organisierter Massenmord an Juden in nationalsozialistischen Vernichtungslagern. Ein Beitrag zur Richtigstellung apologetischer Literatur," *Vierteljahrshefte für Zeitgeschichte* (hereafter *VfZ*) 24 (1976): 105–35, also for the following paragraph.

fundamental inhumanity of which so many human beings everywhere are capable. The various resistance movements against state
atrocities and crimes – in South America, in Africa, in America
during the Vietnam War – are similar responses; manipulation or
exploitation by outside agencies does not change the subjective
position. These resisters were minorities. But there lies a paradox in
the fact that before such a war begins, the majority in the concerned
population appears to be opposed to it. For example, President
Roosevelt initially experienced difficulties similar to those encountered by Chancellor Hitler in marshaling support for war.

In November 1937, Hitler announced plans for conquest to the
heads of the armed forces, much in the manner of Frederick the
Great's "Träume und chimärische Pläne," as political dreams to be
realized when the opportunity arose.[2] But as Hitler spoke, his war
minister Field Marshal von Blomberg, his commander-in-chief of
the army General von Fritsch, and his foreign minister Baron von
Neurath objected; the commander-in-chief of the navy, Grand
Admiral Raeder, is not recorded as having said anything, but the
commander-in-chief of the air force, General Göring, raised indirect
objections. The bare fact was that Hitler had not received any
support for his ideas at this level of society. He concluded he would
have trouble with this crew, and by February 1938 the three prin-
cipal objectors – Blomberg, Fritsch, and Neurath – had lost their
posts.[3]

The response of the population at large was similar to that of the
chief military and political leaders. Berliners flatly refused to cheer
when the Second Motorized Division from Stettin was marched
through the streets of Berlin on September 27, 1938. The "hundreds
of thousands of Berliners pouring out of their offices ... ducked
into the subways, refused to look on, and the handful that did stood

---

2 *Documents on German Foreign Policy*, ser. D, (London, 1949), 1:29–39; Friedrich der Grosse,
  Die politischen Testamente (Berlin, 1922), 63–9 ("Politische Träumereien"), 229–40 ("Träume
  und chimärische Pläne").
3 *Documents on British Foreign Policy, 1919–1939*, ser. 3, vol. 7 (London, 1954), no. 314, pp.
  257–9. See also versions in *The Trial of the Major War Criminals before the International Military
  Tribunal*, vol. 26, Nuremberg 1947, documents PS 798 and 1014; *Trial* 41 (1949), document
  Raeder–27; *Nazi Conspiracy and Aggression* (Washington, D.C., 1946), vol. 7, document L 3;
  Winfried Baumgart, "Zur Ansprache Hitlers vor den Führern der Wehrmacht am 22.
  August 1939: Eine quellenkritische Untersuchung," *VfZ* (1968): 120–49; Peter Hoffmann,
  Widerstand, Staatsstreich, Attentat: Der Kampf der Opposition gegen Hitler, 4th ed. (Munich,
  1985), 143, 702 note 55; Peter Hoffmann, *The History of the German Resistance, 1933–1945*
  (London, 1977), 109, 566 note 56.

at the curb in utter silence.... It has been the most striking demonstration against the war that I've ever seen.... They are dead set against war." So wrote American correspondent William L. Shirer in his diary.[4]

Hitler knew he must do something about this situation, and he addressed members of the press on November 10, 1938, in Munich: "Circumstances have forced me to speak almost only of peace for decades.... Somehow I believe that this gramophone record, the pacifist gramophone record, has played itself out here.... Now the truth must be stated, and the entire people must learn to believe so fanatically in the final victory that any defeats we might suffer would be viewed only from the superior consideration that this was temporary."[5]

In the course of war, military methods become increasingly brutalized, in geometric progression. In World War II this was in part attributable to the growth in technological potential – to more powerful explosives, greater firing power. It was also a result of the greater numbers of people involved in the war, because the population of Europe had grown vastly since the nineteenth century. But the fundamental factor is precisely the popular support that governments have such difficulty in finding initially. In the course of war, demonic forces are unleashed in nationalized, universal-draft armies – the forces of the depths (which King Frederick William III of Prussia had feared when universal military service was advocated by Scharnhorst and Gneisenau).[6] Restraint had been a necessity when professional armies were small and expensive, when professionals confronted professionals. Now the manpower reservoir was almost inexhaustible. Worse still, amateurs now fought amateurs; and people became intoxicated with killing and with the justice of their cause, their nation. It was this very brutality, however, and ultimately the nonmilitary killing operations, which, in the case of Germany, produced an opposition to the government from within on fundamental moral grounds.

4 William L. Shirer, *Berlin Diary: The Journal of a Foreign Correspondent, 1934–1941* (New York, 1941), 142–3; see also Alfred Ingemar Berndt, *Der Marsch ins Grossdeutsche Reich,* 4th ed. (Munich, 1940), 222; Paul Schmidt, *Hitler's Interpreter* (New York, 1951), 105.
5 Wilhelm Treue, "Rede Hitlers vor der deutschen Presse (10. November 1938)," *VfZ* 6 (1958): 175–91.
6 G. H. Pertz, *Das Leben des Ministers Freiherrn vom Stein,* vol. 2 (Berlin, 1850), 178–88; vol. 3 (Berlin, 1851), 298–322; Peter Paret, *Clausewitz and the State* (New York, 1976), 138.

II

No regime ever governs unopposed. A dictatorship forces opposition underground, where it may be residual or may crystallize into a dangerous conspiracy designed to overthrow the government.

There was an early phase, in the months after Hitler's appointment as chancellor, in which the opposition that had functioned under the liberal republic continued to function, but it was soon suppressed, outlawed, and destroyed by the police. Communists and socialists were rendered ineffective as organized sources of opposition, although numerous individuals carried out heroic acts of defiance, resistance, and sabotage against the Nazi regime. Between 1933 and 1945, about 3 million Germans were held for political reasons in concentration camps and prisons. Tens of thousands were executed, after being sentenced to death by a court; more were simply murdered in camps and prisons.[7] These numbers reveal the potential for popular resistance in German society – and what happened to it.

A few resistance groups managed to remain intact beyond the 1930s, such as those connected with the Rote Kapelle, the Soviet military intelligence service, which operated for about a year (1941–42) with fair success, before it was destroyed by the Gestapo. Other organizations which can be said to have presented something more than sporadic opposition – but not much more – were the Catholic church and the Lutheran Confessing Church.[8] This sort of opposition was no more than an irritant to the regime. No dictatorial regime in the twentieth century has been overthrown from within so long as it has commanded the loyalty of its armed forces.

A new political resistance crystallized in 1938. The new center formed around the chief of the general staff of the army, General Beck, and in the military counterintelligence agency of Admiral

7 Günther Weisenborn, *Der lautlose Aufstand: Bericht über die Widerstandsbewegung des deutschen Volkes 1933–1945* (Hamburg, 1962), 30–2; Eric H. Boehm, ed., *We Survived: The Stories of Fourteen of the Hidden and the Hunted of Nazi Germany* (New Haven, 1949), viii; Gabriel A. Almond, "The German Resistance Movement," *Current History* 10 (1946): 409–527; *Trial* 38:362–5; Rudolf Pechel, *Deutscher Widerstand* (Erlenbach, 1947), 326–38; Walter Hammer, *Hohes Haus in Henkers Hand: Rückschau auf die Hitlerzeit, auf Leidensweg und Opfergang deutscher Parlamentarier*, 2nd ed. (Frankfurt, 1956), 114; Annedore Leber, *Das Gewissen entscheidet: Bereiche des deutschen Widerstandes von 1933–1945 in Lebensbildern* 4th ed. (Berlin, 1960), 21.

8 John S. Conway, *The Nazi Persecution of the Churches, 1933–45* (London, 1968); Eberhard Bethge, *Dietrich Bonhoeffer* (London, 1970); Heinrich Portmann, *Cardinal von Galen* (London, 1957); Gerhard Schäfer, ed., *Landesbischof D. Wurm und der nationalsozialistische Staat 1940–1945* (Stuttgart, 1968).

Canaris.[9] In August 1938, Beck moved to lead senior commanders in a coup d'état against Hitler by forcing a confrontation but failed because General von Brauchitsch denied Beck his support, whereupon Beck resigned. His successor, General Halder, carried on with plans to topple the regime if Hitler drove Europe to war, but the unreadiness of the British government for war led to compromise on September 15 and 29, so that Halder's plans were frustrated.

The most active (and a continuously active) center of resistance during the war was in the Abwehr, the military counterintelligence agency. But they were frustrated by lack of military support. How the mood had changed in the army leadership since 1938 was illustrated in November 1939 by General Halder, chief of the general staff of the army from 1938 to 1942. Halder had risked his life by conspiring to overthrow Hitler in 1938, but in November 1939 he told one of the conspirators, Brigadier Thomas, who pressed him to take action against Hitler, that he could not, for these reasons:

1. It violates tradition. 2. There is no successor. 3. The young officer corps is not reliable. 4. The mood in the interior is not ripe. 5. "It really cannot be tolerated that Germany is permanently a 'people of helots' for England." 6. Concerning taking the offensive: Ludendorff, too, in 1918 had taken the offensive, against the advice of everyone, and historical judgment was not against him. He, Halder, therefore did not fear the judgment of history either.[10]

The Abwehr plotters therefore ultimately planned to kill Hitler first, then move Home Army units to take over the government. In the meantime, the center was active in saving Jews and other potential victims and in maintaining and establishing contact with enemy powers. But saving Jews became its undoing: The center was broken up by arrests in April 1943.[11]

Another resistance center, especially during 1942–3, was in the high command of Army Group Center in Russia, headquartered near Smolensk. They cooperated closely with the Abwehr center, and members were instrumental in bringing about two assassination attempts against Hitler in March 1943.[12]

9 Cf. Peter Hoffmann, "Ludwig Beck: Loyalty and Resistance," *Central European History* 14 (1981): 340–8; Hoffmann, *History*, 69–96.
10 [Franz] Halder, *Kriegstagebuch*, 3 vols. (Stuttgart, c. 1962), 1:133; Helmuth Groscurth, *Tagebücher eines Abwehroffiziers 1938–1940* (Stuttgart, 1970), 236–7.
11 Hoffmann, *History*, 292–5.
12 Ibid., 278–89.

The Kreisau Circle had formed around Count Helmuth von Moltke, in the Armed Forces Supreme Command, and some of his friends, including Count Peter Yorck von Wartenburg. The members, unable to engage in direct action against the regime, concerned themselves with preparing for the time after Hitler's death. Nine of the nineteen members were socialists; five were clergymen. Several were currently serving in the armed forces.[13]

As a moving conspiratorial force, the Abwehr center was succeeded, from August 1943 to July 1944, by the Home Army center, as Count Claus von Stauffenberg became active in the opposition. The basic method was the same that the Abwehr group, the group in the Army Group Center command, and the conspirators in the Home Army had envisioned but had not yet refined: to deploy the Home Army against the regime once Hitler had been killed.[14]

In the last months before the final coup attempt, efforts were made to broaden support for a coup and contact was made with the Communist underground, weak though it was. There was no unanimity concerning this contact, neither in the military nor in the civilian wing of the resistance conspiracy, but the contact was made.[15]

This points to an important issue: Sociologically, all categories and levels of the population were represented in the resistance: ordinary soldiers, professionals, factory workers, trade-union leaders, diplomats, government ministers and civil servants, generals, Catholic priests, Lutheran ministers. Politically, the entire spectrum from left to right was represented. But quantitatively, representation was insignificant. The resistance did not represent the nation like an underground parliament. Broad support was lacking, and it could not be generated in the existing conditions. In general terms, the regime was accepted. The true nature and magnitude of its crimes eluded the comprehension of the majority.[16] The war was sustained by nationalism, by an effective propaganda machine, and by secret-police terror.

13 Ger van Roon, *Neuordnung im Widerstand: Der Kreisauer Kreis innerhalb der deutschen Widerstandsbewegung* (Munich, 1967); Engl. abridged ed., *German Resistance to Hitler: Count von Moltke and the Kreisau Circle* (London, 1971). See also Michael Balfour and Julian Frisby, *Helmuth von Moltke, a Leader against Hitler* (London, 1972).
14 Hoffmann, *History*, 278–311.
15 Roon, *Neuordnung*, 589–90; Hoffmann, *History*, 362–4.
16 Moltke to Lionel Curtis, March 25, 1943, in Balfour and Frisby, *Helmuth von Moltke*, 215–24; Lawrence D. Stokes, "The German People and the Destruction of the European Jews," *Central European History* 6 (1973): 167–91.

Attempts to find broad-based popular support, underground, for antigovernment action were made throughout the twelve years of Nazi rule, only to be outflanked again and again by the Gestapo machine. In the Kreisau Circle, for months in 1943 Carlo Mierendorff called for cooperation with the Communist underground.[17] A final, dramatic effort to establish a broad base of support for the overthrow of the Führer was made on June 22 and July 4, 1944,[18] when socialists and Communists met in a Berlin physician's apartment, but this rudimentary underground "popular front" remained elitist. Neither the socialists nor the Communists commanded a mass following, and through an infiltrator present at the meeting the Gestapo was able once again to control attempts of this kind: The conspirators were arrested on July 4 and 5.

Such were the prospects of domestic support for Hitler's overthrow. One feature of the method envisioned for the coup d'état reveals a great deal about the state of mind of German society and about the conspirators' judgment of it. The Home Army was to be mobilized (Operation *Walküre*) on the pretext that corrupt elements within the Nazi party and the SS (Schutzstaffel) had assassinated the Führer in order to put themselves in power, "stabbing in the back" the soldiers who were fighting the enemy. The army had therefore been forced to assume executive power so that it could maintain order and to protect the nation. But the first general orders and proclamations that were to be sent out by teleprinter and to be broadcast by radio would express a profound repudiation of all that the previous regime had done and stood for. One is faced again with the paradox of a society at once repudiating crime and bound in loyal support to the chief criminal.

III

Several assassination plans and efforts were launched in February, March, and December 1943, and in February, March, and July 1944. They were based on the conviction that someone must act to end the killing and that the honor of Germany demanded such an act, even if the territorial integrity and independence of Germany could not be preserved – as indeed it could not be if the Allied war aims were

17 Roon, *Neuordnung* 589–90.   18 Hoffmann, *History*, 362–4.

achieved.[19] If nothing else, the uprising would document the existence of a Germany that did not acquiesce in the crimes committed in
its name.[20]

This view is reinforced by a look at the manner in which the leader
of the conspiracy of July 1944 proposed to proceed.[21] He was Count
Claus von Stauffenberg, chief of staff of the Home Army Command. He had been preparing to lead the Home Army to support a
coup d'état once a member of the conspiracy had assassinated Hitler.
There was no lack of volunteers, but there was a lack of individuals
who possessed access to Hitler as well as the willingness to assassinate him. By July 1944, it had become clear that the assassination –
the key to everything else – would not be carried out at all unless
Stauffenberg himself acted as assassin. But the odds against Stauffenberg were staggering.

The plan required Stauffenberg to move Home Army units into
government centers at once, as soon as Hitler had been killed.[22] The
Home Army command and the government centers were in Berlin;
Hitler's own two headquarters were near Salzburg, in Austria, and
near Rastenburg in East Prussia – in either case, about 300 miles from
Berlin. From a military standpoint, Stauffenberg's plan to act in both
roles was absurd. A commander was to carry out his own orders at
the front; then, three hours would elapse between the assassination
and the return of the assassin to Berlin – if he did return. He had to
try to survive the assassination attempt and return to the coup d'état
center, because no one could lead the coup in his absence.

Stauffenberg was forced to use explosives with a timed fuse.
Wounded in Africa, he had lost one of his hands, two fingers on the
other hand, and an eye. He would therefore have been unable to use a
pistol with any confidence, apart from having to survive and to leave
unobtrusively. As it turned out, he was interrupted by an orderly
while setting his fuse; it is likely that this caused the bomb to go off
with only half of the explosives he had brought with him. The
bomb, which had been designed to kill all those present at Hitler's
situation conference, including Hitler, killed only one person immediately, although three died later.[23]

There was no reasonable hope that an assassin could escape from

19 Ibid., 263–89, 322–32; 373–94.   20 Ibid., 373–94.   21 Ibid.   22 Ibid., 301–11.
23 Ibid., 373–411; Peter Hoffmann, "Warum misslang das Attentat vom 20. Juli 1944?", *VfZ*
   32 (1984): 441–62.

the security zones of Hitler's headquarters after an assassination attack or even after any sort of explosion. Stauffenberg did escape, against all odds, through sheer bluffing. No attempt was made to intercept the airplane that carried him to Berlin. Unpredictably, dangerous obstacles were overcome on July 20, 1944, but the built-in delay and the survival of Hitler could not be compensated for.

Despite initial successes, particularly in Paris and in Vienna, the coup d'état never gained enough momentum. Late on July 20, Stauffenberg and three of his comrades were shot in Berlin. General Beck took his own life. Nearly two hundred other resisters were subsequently hanged. Claus von Stauffenberg's brother Berthold was hanged, resuscitated, and hanged again, several times, and the hangings were filmed for Hitler's personal viewing.[24]

Stauffenberg and his friends knew that their chance of success was as good as naught. They acted in the face of overwhelming odds, without substantial hope of succeeding in killing Hitler or in seizing control of Germany. They had even less hope of surviving politically more than a few days or weeks, no hope therefore of putting into effect their reconstruction ideas, for they saw no way of avoiding the occupation, amputation, and division of Germany by enemy forces. But General Beck, Brigadier von Tresckow, Dietrich Bonhoeffer, Claus and Berthold von Stauffenberg all agreed: The assassination had to be attempted at all cost. Even if it failed, the attempt to seize power in Berlin had to be made. What mattered in 1944 was no longer the practical purpose of the coup but to prove to the world that the men of the resistance had dared to take the decisive step and had given their lives for their beliefs. It was a tragic fall, with all the dimensions of a poetic tragedy: They sacrificed their personal honor for the honor of Germany. As Berthold von Stauffenberg put it, "The most terrible thing is knowing that it cannot succeed and that we must still do it for our country and our children."[25] His brother Claus put it similarly: "I know that he who will act will go down in German history as a traitor; but he who can and does not, will be a traitor to his conscience. If I did not act to stop this senseless killing, I should never be able to face the widows and orphans of the war."[26]

24 Hoffmann, *History*, 412–534, for the course of the coup d'état and its aftermath.
25 Annedore Leber, ed., *Das Gewissen steht auf: 64 Lebensbilder aus dem deutschen Widerstand 1933–1945*, 9th ed. (Berlin, 1960), 126; Engl. ed., *Conscience in Revolt* (London, 1957), xxx.
26 Joachim Kramarz, *Stauffenberg: The Life and Death of an Officer. 15th November 1907–20th July 1944* (London, 1967), 122, 185.

The self-sacrifice made by the resistance gave German society no alibi but did provide Germany with a moral perspective through which it could face up to its recent history. The conspirators of July 1944 became the most visible representatives of the thousands who stood up against crime and evil. Despair is at least tempered by a glimmer of faith in human decency.

The Solitary Witness:
No Mere Footnote to Resistance Studies

KLEMENS VON KLEMPERER

There is general agreement that, by contrast to the resistance movements in the occupied countries and outside Germany, there was no one German resistance movement. As Richard Löwenthal has rightly pointed out, the Nazi dictatorship in Germany, being native (*bodenständig*),[1] came closer than elsewhere to approximating the exercise of total control. All the more was resistance in Germany bound to be "resistance without 'the people'" (Hans Mommsen); the resisters were "'strangers' among their own people."[2]

I am of course aware of the fact that in turn the viability of totalitarianism as a concept has been increasingly questioned, even among non-Marxist scholars. But if total control was not in fact fully realized in Nazi Germany, if we can talk of a "polycracy," and if there were pockets of privacy – more than Robert Ley's "person asleep" – the dynamics of Nazism, the party's and the state's claim to rule, were totalitarian. Moreover, of course, the identification of the Nazi regime with the national cause before – and even more strongly after – the outbreak of the war discouraged the formation of a resistance movement and deprived resisters of what Barrington Moore called that "social support"[3] which was available, at least latently, to resistance movements elsewhere.

Of course there were remnants of the old parties of the Left, the Social Democrats and the Communists, but they were effectively neutralized at the very start, early in 1933, by Nazi terror. There were of course the groups which hitherto, for good reasons, have

---

1 Richard Löwenthal, "Widerstand im totalen Staat," in Richard Löwenthal and Patrick von zur Mühlen, eds., *Widerstand und Verweigerung in Deutschland 1933 bis 1945* (Berlin, 1982), 12.
2 Hans-Adolf Jacobsen, ed., *"Spiegelbild einer Verschwörung." Die Opposition gegen Hitler und der Staatsstreich vom 20. Juli 1944 in der SD-Berichterstattung* (Stuttgart, 1984), 1:xxiii.
3 Barrington Moore, Jr., *The Social Bases of Obedience and Revolt* (London, 1978), 97.

been at the center of resistance studies: the varieties of conservative resistance, the Beck–Goerdeler group, the Abwehr group, the
Kreisau Circle, to name but a few, and a number of circles of
friends (*Freundeskreisen*), like the one in the Foreign Office. And
there were, last but not least, individuals, more or less "solitary
witnesses," to whom I propose to devote my essay.

My purpose here is not to present some marginal figures who
also should have been included in resistance studies. Instead I shall
attempt to move the solitary witness to center stage of the resistance
experience. I name here Johann Georg Elser, Kurt Gerstein, Franz
Jägerstätter, Fritz Kolbe (alias Georg Wood), Michael Lerpscher,
John Mittmeister, Eduard Schulte – and there were many more.
"Wir waren Einzelkämpfer" ("We were solitary fighters") remi-
nisced Chaplain Carl Klinkhammer, who was repeatedly sentenced
to jail by the Nazis. His bishop was all too eager to disavow him: "I
have nothing to do with this."[4] In the last analysis they all were
Einzelkämpfer – an Axel von dem Bussche, a Trott, a Moltke, a
Henning von Tresckow. The solitary witness, then, may emerge
from my argument as prototype of the German resister: Almost
every German resister was a solitary witness.

As I was preparing this essay, I thought I might open up once
again Ernst Jünger's *Der Waldgang*, which I had read years ago. It
occurred to me that Jünger, though by no stretch of the imagina-
tion belonging himself to the *Widerstand*, was and is one of the most
perceptive and profound interpreters of the resistance problem,
especially in the German context. "One could substitute for the
'No' – which was, incidentally, also the 'No' of Albert Camus'
Rebel – one single letter," Jünger wrote, "the *W*, which might
stand for We, Awake, Weapons, Wolves, *Widerstand*."

"It might also stand for *Waldgänger* (woodsman)."[5] The woodsman is a sovereign person who goes his own way. Perhaps I should
say with caution only "who decides to go his own way," because
resistance is not always a matter of a conscious decision; he goes his
own way and stands up for what he thinks right, even at the risk of
suffering and sacrifice. He does not look to the right or left. "The
church," as Jünger put it – and he might have added the army, the

4 "Bericht von Kaplan Carl Klinkhammer," In Christoph Klessmann and Falk Pingel, eds.,
   *Gegner des Nationalsozialismus. Wissenschaftler und Widerstandskämpfer auf der Suche nach
   historischer Wirklichkeit* (Frankfurt, 1980), 261.
5 Ernst Jünger, *Der Waldgang* (Frankfurt, 1951), 25.

civil service, in general the group, the institution – can give under these circumstances at best assistance, but no *"Existenz."*[6] Entering into resistance entails taking an existential step, and it is primarily the individual's. In an extreme situation, in the setting of Nazi terror backed up by an ugly mass consensus, man's place is in the solitude of the forest, where the decision falls within himself, a decision that nobody can relieve him of. Karl Dietrich Bracher picked up on this theme, writing about the "terrible loneliness" which the move into resistance entailed, "the terrible loneliness in the midst of a mass society,"[7] a loneliness that might be shared with a friend, or at most with a group of friends, but not with a larger group or institution.

The epithet which always accompanies the memory of Johann Georg Elser, who staged that unsuccessful Munich Bürgerbräu attempt on Hitler's life in November 1939, is that he was an *Einzelgänger.*[8] This humble and silent Swabian carpenter, who joined the Rotfrontkämpferbund in 1928 or 1929, knew nothing about Communist ideology. He had no friends. He had strong feelings, however, about the dignity of the individual, which he saw threatened in the Nazi state, and about the danger of a European war as a result of Nazi aggression. Elser planned and prepared the attempt all by himself over a period of more than one year. Then, after years in concentration camps, he, this silent man, was finally executed on April 9, 1945, the same day as were Admiral Canaris, General Oster, and Pastor Dietrich Bonhoeffer. One wonders whether it is the same for an admiral, a general, a Bonhoeffer, to go to his death as for an anonymous man like Elser.

Michael Lerpscher and Franz Jägerstätter, both deeply religious, went to their deaths as conscientious objectors, Lerpscher in 1940, Jägerstätter in 1943. Lerpscher was the son of a peasant from Missen-Wilhams in the Allgäu, Jägerstätter a peasant from St. Radegund in Upper Austria, not far from Braunau, where Hitler was born. Said the mayor of Missen-Wilhams to the obstreperous Brother Michael: "Dummer Bua – wärst halt mitganga" (Silly boy, had you only

---

6 Ibid., 85–6.
7 Karl Dietrich Bracher, "Anfänge der deutschen Widerstandsbewegung," in *Deutschland zwischen Demokratie und Diktatur* (Bern, 1964), 263.
8 See Anton Hoch, "Das Attentat auf Hitler im Münchner Bürgerbräukeller 1939," *Vierteljahrshefte für Zeitgeschichte* 17 (1969): 383–413; Lothar Gruchmann, "Georg Elser," in Hermann Graml, ed., *Widerstand im Dritten Reich. Probleme, Ereignisse, Gestalten* (Frankfurt, 1984), 183–9.

obeyed).[9] And Jägerstätter was besieged by his priest, himself a critic of the regime, and by his bishop to do as everybody did, namely to serve, and furthermore not to forsake his wife and three daughters. But Franz thought, so he wrote to Father Karobath, the priest, in his simple but direct language, that the sacrifices of the soldiers in Stalingrad, among whom, he figured, there were four or five from his village, were to be in vain. His own sacrifice would at least not be preceded by the commission of sin. He asked the priest to pray for him. "God protect you, like all priests," he finished his letter; "this is to a happy reunion in heaven."[10]

Fritz Kolbe was a resistance fighter on his own hook altogether. In a responsible Foreign Office position, he was a lonesome man, alone with his conscience. He was not part of the *Freundeskreis* which, under the protection of State Secretary Ernst von Weizsäcker, consisted of men like the brothers Theodor and Erich Kordt, Adam von Trott, Albrecht von Kessel, and Gottfried von Nostitz. Beginning in August 1943 he served as courier, carrying vital diplomatic and strategic intelligence across the Swiss border to President Roosevelt's special representative, Allen W. Dulles. "Operation Kappa" proved to be of vital help to the Allies. As Dulles saw him, he was intelligent but "somewhat naive," and not qualified to pull off a game of double-cross.[11] Why did he do it? Not for money, surely, but to shorten the war and to save further suffering to the unfortunate ones in the concentration camps. When asked about his motives, he quoted Matthew 16:26: "For what is a man profited, if he shall gain the whole world, and lose his own soul?"

And John Rittmeister was an odd fellow. The scion of a Hamburg patrician family and himself of patriotic, conservative bent, in his early years part of the youth movement, he ventured into the study of Marxist philosophy. Of distinctly neurotic disposition, he became a distinguished psychiatrist. He finally struck a connection with Harro Schultze-Boysen's Red Orchestra group, without, however, getting entangled in its espionage network, and he vacillated be-

9 Stefan Stremel, "Der dumme Bua," *Die Zeit*, June 5, 1987; see also Ernst T. Mader and Jakob Knab, *Das Lächeln des Esels* (Blöcktach, 1987).
10 Gordon C. Zahn, *Er folge seinem Gewissen. Das einsame Zeugnis des Franz Jägerstätter* (Graz, 1978), 71–2.
11 Telegram from Allen W. Dulles to the Secretary of State, April 26, 1944, National Archives G. R. 226, Entry 121, Box 19.

tween an attraction to Communism and the search for an under-standing of the mystery of Christ. "Away from trodden paths," as he himself put it, he tried to chart his way in the Nazi landscape which he detested, trying to find clarity within himself and to help the persecuted, and he went to his death, early in 1943, convinced that by the grace of "the righteousness of the one" (Romans 5:18) he would emerge triumphant.[12]

And Kurt Gerstein, "the spy of God," set out all by himself to expose Hitler's euthanasia drive, which, as we know, served as rehearsal for the "Final Solution."[13] And Generaldirektor Eduard Schulte – not a particularly politically minded man, who belonged neither to a persecuted group nor to any of the opposition circles – took information abroad about the "Final Solution" and about German military plans.[14] His motives, the *New York Times*'s James M. Markham later reported, remained an "enigma."[15] Why did he act? He abhorred Nazism and was guided by his own conscience. But he did what he did alone. He was a *Waldgänger*, a solitary witness.

I should, before I enter into my argument, comment on the meaning and implications of the word "witnessing." The definition of "witness" in *Webster's Ninth New Collegiate Dictionary* speaks of "attestation of a fact or event," of "testimony" and "testifying." The cases that I have just presented were of individuals who acted in solitude, but they gave "testimony," just the same to a fact or event. They acted in the face of, and despite, overwhelming terror. Neither a Jägerstätter nor a Gerstein could have expected to overturn the regime; Jägerstätter certainly not, and Gerstein could at best have hoped for an exposure of the deadly practices of the Nazis. Elser acted to testify to the fact that "justice was denied to the oppressed and the burden [had become] insupportable": He acted in an extreme situation. The latter, while it gave his act legitimacy, held out by definition little or no hope for the success of his venture. The attempt amounted to, not a political statement but essentially a gesture. For to expect even a limited political impact from the deed was out of the

---

12 See especially Walter Bräutigam, *John Rittmeister – Leben und Sterben* (Ebenhausen, 1987); W. Kemper, "Aus den Tagebuchblättern des Dr. John Rittmeister," *Zeitschrift für Psychoanalyse* (1949): 60–6.
13 See Helmut Franz, *Kurt Gerstein: Aussenseiter des Widerstandes der Kirche gegen Hitler* (Zürich, 1964); Saul Friedländer, *The Ambiguity of Good* (New York, 1969).
14 See Walter Laqueur and Richard Breitman, *Breaking the Silence* (New York, 1986).
15 James M. Markham, "An Unsung 'Good German'," *New York Times*, November 9, 1983.

question. All this, of course, makes one wonder whether all resistance in a totalitarian setting is witnessing – is the gesture, no more
and no less. A clear-cut instance, I might add, of such witnessing has
been attributed to the Jewish historian Simon Dubnow, who, in
December 1941, at the age of eighty-one was apprehended by the
Nazis during the evacuation of the Riga ghetto, and, before being
shot, exclaimed to his fellow Jews: "Schreibt un farshreibt!" (Yid-
dish for "Write and record!").[16] In the face of utter hopelessness, he
still conjured up the weapon of memory, of knowing, of witnessing.
In the Pascalian sense ("Man is but a reed . . . , but he is a thinking
reed"), the mere call for recording and witnessing gave dignity to
resistance.

We are now in the midst of the argument. I have proposed to
move the solitary witness to the center stage of resistance studies. In
this case my argument must be a double one: (1) that in Germany the
resister was first and foremost a *Waldgänger*, a *solitary* witness; and (2)
that resistance in the German setting could be a matter of political
calculation only up to a certain point: that the totality of state control
imposed upon the resistance effort the function of the gesture, thus,
as it were, degrading it politically and condemning it to impotence,
but upgrading it ethically to a point at which witnessing – the
testimony, then, itself – became the raison d'être at the price of
sacrifice.

As for the first proposition, it seems to fly in the face of the
direction which resistance studies have taken in the last three decades. Resistance – in our case *Widerstand* – has become the object of
"historicization," whose primary thrust has been precisely to de-
mythologize and to demonumentalize resistance and to identify its
societal, supraindividual preconditions. Certainly Hans Rothfels's
and Gerhard Ritter's perhaps too one-sided emphasis on the "other
Germany's" ethical impulses has yielded to a scrutiny of the ambiguity of motivation among the resisters. Moreover the general
debate, especially among West German historians, concerning
whether National Socialism can be identified with the policies of
the Nazi elite or whether it must be seen in the structural context
of German history and society – the tiresome feud between the
so-called intentionalists and structuralists – has naturally had rever-
berations in the field of resistance studies. Here too motives were

16 Michael R. Marrus, *The Holocaust in History* (Hanover, N.H., 1987), xiii.

deemphasized in the course of argument, and in turn the connections, especially of the conservative resistance, with the infrastructure of history and society were stressed. High-flown heroism, then, or *Widerstand*, while never wholly questioned, was brought down to earth and was found joined with attitudes and positions rooted in traditionalist, but not really liberal-democratic, notions.

Also the studies of the Munich Institut für Zeitgeschichte have furthered our grasp of resistance studies by identifying the halfway concept termed *Resistenz*[17] – to which Richard Löwenthal, for good reasons, prefers the term "refusal" (*Verweigerung*)[18] – a restricted resistance which was a matter not primarily of principle but of less spectacular forms of nonconformance, like listening to the BBC or not participating in Nazi rituals. Alongside the widespread incidence of individual acts of *Resistenz*, institutional *Resistenz* or refusal was generally offered by the traditional establishments with the aim of preserving their special interests – that is, their autonomy vis-à-vis the regime and the process of "coordination" (*Gleichschaltung*). *Resistenz* was a value-free resistance of sorts, and institutional *Resistenz* in particular had a tendency to obviate the need for outright resistance.

But historicizing resistance, however necessary, should not stop short of the dimension of individual motivation. Large groups as such did not and could not offer resistance. The assumption that one can expect resistance *en bloc* from industrialists, officers, or the clergy is altogether fallacious. If anything, such groups are disposed to conform, if not to collaborate. At best they practiced this partial *Resistenz*. But the latter, we must visualize, was a weed of sorts, which may look to us historians like the real stuff, namely resistance, but is not the real stuff, and we should not allow the weed to take over and to smother, as it always has a tendency to do, that precious plant in our garden, true resistance to tyranny.

What Peter Hüttenberger called the *Repräsentationstheorie* of *Widerstand*[19] – that is, the predominantly sociological approach to resistance – tends to stop short of the existential resistance dimension. I enter a caveat, then, against the all too pervasive reliance on the part of historians of resistance on group or class action. Resistance in

---

17 Martin Broszat, Elke Fröhlich, and Anton Grossmann, eds., *Bayern in der NS-Zeit*: vol. 4, *Herrschaft und Gesellschaft im Konflikt*, pt. C (Munich, 1981), 691–709.
18 Löwenthal, "Widerstand im totalen Staat," 14.
19 Peter Hüttenberger, "Vorüberlegungen zum Widerstandsbegriff," in Jürgen Kocka, ed., *Theorien in der Praxis des Historikers* (Göttingen, 1977), 118.

Germany remained the preserve, above all, of individuals and small groups. Of course for their behavior, too, it can and must be argued, certain historical and sociological determinants came into play, but these mostly point in the direction of conformance or *Resistenz*. All the more does the move into true resistance constitute an extraordinary leap into an existential situation that defies historical and social stereotypes. In resistance the individual emerges, though often unpredictably and not always unequivocal in his or her motivation, sovereign. Yes, and here we come back to the *Waldgänger*: the officer as *Waldgänger*, the churchman as *Waldgänger*, the civil servant as *Waldgänger*.

"Opposition to Hitler," wrote Fabian von Schlabrendorff (and he meant resistance), "began . . . not as an organized political movement, but as the reaction of individuals with religious and moral convictions to the theories, and later to the practices, of National Socialism."[20] Indeed Axel von dem Bussche explicitly cautioned us historians against sociologizing resistance studies, against connecting resistance – and undoubtedly he had *Widerstand* in mind – with group action.[21] In France, in Norway, where national interest created a bond among individuals, this may have been a different matter. But in Germany, von dem Bussche wrote, "the individual must decide, and he decides on the grounds of experiences and motivation." In his own case, his motivation was derived from his Polish experience, as was that of General Helmuth Stieff.

The next step was the small group: the group of friends, the circle, the regiment. In the case of von dem Bussche, it was the renowned Ninth Infantry Regiment from Potsdam, which was also Henning von Treschkow's and Fritz-Dietlof von der Schulenburg's regiment. But the small group has to remain the nucleus of resistance. It was Helmuth James von Moltke who so insistently referred to the solitude, the isolation, of the German resister, in writing to his English friend Lionel Curtis. In November 1937 he cited the "absolute loneliness in major questions" that "harassed" him,[22] and in a letter of March 1943, which finally reached its destination in July, he lamented the lack of unity, the lack of men, and finally the lack

---

20 Fabian von Schlabrendorff, *The Secret War against Hitler* (New York, 1965), 34.
21 "Bericht von Axel von dem Bussche," in Klessmann and Pingel, eds., *Gegner des National Sozialismus*, 272.
22 Helmuth James von Moltke to Lionel Curtis, Berlin, November 11, 1937, Curtis Papers, Box 28, Bodleian Library, Oxford.

of communication that plagued the German resistance, citing in particular his inability to use the telephone or the mail, to send a messenger, or even to speak with those with whom one is completely in accord.[23] Isolation, we might summarize, was a major problem for the German resistance, but it, in turn, lent it the strength of conviction.

In the reflections which Dietrich Bonhoeffer wrote down at Christmas 1942 for his friends Hans von Dohnanyi, Hans Oster, and Eberhard Bethge, surveying the past decade of trials, he asked the question "Who stands fast?", and he wondered what scope was left to the "silent witnesses of evil deeds." His answer to the latter question – "free and responsible action,"[24] – leads us into the second phase of our argument, the calculation of success and failure in resistance. By "free and responsible action" he meant not success but accountability to God for the necessary deed. What he was ready to do, and what he indeed did, was, as he outlined it to Bishop George Bell of Chichester, in Stockholm in May 1942, an act of penance: "Christians do not wish to escape penance, or chaos, if it is God's will to bring it upon us. We must take this judgment as Christians."[25] Success, no doubt, Bonhoeffer recognized, in the last resort makes history. But in his and his friends' particular predicament – as the outcasts, the suspects, the maltreated, the powerless, the oppressed, the reviled – the affirmative, responsible action was to bear witness and to have the necessary action understood as an act of penance.[26]

A few months later, in September 1942, also in Sweden, Adam von Trott, who dedicated his part in resistance to building bridges to the outside world and negotiating terms with the Allies that would facilitate a coup in his own country, confided to Dr. Harry Johansson, director of the Nordic Ecumenical Institute in Sigtuna, that he and his friends did "not intend to plead for support or even encouragement, from friends on the other side" but that they wished (he continued, in his rather awkward English) "to deposite [*sic*]" their faith "in the necessity of some such movement springing

---

23 Moltke to Curtis, Stockholm, March 25, 1943, in Michael Balfour and Julian Frisby, *Helmuth von Moltke: A Leader against Hitler* (London, 1972), 214–24.

24 See Dietrich Bonhoeffer, "After Ten Years: A Reckoning Made at New Year 1943," in Dietrich Bonhoeffer, *Letters and Papers from Prison* (New York, 1971), esp. 4–6, 16.

25 Quoted in Ronald C. D. Jasper, *George Bell, Bishop of Chichester* (London, 1967), 269.

26 Bonhoeffer, "After Ten Years," 7, 17.

from solidaric and representative minds in the whole of Christian Europe to make salvation possible."[27]

And then there was Treschkow's often quoted message to Stauffenberg, sent early in June 1944, after the Allied invasion of Normandy had begun:

The assassination must take place *coûte que coûte*. Even if it does not succeed, the Berlin action must go forward. The point now is not whether the coup has any practical purpose, but to prove to the world and before history that German resistance is ready to stake its all. Compared with this, everything else is a side issue.[28]

Stauffenberg then staged the attempt in the same spirit: He acted, in the face of utter hopelessness, to save the honor of his country.

In conclusion: I have merely set certain accents to the story of the German resistance which the evolving discussions on *Widerstand* should not lose sight of. First, the historicization of the resistance should not stop short of the individual; it must penetrate to the singularity of the act of resistance. If anything, conformity, collaboration, and *Resistenz* are of one and the same order; resistance is of a unique order. While I should be ready to endorse wholeheartedly the historicization of resistance, I see the need to voice a caveat to the excessive sociologization of resistance. Sociological analysis comes in a subsidiary way in the course of an examination of programs, war aims, peace aims, and the like. As for the question of motivation, we cannot settle on a simple equation between any group – occupational, social, economic, religious – and resistance. Jägerstätter, then, the *Waldgänger*, emerges as the prototype of the resister. Second, in the German setting resistance was only up to a certain point a matter of political calculation. The countermodel elsewhere for *Widerstand* would clearly be the Chetniks and the partisans in Yugoslavia and the partisans in Russia. The chances for resistance in the setting of nearly total dominion of Nazism as it prevailed in Germany were minimal. Certainly the combination of conformity, collaboration, and *Resistenz* did account for what Father Max Pribilla called "the weakness of the beginning."[29] But what had been the chance for

27 Quoted in Henrik Lindgren, "Adam von Trott's Reisen nach Schweden 1942–1944: Ein Beitrag zur Frage der Auslandsverbindungen des deutschen Widerstandes," *Vierteljahrshefte für Zeitgeschichte* 18 (1970): 274–91, 274.

28 Quoted in Joachim Kramarz, *Stauffenberg: The Architect of the Famous July 20th Conspiracy to Assassinate Hitler* (New York, 1967), 172.

29 *Vollmacht des Gewissens*, Europäische Publikation, ed. (Frankfurt, 1960), 21–2.

political resistance even in the early years, between 1933 and 1938 or 1939? Certainly after the outbreak of the war and especially after the launching of the campaign in the West, resistance increasingly took on the nature of the grand gesture transcending political consideration or realistic consideration of success or failure. It became a matter of bearing witness through acting as well as recording.[30] In this respect, Simon Dubnow, like Jägerstätter, might well move to center stage, together with Stauffenberg, with the message "Shreibt un farshreibt!."

---

30 As for documentation, it is known that Gen. Ludwig Beck strongly opposed destruction of documents exposing the Nazis and that on his urging Hans von Donnanyl assembled a dossier for posterity on Nazi crimes, at the risk of self-incrimination of the opposition in case of its discovery by the authorities.

10

The German Resistance in Comparative Perspective

CHARLES MAIER

I

I am writing about the German resistance not because I am an expert on the subject – I am not – but because brave men and women deserve to be commemorated and because I feel that once again the German resistance might be under attack. It is easy to minimize the accomplishments of the resistance in Germany. More precisely, it is easy to point out that there was little enough resistance there. Of course, we cannot tax those Germans who went to their deaths for their opposition with the passivity of those who did not suffer. Nonetheless, the German resistance has always had to fight for historical legitimacy. May it not have to struggle again? Ernst Nolte has argued that emphasizing "the guilt of the Germans" makes it impossible to give a fair hearing to those who did not choose to resist. Even so scrupulous and critical a historian as Andreas Hillgruber suggested in early 1986 that the resistance, if successful, might have wrought more harm than good by disorganizing the defense at the eastern front: "Might it not be expected that even the case of a successful coup d'état would result only in wretched confusion among the German leadership, a debacle that would press the Soviets to an even quicker victory?"[1] In more demagogic hands, such a line of inquiry can too easily degenerate into a renewed "stab-in-the-back" thesis. No respectable commentator, naturally, would openly impugn the motives of the resisters, but the consequences of their conspiracy (so it could be suggested) might have hastened the collapse and led to the division of the Reich. As in the recent

---

1 "War nicht selbst im Falle eines Gelingens des Staatsstreiches nur ein heilloses Durcheinander in der deutschen Führung zu erwarten, ein Debakel, das die Sowjets nur zu noch schnellerer Kriegsentscheidung vorantreiben würde?" *Zweierlei Untergang. Die Zerschlagung des deutschen Reichs und das Ende des europäischen Judentums* (Berlin, 1986), 22.

Historikerstreit, such a claim would not be asserted outright but merely implied, by open–ended questioning; a moral commitment is deprecated by taxing it with strategic misjudgment. And critics, naturally, will suggest once again that the wrong enemy was being fought by the Western Allies. But the point, of course, is not whether a successful coup on July 20, 1944, would have accelerated German defeat, whether in the East or West. The resistance (and here I refer to all who resisted after 1933, not just the July plotters) is commemorated because its protagonists alone understood that some effort to bring down a monstrous regime must be undertaken by the people whose adulation had facilitated its triumphs.

II

I cannot provide expertise on the German resistance; the other contributors to this volume know far more than I do. But I would like to look at the German resistance in the perspective of the other European resistance movements. Comparison reveals obvious differences; it also allows us to notice traits that we otherwise might undervalue. It further permits us to ask what difference the resistance made, what legacies it left.

Clearly there is one major difference from the other resistance movements, which historians always cite. Elsewhere in Europe the other resistance movements were arrayed against German occupiers and domestic collaborators. Even in Italy, although illegal opposition existed from the time that fascism seized power, mass resistance began only after the war began to turn against Italy. The semiclandestine opposition parties began to meet together in the fall of 1942. There were major strikes at the Fiat works in Turin in the spring of 1943 – the only mass strike organized in Western Europe. But the mass resistance began after the Germans occupied most of Italy, in September 1943. The situation in Germany was unique. Only the Germans had to resist a government of their own, which had been confirmed by elections, plebiscites, and periodic jubilation.

This circumstance helps explain, I believe, one of the unique aspects of the German resistance, at least the non-Communist resistance. In Germany, the resistance was characterized by an existential loneliness, a conviction that even if successful, the collaborators would be despised for treason. To be sure, the social status of the resisters, their political nurturing on the anti-party attitudes of the late Weimar Republic, led to a conspiratorial mystique. But their isolation was political as well as social. In other countries, clandestinity was bonding. Danger and risk enhanced the fraternity of the small group in peril. But in Germany, I believe, clandestinity was atomizing; the resistance vocation (I use the biblical language deliberately) meant separation from one's countrymen. Only primary groups, lovers, family, and cell mates remained. And this loneliness also helps to explain why in some ways the German resistance was so apolitical – or perhaps, more precisely, infrapolitical. The German resistance conveys the sense of a radical Protestant (or, in a Catholic context, Augustinian) confrontation: the individual man or woman of conscience against an inscrutable authority. It is doubtful that elsewhere in Europe a phenomenon such as the Kreisau Circle could be remembered so prominently.

To be sure, I am referring here to the wartime resistance, preeminently the men and women behind the assassination attempt – not to the leftist opposition of the 1930s, the Communist and Socialist organizations that sought to fight a rearguard action after 1933. Nor am I am speaking of what might be called the *petite resistance*,[2] the selective noncompliance of workers, women, and various stubborn and decent individuals who did not want to knuckle under. I am talking of organized networks and plans. For the Socialists and Communists in the 1930s, resistance activities could still be informed by comradeship, and the regime, while brutal, still had not gotten its coercive apparatus fully in gear. We know, for instance, that the People's Court delivered sixteen thousand or more death sentences, of which three-quarters were given after 1940. (Let me interject a personal reaction here: It is a curious fact that when one reads about most horrendous episodes in human history, the more one reads the less exceptional the horrors seem, and they become historically and psychologically graspable. Precisely the opposite is true with the Third Reich: The more one reads, the worse it becomes; the more one learns, the more obscene seems the regime's will to hatred and violence.)

---

2 By this term I mean still more defiant a stance than suggested by the recent German concept of *Resistenz*, which seems so elastic that it can cover almost any gesture of nonenthusiasm. I am referring to outright gestures of opposition, but of a decentralized and nonconcerted origin.

The major consequence of this atomization, this radical loneliness, was a political one – or, more precisely, the absence of a political legacy. What strikingly differentiates the German resistance from the resistance elsewhere is that in Germany the resistance provided so little basis for postwar politics. That statement, of course, requires justification. The opposition to the Nazi regime certainly conveyed a title of legitimacy after the war. But resistance did not benefit participants per se. The Communist party had suffered, but the Communists in Moscow, and later in the German Democratic Republic, were largely the beneficiaries. Socialists had been martyrs of the German resistance – Carlo Mierendorff and Julius Leber were killed; Kurt Schumacher had been in a concentration camp. But even without their personal roles, the Social Democratic Party (SPD) would have been a major candidate for postwar power in any case. And it is arguable that the legacy of the resistance for the SPD became important only in the late 1950s, with the Bad Godesberg program. Before then, the Social Democrats had been preoccupied with other matters: a programmatic collectivism such as that sponsored in the late 1940s, by Viktor Agartz; the struggle in Berlin against the Communists, waged by Ernst Reuter; and finally, the opposition to Konrad Adenauer's integration of West Germany into the Western bloc, led by Kurt Schumacher. But these three struggles were not agendas suggested by the resistance. The SPD, in effect, did not require the aura of the resistance. It had retained legitimacy because of its record before the Nazi period and also because it had voted against the Enabling Act on March 23, 1933.

Nor can it be claimed that the Christian Democrats were identified as a resistance party. At best this was a party of the "inner emigration" (as in the case of Adenauer), not a cadre of resisters. Organized Catholicism, moreover, had too ambiguous a record vis-à-vis the National Socialist regime. Brave priests had gone to concentration camps, and Cardinal Galen had denounced euthanasia, but there had been too many compromises during the 1930s and too resounding a silence at critical times. No – the postwar parties hardly drew upon a resistance legacy. Nor did the resistance groups leave a viable political agenda. In fact, they were a problem in their own right; their opposition was too radical to serve the parties that had to pick up the pieces after 1945.

III

Why was that? This absence of legacy – harsh judgment though it may seem – is best understood in light of some differences from other national groups. Let me read parts of a document that I found in the Partitod'Azione archives in the Centro Gobetti of Turin. It is a political essay, dating from September 1944; I cannot ascertain the authorship precisely, but perhaps it was written by Leo Valiani. In any case, the author writes: "The war, in its concluding phase, increasingly highlights the insurrections of the Continental peoples or at least emphasizes the participation of the masses alongside the great victorious armies of the united nations." The writer then evokes the liberation of France and Belgium, and the Warsaw rebellion.

The enthusiasm of the struggle has been projected everywhere beyond its immediate objectives toward the new society that must arise from the ruins of Fascism. The sense of anti-Fascism as a European revolution has been brilliantly confirmed in the devastation of a war that had opened as a simple struggle among the powers. . . . Every event tends to demonstrate that the social contrasts are those of a war deepened sufficiently to become a true civil war. A civil war characteristically reveals the disintegration of the dominant classes, the shattering of their internal solidarity, and the necessity on the part of the parties to seek their salvation by appealing to yesterday's enemy, i.e., to the popular masses. . . . Fascism is not a disease that can be cured with the normal medicine of the arts of government: A totalitarian disease can be wiped out only by adequate means of total mobilization and war to the utmost. . . . The successive efforts in the other states have utilized the Italian experience: the mobilization of the masses and the formation of democratic governments follows an accelerated rhythm; the monarchs, generals, landlords, and industrialists have come to understand, regretfully, that to save themselves from Hitler they must appeal to peasants and workers, even with the consequences that may follow.

What strikes me about this passage is its contextualization of the resistance in the panorama of an international civil war, whose end result is the triumph of mass democracy. The resisters of the Piedmont thus saw their own resistance as giving them a role in the political reconstruction of Europe. Cut off from the Allies and beset by the Germans during the winter of 1944–5, they still felt part of a regeneration affecting all of Europe. The resistance of the elites in Rome, it was felt, was condemned to failure; one could not arrange a managed transition to the old conservatives.

For the non-Communist resistance forces who aspired to a democratic revolution, the major issue was the future role of the Communist cadres. What could prevent this newly legitimated mass party, so central in the partisan organizations, from becoming the source of a new tyranny? (In effect, in terms of ability to mount resistance the Communist party was the opposite of the Kreisau Circle. Politics was so total a commitment that arms could be taken up even when dreadful reprisals were certain to follow.) For the writer of the manifesto just quoted, the role of the non-Communist resistance parties, especially his own Party of Action, was crucial. It would prevent a new totalitarianism: "All revolutionary parties must throw themselves, without reciprocal jealousies, into the movement; the presence of the Party of Action alongside the Marxist parties provides a guarantee of democratic success and an obstacle to a totalitarian outcome, provided its presence is effective and rich with initiative." Such a calculation suggests a major difference between the Italian and German resisters. No German could take comfort in the concept of an international civil war. Italians, French, Yugoslavs, and Greeks might participate, but Germans could not. They had sought links with the British political class in 1938 but with little result. The English were either too appeasement-oriented, too skeptical of the German efforts, or too anti-German without discrimination. In effect, there was no real Europeanization of the resistance that could help the Germans, for the Europeanization of the resistance would be directed entirely against the Germans.

To be sure, the members of the Kreisau Circle likewise came to understand the need for a reaching out, even to the Communists. But if admirable, the Kreisauers still were only a tiny circle of elites, and their major institutional connections remained the dissenters of the military and the Foreign Office. There was no equivalent in Germany of the Party of Action or of the democratic current that had begun in Italy with the exiles of the 1930s, Giustizia e Libertà. There was no counterpart for the tradition represented in France by the Combat group (of which Albert Camus was a leading spokesman) or the center-left groups that formed the Parti Democratique et Social de la Résistance (of which the youthful François Mitterrand was a member in the late 1940s).

Is this just to argue that the German resistance did not have a bourgeois-leftist component? That would be too simple. It is also true that Germany did not have a partisan army. France, Italy,

Yugoslavia, and Greece each boasted significant partisan forces –
between one and two hundred thousand, in the case of Yugoslavia
and Italy. To maintain such a force required a large territory of
mountains or broad forests (as in Poland). Usually the Communists
dominated these armies, at least numerically. Nonetheless, by vir-
tue of their participation, even the small bourgeois-leftist elites
in these countries – what I like to think of as the resistance of the
historians – gained the moral entitlement to participate in postwar
reconstruction. This moral entitlement was crucial in 1944–5, although it conferred a disappointingly meager outcome in terms of
postwar electoral results.

Participation in the resistance in these countries meant the right to
help draft charters for the coming liberation. In Italy and France these
charters were the products of compromise. They included some
social and economic planks, usually demanding an end to mono-
polies and nationalization of collaborationist firms, of banks, and
sometimes of industry. They asked for the establishment of a social
welfare system. They appealed to a thoroughgoing democratization
of institutions. Ironically, these charters were necessitated by the
fact that Vichy and the other Fascist governments had imposed their
own "charters of labor" in an effort to control labor organization.
Nonetheless, even the Fascist charters of labor had accepted the idea
of collective bargaining and labor relations. The resistance could do
no less. Agreement on its charters was also made possible by the fact
that in 1944 the Communists (following the line initiated by the
Popular Fronts after 1935) no longer insisted on collectivization,
while the representatives of the bourgeois Left and the future Christian Democrats were now enthusiastic about inscribing the guaran-
tees of the welfare state. No party sought a return to laissez-faire.
Still, important differences separated the resistance parties and would
become more acute after the Allied victory in Europe.

What bridged the differences, during 1944–5, was the conviction
that the resistance forces had a moral claim to lead postwar Europe.
The plank that most united them, in fact, was the demand for a
purge of Fascist collaborators from political and economic life. In
concrete terms, according to the Italian memorandum, moral
renewal meant replacing the reactionary cadres of Europe, precisely
those then seeking to save themselves through opportune changes in
alliance.

What is the difference between such ideas and those, say, of the

Kreisau Circle, or of the projects drawn up by Carl Goerdeler? Certainly the resistance's proposals in France and Italy differed from the quasi-authoritarian schemes of Hassell and Popitz. But even as Kreisau participants reached out to the Left, its leaders knew that they had no popular base; they could not talk of freeing their country from foreigners or just emphasize the need to renew the elites. They had to exercise a trusteeship on behalf of a civic community that no longer existed. In its place they had to appeal to the model of the allegedly apolitical Prussian military or civil service – or even to the nonpolitical forces of the church and trade unions. For the German resistance there remained no social or civic contract to invoke; at best they might recall the supposedly nonpolitical legacy of the *Rechtsstaat*. The French and Italians could remain confident that a democratic foundation was already in place, suppressed by collaborators and Nazis but ready to be built upon once again. Here too the French and Italian resisters felt (even as leftist liberals) that they were the vanguard of a European movement. That confidence could not mark the German conspirators.

Expressed another way, the French and Italian resistance movements presupposed that political-party cadres were the natural basis for organization. These parties had fielded the major partisan forces: in France, Franc Tireur, Combat, and the FFI (Forces Françaises de l'Intérieur); in Italy, the Garibaldi brigades and other units. The diverse resistance forces accepted the associational basis of a future democracy. The political world had always to be constructed on the basis of collective efforts and sodality. The German resistance could not really start from this premise. Weimar, after all, had been constructed on the basis of party pluralism but remained discredited. The only resistance parties were in exile. For the resistance in the occupied countries of Europe, the task ahead was to remove tainted governments and try collaborators. For Germans, according to the Kreisau Circle, the task was to rebuild politics from the ground up on an individualistic basis – testimony to the National Socialist pulverizing of civil society.

There was a further distinction, and it pertained to the tasks imposed by the international situation. The Kreisauers or the generals had to extricate Germany from a war. This meant trying to minimize the consequences of defeat, and we know that the goals proposed were often unrealistic in the extreme. The international task, its conservative members often suggested, was to preserve the gains that Hitler had made from 1933 to or through 1938. For the resistance forces in France and Italy (with the exception perhaps of de Gaulle), the international challenge did not consist of restoring the power of their respective states; it involved bridging the gap between Russia and the Anglo-Saxons. They had to mediate so as to avoid a future East–West conflict. This aspiration also surfaced among members of the German opposition; the "bridge" concept had many German roots. But mediation, for the Germans, was not intended to forestall a future Cold War but to endow Germany with a renewed great-power mission, a task that still is yearned for among some elements of German conservativism.

IV

In the end, however, the historian must ask, Did the resistance really succeed in France or Italy, except at the level of myth? The military accomplishments were minimal. Resistance forces could not stand up to organized German military units. Its political results were doomed to disappointment. The problem of the purge (or *épuration*) seemed intractable; once summary lynchings ended, the purges bogged down in cumbersome judicial procedures. The leftist bourgeois parties tended to evaporate at the polls, winning less than 10 percent of the vote in the early postwar elections in France, Belgium, and Italy. Politics assumed anew the humdrum, deal-making quality that had characterized it in the prewar period. "The Fourth Republic is dead," wits said, in France; "Long live the Third." The characteristic political legacy of the resistance was "tripartism," the coalition of Communists, Social Democrats, and Christian Democrats, with a sprinkling of leftist-liberal intellectuals and maverick democrats. By 1948, tripartism had largely collapsed. The most promising change in postwar politics seemed the new role of Christian Democracy. In this sense West Germany did not end up much differently from the countries where the resistance had mounted such intense claims and hopes. In France and Italy, the Communists were confined to a thirty-year opposition; in Germany, they became segregated in the Soviet Zone.

But the mythic role of the resistance remained vitally different in Germany and the formerly occupied countries. In the Federal Republic, the resistance has served to show that not all the nation applauded National Socialism; it served as a moral protest, a form of witness, all the more significant because the conditions under which it operated were so brutal, harsh, and lonely. No one who has a commitment to maintain the possibilities of liberty can fail to be grateful for this achievement. But in Western Europe outside of Germany, the resistance was not only a moral achievement; it was a political one as well. It was a claim on power. It outlined a coalition of emancipation, an institutionalization of democratic potential, a belief not just in moral action but a high confidence in collective political reconstruction. For the Germans, little had been left as a basis for resistance but individual conscience. That became important but represented only half of a political concept. It was resistance as witness, but not as revolution, nor even as positive transformation. Politics in the modern era is about party and association. The resistance in Italy, France, and elsewhere incorporated a discourse about politics; it recognized the need for force in politics but also expressed a faith in purposive association. Outside the working-class parties in Germany, that discussion was largely lacking. Yet outside Germany, too, the resistance faltered. If we look back on the postwar era, it is hard to discern a continuing resistance input into institutions. The resistance remained important as experience, as engagement, as a declaration that Fascism might be seen as aberrant and not as the historical necessity that the disillusioned of the 1930s and 1940s had come to accept. To that legacy, important if elusive, the German resistance also contributed.

11

The Political Legacy of the German Resistance: A Historiographical Critique

HANS MOMMSEN

It seems significant that the historiographical interest in the German resistance movement against Hitler lost much of its impetus in the early 1960s, years before the influence of the Critical Left in West Germany substantially altered popular preferences in historical subjects. Previously the legacy of the resistance had served as a source of secondary legitimization for the democratic restoration of the Federal Republic, but the growing self-consciousness of the West German political elites and the country's obvious political and economic success after the Korean War made it less desirable to refer to the resistance as a precursor of postwar German democracy. Moreover, critical evaluations of the national-conservative resistance had gained increasing prominence. Although pointed attacks by Hannah Arendt, George Romoser, Henry Pächter, and others did not affect the official state-sponsored interpretation of the resistance – an interpretation ritually repeated at annual commemorations of the Twentieth of July assassination attempt – their contributions initiated more careful and systematic study of the resisters' political and social philosophy. Works such as Gordon Craig's *German History, 1866–1945* and Sebastian Haffner's *Anmerkungen zu Hitler* suggested that the original portrait of the resisters as unambiguous proponents of mainstream democracy fell quite far short of the mark. They argued convincingly that the national-conservative resistance was not – as originally depicted in pioneering accounts by Hans Rothfels, Eberhard Zeller, and Fabian von Schlabrendorff – an internally consistent and "unpolitical" movement, informed largely if not exclusively by ethical values. Beyond such reinterpretations of the Twentieth of July movement, historical research in the 1960s also resurrected hitherto neglected dimensions of the resistance scene, including the Communist and the Socialist opposition, the role of the

151

German émigrés, and everyday popular "dissent" within the Third Reich. In conjunction with this trend, marginal phenomena like the Red Orchestra – originally excluded from the resistance canon because it supported a competing totalitarian system – finally found adequate scholarly treatment.

Notwithstanding the annual commemorations at the Plötzensee Memorial in West Berlin, popular interest in the Twentieth of July movement is now apparently declining. Interest in various forms of local resistance and in leftist opposition, on the other hand, is rapidly gaining ground, especially among younger people. It strikes me as deplorable that the psychological need to identify with historical models like these should be exploited exclusively by Communist or Marxist groups, while the official institutions of the Federal Republic continue to ignore them. Instead of catering to this interest, indeed, local authorities in West Germany deliberately destroy the remnants of concentration camps and graveyards of camp inmates and Soviet prisoners of war, while transforming surviving monuments of Nazism into innocuous or politically acceptable memorials – as was achieved, for example, by converting Himmler's Wewelsburg Castle into a historical museum celebrating Germany's "lost" territories in the East. The current debate over the construction of a World War II memorial in Bonn also reflects this inclination to repress or safely rechannel public memory of the Nazi past.

Because the political legacy of the German resistance is by no means uncontroversial or politically neutral, serious research on this topic is obliged to fight a two-front struggle. On the one hand, the necessarily more critical evaluation of the resisters' political goals seems to conflict with the recollections of the survivors and the protective views of their families. Issues like the national-conservative resisters' somewhat ambivalent position on the "Jewish question," their partial collaboration with the Nazi regime, and their problematic foreign policy goals are still taboo in many circles. On the other hand, there exists an increasing tendency to dismiss the conservative opposition as a rather meaningless interlude within the inexorable collapse of National Socialism. Despite numerous publications and special emphasis on the conservative resistance in West German public schools, the Twentieth of July legacy remains far from securely rooted in the national consciousness. Count Claus von Stauffenberg's desperate attempt to kill Hilter and overthrow his regime is less familiar to the average German than General Erwin Rommel's much-celebrated North Africa campaign.

Among the many reasons for the declining interest in the conservative opposition, one is of particular significance. Traditional histories of the resistance, written primarily by and for members of the prewar generation, ritualized the conservative resisters' ethical stance in ways that could hardly appeal to skeptical postwar generations lacking in strong moralistic assumptions. To younger critics, the traditional histories seemed apologetic in tone, their central purpose to argue that resistance to Nazism was indeed legitimate. For the postwar generations who grew up under the influence of the Cold War and theories of totalitarian dictatorship, such questions of legitimacy lacked substance. Unlike their fathers, they were not concerned about whether it was permissible to break one's oath of allegiance to the Führer or whether resistance was a necessary response to the criminal character of the Third Reich. Their central preoccupation was not the acceptability or legitimacy of resistance in extreme circumstances but the questions of why resistance occurred so late, why it was so restricted in scope, and why the conservative opponents of Hitler hesitated to kill him with all the means at their disposal.

In order to comprehend the fundamentally different perception of the legacy of the German resistance by the present generation, one has to be aware that traditional nationalist values no longer prevail and that the basically nationalistic position of much of the resistance is not automatically accepted by those whose attitudes are characterized by a considerable indifference to nationalism. Any attempt to draw direct political conclusions from the experience of the German resistance unavoidably creates a feeling of distrust among many young Germans, although they often feel a psychological need to identify with anti-Fascist traditions. In conjunction with this, it is remarkable that studies dealing with broader political dissent and opposition (the German term is *Verweigerung*) meet with far greater interest than those focusing on the plot of July 1944 and its precedents. Recent publications by Martin Broszat, Ian Kershaw, and others on public behavior under Nazi rule have been warmly received. In some respects, this form of political dissent is less distant from contemporary experience: It resembles the call for civil disobedience that is familiar to many of the younger generation, especially to those who engage in public affairs. They like to think that their own experiences with ecological protest and opposition to the computerization of public and private life bear connections to acts of civil disobedience in the recent past.

In other respects, however, the progress of scholarly research supports the already-mentioned change in the main paradigms regarding the legacy of the German resistance. This is not so much an outcome of the increasing number of publications dealing with the leftist resistance, which argued that the impact of Communist and local radical opposition groups could no longer be ignored in West Germany, as they had been throughout the Cold War period, when even marginal remarks on the Communist resistance disappeared in new editions of leading publications. Symptomatic of this trend was that even a progressive politician like Klaus von Dohnanyi, then mayor of Hamburg, mentioned the Communists as victims, but not as part of the resistance, in his commemorative speech on the resistance in the Bendlerstrasse in July 1984. Hence – as could be proved by many other examples – the efforts of leftist-oriented historians to defend the Communist and Socialist resistance per se had a rather limited influence. Moreover, their contributions suffered in some respects from the same shortcomings that marred many histories of the bourgeois opposition: They isolated their topic from the general political process of the Third Reich and celebrated the moral legacy of the dedicated, but inevitably abortive, Communist attempts to maintain a conspiratorial network that eventually could serve as the basis for a mass revolt against the Nazi regime.

Scholarly treatments of the German resistance used to begin with the assumption that there existed a basic dualism between the structure of the Nazi political system and allegiance toward its rulers. It is worthwhile to note that the concept of "the alternative Germany" (*das andere Deutschland*) was originated by German émigrés. National-conservative resisters like Carl Goerdeler, who stayed in Germany, may have hoped to resurrect a "true" Germany, but they did not see their goal as that of providing a fundamental alternative to the Third Reich. It took years of bitter experience before they recognized the total breakdown of Germany and accepted the necessity of a putsch to change the authoritarian foundations of government. Few of the conservative resisters were ready to accept that this break with the past might require sacrificing the foreign policy gains that Hitler had achieved prior to the Munich Conference of 1938. In fact, except for the Kreisau Circle, whose perception of Nazism as the culmination of historical trends toward absolutism prompted their demand for a fundamentally new form of government, the national-conservative opposition hoped to preserve the inherited nation-state and its authoritarian Prussian traditions, which it believed had been abused or distorted by the Nazis. Visiting the grave of Col. Werner von Fritsch, an old opponent of Hitler's, nationalist resister Fritz-Dietlof von der Schulenburg spoke tellingly of "the coming Reich" – a binding ideal for him. Schulenburg was one of those neoconservatives who believed that the Nazis had betrayed the "national awakening" of 1933. Other nationalist opponents of Hitler, such as Ludwig Beck, Carl Goerdeler, Ulrich von Hassel, and Johannes Popitz, thought in more traditional, authoritarian terms and hoped for the restoration of a refurbished Bismarckian Reich. But almost none among the national-conservative resisters – with the exception of Julius Leber, a right-wing Social Democrat – expected a total breakdown of the inherited national state or its disappearance as a European great power.

Not surprisingly, this dualistic approach, which starkly contrasted resisters with the leading Nazi clique, tended to obscure the extent to which the majority of the nationalist opposition shared assumptions held by more moderate Nazis and their conservative supporters. In fact, not even the Socialists within the Goerdeler circle expected that there would be either the opportunity or the desire to return to the Weimar parliamentary system. Labor leaders like Wilhelm Leuschner were willing to accept the Nazis' replacement of free unions by the government-controlled German Labor Front as a step toward achieving the long-cherished unity of the German labor movement – even if this meant abandoning an independent Social Democratic party. Christian trade unionists within the Goerdeler group shared Leuschner's conviction that the Communists would play no significant role in a provisional government. Indeed, not before 1942 did the majority of national-conservative resisters begin to realize that they would have to reckon with a strong Communist movement in a post-Nazi Germany. Fully expecting a German victory over Russia in 1941, Goerdeler continued to believe until the last possible moment that the Red Army could be stopped at the German border, perhaps with the help of the Western powers. In essence, then, it would seem that the assumptions and strategies of the national-conservative resistance (at least as they were articulated in the period before the Reich's collapse became inevitable) must be placed in a new perspective; the original postwar interpretations simply will not do.

These traditional interpretations contain another, related, deficiency. They perceived the resisters' actions exclusively within the context of increasing Nazi terror and the impediments this placed in the way of a successful opposition, rather than in the framework of changing political expectations growing out of the Nazis' strategic and political failures. Thus they focused almost entirely on the role of the desperate military resisters, ignoring the participation of political figures from the Kreisau Circle in the conspiracy against Hitler. (True, Helmuth James von Moltke claimed, shortly before his death, that the Kreisau Circle had confined its activities to political contingency planning and did not directly participate in the Twentieth of July plot, but since this was presumably his defense before the Gestapo it should not simply be passed down as an accurate statement of the facts.) Indeed, leading representatives of the Kreisau group certainly did belong to Count von Stauffenberg's inner circle at the time when he decided to attempt the putsch. In addition to neglecting this facet of the Twentieth of July movement, traditional resistance historiography (with the exception of some early publications by Emil Henk) ignored the political networks built up by Socialist members of the national-conservative opposition. Hence the crucial debate between the various resistance camps over the possible establishment of a nonpartisan people's movement did not receive much attention. Perhaps an additional reason for this was that the leading conspirators entertained considerably divergent ambitions for the future of Germany – an awkward reality that conflicted with received wisdom regarding the monolithic unity of the nationalist resistance.

To sum up: Three things – the unhistorical perception of the resistance as a consolidated countermovement; the general tendency to overemphasize the resisters' ethical (and not political) motivation; and, finally, the inclination to place in the foreground the abortive assassination attempt against Hitler – all combined to separate the national-conservative resistance from the complex and changing political context in which it operated. This historiographical pattern, which reflected both the authoritarian style and the political needs of Konrad Adenauer's *Kanzlerdemokratie*, made resistance studies vulnerable to attack from both the neo-Nazi Right, which resented the "glorification of traitors," and the anti–Fascist Left, which resented the exclusive focus on groups with a strongly nationalistic bias. Other critics, most notably Hannah Arendt, pointed to the Twentieth of July resisters' ambivalent position on the Jewish issue, a problem delicately glossed over in traditional resistance historiography.

With time, however, new research on the broader history of National Socialism began to show the German resistance in a more positive light. Pathbreaking studies on the role of the Wehrmacht leadership in preparing and executing Operation Barbarossa, for example, placed some of the resistance generals in a fatal twilight. Gerhard Schulz's pioneering work on national patriots in the resistance (*Nationalpatriotismus im Widerstand*) pointed up the problematical role and views of General Franz von Halder, while Christian Streit's analysis of the treatment accorded Soviet prisoners of war by the German military command (*Keine Kameraden*) showed that leading generals in the military opposition were also deeply involved in the war crimes of the Third Reich. No doubt the generals' fanatical antibolshevism and undeniable anti–Semitism strongly influenced their behavior. Of course these prejudices were not simply induced by the war; General Fritsch's letters, recently published, reveal that he had long harbored anti–Semitic views and indeed continued to do so even after he was dismissed by Hitler in 1938. Klaus-Jürgen Müller's reevaluation of General Beck, along with the Militärgeschictliche Forschungsamt's monumental works on the staging of World War II, also cast the Wehrmacht leadership in a rather less favorable light than had been evident in earlier studies by uncritical authors like Wilhelm Ritter von Schramm.

The stance of the conservative resisters on the Jewish issue is therefore problematical, and we might note that although the anti-Nazi opposition clearly disapproved of openly punitive measures like the *Kristallnacht* pogrom of November 1938, the Nazi persecution of the Jews was by no means the primary motivation pushing most of the resisters (Moltke and Yorck perhaps excepted) to more fundamental forms of opposition – to the conviction, that is, that the Nazi state had to be replaced rather than merely reformed. Although their attitudes differed in detail, men like Popitz, Goerdeler, and Schulenburg apparently supported a general strategy of segregating "nonassimilated" Jews from the German community.

Although the question of the racism of some of the resisters is still highly controversial and insufficiently researched, its revelation nonetheless undermined ongoing attempts to keep the conservative resistance securely and unambiguously within the modern German pantheon. This effort was also vexed by new work in the field of National Socialist foreign policy. Recent studies embracing both the Nazis' foreign policy goals and various resisters' attempts to negotiate with the Western Allies between 1938 and 1940 clearly pointed up the need for a critical reevaluation of the relationship between resistance and official Nazi foreign policy. Alfred Kube's work on Hermann Göring, for example, made clear that Goerdeler's attempts to achieve an understanding with Great Britain were remarkably similar to the intentions of the Reichsmarshall, who obviously feared Hitler's aggressive designs. New and careful analysis of the relationship between representatives of the British Foreign Office and their German resistance contacts, including figures like Schacht and Joseph Müller, revealed that the German resisters had unjustifiably high expectations for a favorable British reaction to their essentially revisionist proposals. Studies by Gerhard Schulz, Henry Malone, and Leonidas Hill also showed that although the German resisters repeatedly thought that they were making a positive impression on British diplomats, their real negotiating partner was the British Secret Service. (Earlier German research on resistance foreign policy, it might be noted, had severely underestimated the importance of the Allied secret services.) The resisters' diminishing chance of receiving reliable or acceptable promises from the Western powers has been convincingly treated in a number of new studies, most notably those of Peter W. Ludloff, Klaus-Jürgen Müller, Gerhard Schulz, F. H. Hinsley, David Dilks, Lothar Kettenacker, Rainer A. Blasius, and Hedva Ben-Israel. As these works made clear, the attitude of the German resisters toward Great Britain and their attempt to forge a basis for postwar European cooperation turned out to be an indispensable key to comprehending the German anti-Nazis' vision of the Reich's future role.

Studies of the German resistance's economic expectations for the postwar era have also contributed to an ongoing reassessment of the anti-Hitler opposition. Recent research has shown that social-liberal economic concepts (later expressed in Ludwig Erhard's social market economy theory) dominated the economic planning of the Goerdeler and Kreisau groups, as well as that of some Nazi economists. Udo Herbst's impressive analysis of the economic planning for the postwar period initiated by Otto Ohlendorff (a Nazi economist who served both in the SD and in the Reich economics ministry) showed that there were striking similarities between Ohlendorff's position and that of the liberal Freiburg school. The Freiburg economists, in turn, strongly influenced the resisters, though there remained unresolved differences between the former's more pronounced free-market orientation (a legacy of Walter Eucken's theories) and the quasi-Socialist direction taken by resisters like Moltke and Yorck. Still, one is left with a new perception of the essential congruity between the Nazi economic vision and that of the resistance – with the Freiburg school providing the theoretical connections. The resisters' motives may have differed from those of the Nazi planners, and the degree of their capitalistic orientation may have varied according to the Reich's changing military situation, but both they and the Ohlendorff group ignored the role of organized labor and expected to continue the system of the German Labor Front, which assured state control over all laboring classes, blue-collar and white-collar alike. Another economic reform, proposed by the resister Johannes Popitz, also reflected authoritarian traits, for it continued the tradition of the late-Weimar presidential cabinets and assumed that the Nazis' destruction of radical or independent labor had laid the groundwork for a new holistic social order – an ideal that of course had nothing in common with the pluralistic principles familiar in Western industrialized societies. Pluralistic social ideals, indeed, were roundly criticized by all factions of the Twentieth of July movement, both the Socialist wing and the conservative-authoritarian group around Popitz and Hassell. Both camps embraced the Prussian socialism of Oswald Spengler – Hassell and the more leftist-oriented Yorck going so far as to call Goerdeler, who inclined toward more traditional laissez-faire principles, a reactionary.

The new work on resistance economic planning has pointed up a need for more far-reaching and systematic studies on the role of the Socialists within the national-conservative resistance. Although our knowledge of the Socialist resistance groups has been considerably enhanced by a series of recent publications, the impact of this faction on the social and constitutional views of the German opposition after 1943 still tends to be underestimated. It might be noted in this regard that Wilhelm Leuschner obtained provisional approval from Moltke to establish the *Deutsche Gewerkschaft* and that plans to nationalize the raw-materials industries were components of both the Kreisau and Goerdeler economic programs. All this suggests an increasing influence on the part of men like Julius Leber, Hermann Maass, and, in the background, Emil Henk. As a matter of fact, the Social Democratic participation in the final stages of the Twentieth of July movement makes clear that – contrary to the traditional assumption – there was no definite line dividing the Socialist conspiratorial activities from those of the Stauffenberg group. But the extent to which the Socialists within the national–conservative resistance could have expected mass support from the working class and from various local forms of opposition, in the event of a successful putsch, needs further elaboration. This question in turn requires a more systematic assessment of the relationship between resistance in the strictest sense and broader forms of popular dissent.

Another issue requiring explication and reevaluation is the apparent double strategy pursued by the resistance as a whole. With the exception of a few individuals like Ewald von Kleist-Schmenzin and Hans Oster, most resistance leaders accepted certain aspects of National Socialist policy or held responsible positions within the Reich, while at the same time they were working to replace the Hitler government. Their complicity with the regime cannot be explained exclusively as a clever ruse designed to disguise their opposition. More careful examination of the origins of the resisters' ideology in the Weimar period would show that their affinity for authoritarian and radical–conservative ideas had deep and solid roots. No doubt some of the early historians of the resistance – among them Gerhard Ritter – were aware of this fundamental ambiguity, but it tended to be deemphasized in later studies, only to be brought to the fore again in the most recent work.

While historians of late have emphasized ambiguities and conceptual discontinuities within the resistance, a similar historiographical flexibility has replaced older notions of a monolithic Third Reich with new perceptions of competing strategies in Nazi domestic and foreign affairs. Alfred Kube's work made it quite clear that Hermann Göring pursued a fairly independent course in foreign and economic policy and that Hitler did not completely control either sector before 1938. The widespread rumor that Göring would replace Hitler as chancellor, which arose first in 1934 and then again in 1938, surfaced also in the national–conservative resistance's so-called X-Plan, in which Göring was proposed to the British as an alternative to Hitler. That the resistance could cherish the hope for such a high-level restructuring of the regime was a function of a much broader doubt about Hitler's leadership, disillusionment with Nazi foreign policy, and concern with increasing governmental chaos and internecine quarreling.

Given the internal complexity of both the Nazi system and the resistance movement that sought to modify or overthrow it, historians of the anti-Nazi opposition are faced with a number of pressing challenges. They must realize that any attempt to describe the varieties of opposition under Nazi rule as a consistent or coherent political force is doomed to failure – though the conservative resisters' serious efforts, especially after 1942, to unify the various opposition factions deserve more recognition than they have generally received. In essence, it must be seen that the highly fragmented nature of the Nazi political system resulted in a wide-ranging variety of opposition and that ultimately it was primarily the Gestapo that decided what resistance was. Nevertheless, scholars should make an effort to understand what resistance meant in relation to various forms of popular dissent – for example, the Catholic church's struggle to preserve its religious autonomy and social network against Nazi intrusion. They must also see that the selection of those involved in the final conspiracy against Hitler often depended upon rather casual factors that had little to do with the individual's motivation to enter active political resistance. Another challenge involves a clearer delineation of the stages within the resistance project, a demand already advanced, but not adequately disposed of, by Klaus-Jürgen Müller. The essential question remains: At what point did limited opposition to specific aims of the Nazi regime turn into a principled rejection of Nazism's very foundations? To answer this question, it seems advisable to interpret resistance not as a one-time decision by individuals or groups to wage all-out war against Nazism but as an evolving reaction of various factions to the increasingly terroristic and inhumane nature of the regime. If one sees the resistance as a process, rather than as the result of static decisions, then the differing intensity of the opposition over time becomes more comprehensible. In the same vein, the need to offer an integrated picture of the diverse forms of opposition cannot be satisfied by a methodological approach that narrowly locates the resisters' motivation in ethical humanism, independent of social, political, and denominational considerations. Ethical humanism was indeed one source of motivation, but it was not a necessary precondition for joining the ranks of active opposition. The resistance movement as a whole produced an impressive variety of responses to the National Socialist terror regime, and these responses, it must be seen, were in turn a legacy of Germany's traumatic defeat in 1918 and its failure in the subsequent years to stabilize a Western-style parliamentary democracy. It is highly significant that among the alternatives to National Socialism offered by the German resistance, liberal-democratic visions were almost entirely absent.

If the historiography of the resistance needs to encompass the pre-Nazi German past, it also needs to liberate the resistance legacy from the deliberate political demands placed upon it in the present. A judicious and nonexploitative interpretation would allow the younger generation to appreciate the almost insurmountable obstacles that confronted isolated groups of resisters standing against a hostile majority that had been successfully indoctrinated with Nazi propaganda. Certainly no interpretation of the resistance should omit the double legacy left by the opposition: the belief – shared by all but the Communists – in a peculiarly German "way" (*Sonderweg*); and a final willingness, despite internal differences and illusions, to risk failure and death in order to restore a humanitarian politics that transcended individual interests. The basic belief that any policy claiming to represent the public interest had to be founded on humanitarian principles was one of the essential legacies left by all the resistance martyrs killed by the Nazis. This insight, however, can be put in proper perspective only if the relationship between the resistance and the Nazi regime is uncompromisingly laid out and the predominantly political character of the opposition is recognized.

Taking this approach to the history of the resistance – following, that is, Martin Broszat's plea for a "historicization" of the Third Reich – is by no means tantamount to accepting Ernst Nolte's call for a relativization of Nazi crimes. Nor does it amount to an endorsement of Andreas Hillgruber's equally dubious effort to explain Nazi barbarities by emphasizing Germany's pressing need to protect Western civilization from the Red Army. Arguments of this kind finally turn on the concept of *Realpolitik* – the very legitimacy of which the German resistance courageously opposed. Perhaps this was its most important legacy of all.

12

Uses of the Past: The Anti-Nazi Resistance Legacy in the Federal Republic of Germany

DAVID CLAY LARGE

Not long ago the West German historian Michael Stürmer declared, "He who controls the past also controls the future."[1] What he apparently meant by this was that German historians should shape a coherent vision of the national past that might help rekindle a sense of national pride and self-confidence among the German people. This is a very problematical notion, suggesting as it does that there can or should be a coherent national history, and that this interpretation of the past should take a political direction that makes it serviceable to the present and future.

Be that as it may, all nations seem to need a "usable past" with which they can validate their present and inspire faith in their future. Certainly, few nations in recent times have needed this more than the young Federal Republic of Germany, which (like its eastern equivalent) was founded under the auspices of foreign powers, enjoyed for much of its history only limited sovereignty, and suffered from an acute lack of national identity. But if the Federal Republic was to find historical traditions that might give it added legitimacy, where could it look? It could, and did, turn to the Prussian reform movement of the early nineteenth century, to the liberal ideals of the Hambach Festival and the revolutions of 1848, and to the comparatively restrained national diplomacy of Bismarck. But as far as the more recent past was concerned, prospects seemed quite dismal indeed,

---

1 Michael Stürmer, *Aus Politik und Zeitgeschichte*. Supplement to *Das Parlament* (hereafter cited as *Aus Politik und Zeitgeschichte*), 17 (1984). For critical discussions of the call for a more coherent historical identity, see Martin Broszat, "Die Ambivalenz der Forderung nach mehr Geschichtsbewusstsein," in Hermann Graml and Klaus-Dietmar Henke, eds., *Nach Hitler. Der schwierige Umgang mit unserer Geschichte: Beiträge von Martin Broszat* (Munich, 1986), 310–23; Richard J. Evans, *In Hitler's Shadow: West German Historians and the Attempt to Escape from the Nazi Past* (New York, 1989).

with perhaps one glorious exception: the anti-Nazi resistance movement that culminated in the attempt to kill Hitler on July 20, 1944.
Here that "other Germany" – the Germany which so many Germans
wanted desperately to believe was the "real" Germany – had done its
best to eliminate the tyrant who was terrorizing Germany and the
world. Even in failing to eliminate Hitler, and thereby suffering the
tyrant's grisly revenge, the conspirators had "saved German honor."

Or so it was claimed, in the dozens of speeches commemorating
the resistance movement given by political leaders in the Federal
Republic from the mid-1950s down to the present day.[2] In fact,
however, this legacy his proved to be much more complicated and
problematic for the Federal Republic than the commemoration
speeches would suggest. Indeed, attempts to mine it as a source of
political and moral legitimacy have yielded almost as much doubt
and discord as inspiration. I would like to chart, in a more or less
chronological fashion, some of the high points in the Federal Republic's reckoning with this particular aspect of the recent German past.
This will serve, I think, to tell us something not only about changing
German perceptions of the resistance legacy but also about changes
in the West Germans' attitude toward the Federal Republic itself.

In the first years after the end of World War II, the German people
did not pay a great deal of attention – certainly not a great deal of
positive attention – to the resistance legacy and its possible meanings
for the German future. There were several reasons for this. Most
Germans were so preoccupied with the digging out from the ruins
and surviving in the country's shattered economy that they had little
inclination to engage in any soul-searching about the recent past.
As Bertolt Brecht put it, in a different context, "Erst kommt das
Fressen, dann kommt die Moral." With specific respect to the July
20 assassination attempt, German opinion was still to some degree
clouded by the Nazi interpretation of that event, according to which
the conspirators were nothing more than "traitors" who had tried to
stab their leader in the back. The fact that some survivors of the
resistance movement later worked for the Allied Occupation authorities or gave evidence for the prosecution in the postwar trials only
reinforced this image of the resisters as traitors.

Ironically enough, the resisters' reputation among the Occupation

---

2 Ulrike Emrich and Jürgen Nötzold, "Der 20. Juli in der öffentlichen Gedenkreden der
Bundesrepublik und in der Darstellung der DDR," *Aus Politik und Zeitgeschichte*, 26 (1984):
3–12.

authorities was not much better. The Allies had largely snubbed the resistance during the war, considering it a peripheral movement dominated by reactionary aristocrats. When one of the survivors of the military resistance rejected an Allied effort to recruit him for the prosecution at Nuremberg, he was told: "You Twentieth of July people are just as much pigs as the others."[3] Though with more information the Occupation authorities began slowly to revise this view,[4] they continued to believe that they had been correct not to deal seriously with the resistance during the war. When the Adenauer aide and former resister Eugen Gerstenmaier asked Winston Churchill, in August 1950, why Churchill, six years earlier, had not answered the German resistance's call for support, the latter insisted that he could not have acted other than he did. "I'm sorry," he added, and held out a fistful of cigars.[5]

When it came to establishing a West German state in 1949, the German framers of that new political order did not find – indeed they did not look for – a major source of inspiration in the wartime resistance movement. It is true that three of the state constitutions – those of Hesse, Bremen, and West Berlin – contained provisions for "resistance" against unconstitutionally exercised governmental authority, but until 1968 the federal constitution, the *Grundgesetz*, did not. A proposition for such a resistance clause was advanced in the constitutional debates but was rejected on the grounds that it would introduce a plebiscitary element into the governmental system – something that the Weimar experience prompted the framers to want to avoid at all costs. Moreover, opponents of a resistance clause pointed out that it made no sense to enshrine such a "right" in the constitution, since by definition it could apply only in situations where the constitution had broken down.[6]

In one realm, however, the resistance legacy may have found a constitutional echo. This was in the Basic Law's emphasis on the dignity of the individual and on such personal and political rights as freedom of expression, religion, and assembly. A similar catalog

3 Quoted in Georg Meyer, "Zur Situation der deutschen militärischen Führungsschicht im Vorfeld des westdeutschen Verteidigungsbeitrages 1945–1950/51," in Roland G. Förster et al., eds., *Anfänge westdeutscher Sicherheitspolitik* (Munich, 1982), 668.
4 See, for example, Franklin Ford, "The Twentieth of July in the German Resistance," *American Historical Review* 51 (1946): 609–26. Ford was an officer with the American Occupation forces.
5 Eugen Gerstenmeier, *Streit und Friede hat seine Zeit. Ein Lebensbild* (Frankfurt, 1981), 322.
6 On the codification debate, see especially Christoph Böckenförde, "Die Kodifizierung des Widerstandsrechts im Grundgesetz," *Juristenzeitung* 25: 5–6 (1970): 168–72.

of human rights had been contained in the constitutional drafts prepared by members of the so-called Kreisau Circle, an important bastion of anti-Nazi resistance. It is not clear, however, that there was any direct borrowing here: Few of the members of the Parliamentary Council which drew up the Basic Law could have had any detailed knowledge of the constitutional ideals of the Kreisau Circle. Moreover, they could draw on traditions of individual rights and the rule of law contained in previous German constitutions, most recently that of Weimar. But if the personal testimony of some of the framers can be believed, they were mindful in general of the resistance movement's commitment to human dignity and the sanctity of law when they drew up the personal-rights component of the Basic Law.[7]

As for the populace as a whole, public opinion polls taken in the first years of the Federal Republic registered an at best ambivalent attitude toward the German resistance. A survey taken in 1952 showed that only 20 percent of the respondents believed that Hitler's opponents should have resisted during wartime; 34 percent insisted that the resisters should have "waited until after the war," and 15 percent said there should have been no resistance at all. To the question "How should the men of the Twentieth of July be judged?", 40 percent answered positively, and 30 percent answered negatively; the rest had no opinion. Over 50 percent were opposed to naming a school after Count von Stauffenberg.[8] In these same years, liberal newspaper columnists often complained that the resistance cause "had not found a secure place in the German heart" and that the Twentieth of July seemed already "forgotten."[9]

Some Germans, however, appeared to have remembered this dimension of their recent past only to condemn it in the old Nazi fashion. There was now considerable open talk of the July 20 assassination attempt as a "treasonous" act. Right-wing former-officers' associations like Bruderschaft and Freikorps Deutschland took this line; so did respected former generals like Heinz Guderian and Franz Halder. By 1951, West German newspapers were warning

7 Torsten-Dietrich Schramm, *Der deutsche Widerstand gegen den Nationalsozialismus. Seine Bedeutung für die Bundesrepublik in der Wirkung auf Institutionen und Schulbücher* (Berlin, 1980), 47–50.
8 Erich-Peter Neumann and Elisabeth Noelle, *Jahrbuch der öffentlichen Meinung 1947–1955* (Allensbach, 1956), 138.
9 "Gedanken am 20. Juli," *Süddeutsche Zeitung*, July 20, 1951; "Der vergessene 20. Juli," *Schweizer National-Zeitung*, July 21, 1951.

of a "new stab-in-the-back legend,"[10] and in October of that year the federal cabinet in Bonn felt obliged to issue an official statement defending the July 20 resisters against "libelous slander." "The men and women of the Twentieth of July," said the statement, "proved to the world that not all Germans had been taken in by National Socialism. Their act helped establish the basis upon which a Germany could be rebuilt in cooperation with the free world."[11]

In apparent recognition of the resistance's services to Germany, the Bundestag in 1953 voted to include resistance survivors or their families in the Federal Indemnification Law, which materially compensated victims of Nazism. These payments, however, proved small in comparison with the compensation given the so-called *Kriegsgeschädigten*, the people who had been victimized by the war. In order to claim compensation as resisters, potential recipients had to show proof that they had suffered because of their resistance to Hitler, a requirement some of the former resisters found so degrading that they refused to apply for benefits. And then, in 1956, a new provision in the Compensation Law stipulated that Communists who had remained members of the party were not entitled to compensation.[12]

Another source of malaise among the resistance survivors was the conviction that they were not accorded the degree of political influence in the new state commensurate with their services and sacrifices to the nation. They charged that although some of them had found important positions in the government and parties – Jakob Kaiser and Eugen Gerstenmaier were cases in point – all too many of them were being used primarily as "window dressing" (*Aushängeschilder* or *Persilscheinaussteller*). One resistance veteran, Rudolf Pechel, even insisted that former resistance figures were deliberately excluded from real power because they made their colleagues "uncomfortable" – they were a "living reproach" to those who had not stood up against the Nazis.[13]

This complaint sounds somewhat self-serving and should be taken with a grain of salt. It was true, however, that former resisters did

---

10 "Neue Dolchstosslegende im Kommen?", *Welt am Sontag* (Hamburg), February 22, 1951; "Neue deutsche Dolchstosslüge," *Das freie Wort* (Düsseldorf), August 31, 1951.
11 "Bonn bekennt sich zum Widerstand," *Stuttgarter Zeitung*, October 3, 1951.
12 Peter Steinbach, "Widerstandsforschung im politischen Spannungsfeld," *Aus Politik und Zeitgeschichte*, 28 (1988): 6–7.
13 Claus Donate, "Deutscher Widerstand gegen den Nationalsozialismus aus der Sicht der Bundeswehr," Ph.D diss., University of Freiburg, 1976, 394.

not set the political tone or pull the main levers of political power in the new Federal Republic. But this should hardly surprise us: The resistance veterans were few in number and not invariably politically talented. And they did have a way of irritating their colleagues – not always because of their resistance credentials per se but because they sometimes wore these credentials on their sleeves. Yet Pechel's observation that the resistance legacy was a source of discomfort in the new Germany bears reemphasis. If, on the one hand, the exist-ence of an active German resistance could be used by postwar Germans to counter charges of collective guilt, the resisters' example also represented a moral challenge to those – and of course they constituted the overwhelming majority of Germans in the Third Reich – who had done nothing of consequence to oppose Hitler. However flawed and ineffective their opposition, the resisters had shown that there was an alternative to complicity, that one did have a choice.

When resistance figures complained, as they often did, that genuine power in the Federal Republic was exercised by people who had "wintered over" during the Third Reich, they were undoubtedly thinking primarily of Chancellor Konrad Adenuaer. Adenauer, of course, had been no Hitler supporter. He had been thrown out of his job as mayor of Cologne by the Nazis, for whose policies he had nothing but contempt. During his enforced exile from political life he had been in contact with some figures in the Catholic resistance. But when one of them, Jakob Kaiser, told Adenauer of his conspir-atorial plans involving a group of generals and invited Adenauer to join the conspiracy, the latter declined. "Have you ever seen a smart general?"[14] he asked. Clearly Adenauer had little faith in the efficacy of a military resistance, and even less in the machinations of another leading figure in the opposition, Carl Goerdeler, whom he consid-ered a careless fool. Adenauer, on the other hand, was anything but careless. He knew he was being watched by the Gestapo, and he believed – perhaps correctly – that he could not be of much use to the plotters. But whatever the justification for his cautious stance, people who had actually risked their lives in the resistance naturally resented it when Adenauer's party eventually associated him directly with the resistance legacy.

It was Adenauer, however, who took the lead in the Federal

14 Hans-Peter Schwarz, *Adenauer. Der Aufstieg*, 1876–1952 (Stuttgart, 1986), 406.

Republic's belated discovery of the resistance legacy as a source of moral and political inspiration, as well as a kind of ticket for readmission to the community of civilized nations. He and several of his governmental colleagues took the tenth anniversary of the July 20, 1944, assassination attempt as an opportunity not just to honor the anti-Nazi resisters but also to extract some political mileage from their example. Speaking at Bonn's newly constituted Foreign Office, Adenauer declared that the martyred resisters who had belonged to the German Foreign Office in the Third Reich had "given their lives . . . so that the unjustifiable condemnation [of the Foreign Office] at home and abroad might be reversed."[15] He also took pains to recall that Foreign Office personnel like Ernst von Weizsäcker had urged the Western powers to stand up to Hitler, in which case he might have been overthrown from within; the West, however, had chosen to "save" Hitler at Munich. Adenauer's colleague Eugen Gerstenmaier said on the same occasion that it was high time that the Foreign Office be recognized as a bastion of the "other Germany."[16] But it was President Theodor Heuss, speaking at the new Free University of Berlin, who made the most sweeping claim of all: "The blood of the martyred resisters," he insisted, "has cleansed our German name of the shame which Hitler cast upon it." The resistance was therefore "a gift to the German future."[17]

These claims were not without validity, and many people, both in West Germany and abroad, were pleased that Bonn seemed finally to have found something in the recent German past to be proud of, some "tradition" that might help give the young republic an added measure of legitimacy. Bonn's evocation of the Twentieth of July legacy, however, could not simply be applauded as a welcome recognition of the anti-Nazi resisters' tragic service to the nation. The government's expropriation of this inheritance was open to charges of hypocrisy, since some of the chancellor's closest associates, most notably Hans Globke and Theodor Oberländer, were themselves implicated in Nazi crimes. Moreover, in inscribing the resistance movement in the Federal Republic's pantheon, Bonn's leaders were obliged to interpret this phenomenon rather selectively,

---

15 *Bulletin des Presse- und Informationsamtes der Bundesregierung* (Bad Godesberg, July 22, 1954), 1211.
16 Ibid., 1209.
17 Theodor Heuss, *Dank und Bekenntnis. Gedenkrede zum 20. Juli 1944* (Tübingen, 1954), 30, 25.

to downplay its antipluralistic, anticapitalist, and less democratic sides and to overlook the painful fact that some of those who had sought a way out of the Nazi tragedy by trying to kill Hitler had been among those who had helped bring him to power in the first place. In this context, we might recall that President Theodor Heuss himself, who certainly became a committed opponent of the Nazis, was one of those parliamentarians who had voted for the so-called Enabling Act in March 1933, which helped Hitler break through to dictatorial power.

Moreover, however selectively Bonn's leading politicians interpreted the Twentieth of July conspiracy, their almost exclusive focus on this particular dimension of the anti–Hitler opposition betrayed an eagerness to overlook the more prolonged and systematic resistance that had came from the radical Left, particularly from the Communists. And one can sense also in the claims of Adenauer and company a willingness both to shift some of the blame for Hitler from the Germans to the Western powers and to exaggerate the extent to which conservative institutions like the Foreign Office represented cohesive bastions of the "other Germany." In short, what one had here was the beginning of a mythologization of the resistance that was not a great deal more faithful to historical reality than the wartime Allies' all too hasty dismissal of its significance.

But whatever objections we might have to the selective way in which Bonn interpreted the resistance, the various official speeches marking the tenth anniversary of the Twentieth of July attempt seemed to suggest that West Germany's ruling establishment had now taken this legacy warmly to its heart. Another occurrence at that same time, however, showed that memories of the resistance were still capable of arousing passionate controversy. On July 20, 1954, Otto John, a former resister and now president of Bonn's Verfassungsschutz (Office for Constitutional Protection), slipped over the border into East Germany. Immediately thereafter he went on the radio to say that Stauffenberg had not "died for the Federal Republic," which he accused of fomenting a neo-Nazi revival. In the investigation that followed, it turned out that during the war John had worked on behalf of the resistance in Madrid and had been in contact with the British Secret Service. The British, in fact, had recommended him for his post as head of the Verfassungsschutz. He may also have had ties to the underground Communist resistance, the Rote Kapelle.

Revelation of all this inspired a new wave of recrimination in West Germany against the resistance veterans in general, and in particular against those resisters who had operated in foreign countries or later served the Occupation powers. John's bitter rival, Reinhard Gehlen, who headed the Bundesnachrichten Dienst (Federal Intelligence Agency), made the acid comment: "Once a traitor, always a traitor."[18] In the parliamentary debate on the John affair, Hans Joachim von Markatz of the conservative Deutsche Partei declared that a man like John, who had "served the enemy," should have been automatically disqualified from holding any official position. He insisted that an investigation be opened to determine if anyone else with a background like John's was employed in a sensitive position.[19]

These attacks opened the way for a broader witch-hunt directed against Germans who had fled the Reich to work in resistance organizations abroad and then returned, after the war, to join in the effort to rebuild their country. Among this group were prominent figures in the Social Democratic Party (SPD) – Erich Ollenhauer, Fritz Heine, Herbert Wehner, Willy Brandt – and they were now tarred by the nationalist Right with the brush of treason. So vicious was the attack that even some Christian Democratic leaders, including Adenauer and future chancellor Kurt Georg Kiesinger, felt obliged to denounce this slur on the Socialist emigrants. But Kiesinger, interestingly enough, drew the line at those who had given evidence against Germans in postwar trials: Their presence in government, he said, was cause for "grave concern."[20]

If the John affair revealed lingering ambivalence – to put it mildly – about the resistance legacy, it also showed the extent to which this aspect of the recent German past was becoming a bone of current political contention. Adenauer's Christian Democratic Union (CDU) was busy staking its claim to the resistance legacy, or at least to that part of it which the party wished to recognize. The CDU claimed that its "historical roots" could be found in the resistance movement's ecumenical organization and in its commitment to high ethical standards and traditional Christian values.[21] CDU politicians

---

18 See "Ich habe mich ergeben," *Der Spiegel*, December 21, 1955, 11.
19 *Deutscher Bundestag*, 42. Sitzung, September 16, 1954, p. 1985.
20 Ibid., p. 1961.
21 Schramm, *Der deutsche Widerstand*, 65–8.

tended to beat this drum at the annual commemorations of the Twentieth of July attempt in the late 1950s and early 1960s. Helmut Kohl beat it again in his foreword to a collection of documents entitled *Der deutsche Widerstand und der CDU*, where he declared that the men and women of the resistance – here he named early CDU luminaries like Adenauer, Gerstenmaier, Karl Arnold, Hermann Ehlers, Robert Lehr, Otto Lenz, Theodor Steltzer, and Christine Teusch – had carried the moral and political legacy of the resistance into the government of the Federal Republic.[22]

The CDU's main coalition partner, the Free Democratic party (FDP), also claimed to perpetuate certain dimensions of the resistance legacy, particularly its emphasis on individual dignity and personal freedom.[23] But this party was by no means unified on the advisability of honoring the men who had tried to kill Hitler. The FDP's military specialist and chief liaison to the postwar veterans' movement, former general Hasso von Manteuffel, declared that he was proud not to have belonged to the Twentieth of July circle and that he had done his duty to the bitter end. In 1948 he had advised Adenauer to have nothing to do with men who had "broken their oath to the Führer."[24] In order to avoid an open split within the party over the resistance issue, the FDP leadership put together a compromise formula that officially documented its respect both for those who had resisted the Nazi state and for those who had loyally served it to the end.[25] The statement explicitly avoided according a higher moral or political value to the former posture than to the latter. One might argue that the FDP's failure to make this elementary distinction undercut its claim – advanced in the *Freiburger Thesen* – to be Germany's most reliable guardian of the classical liberal tradition.

Meanwhile the chief opposition party, the SPD, was not about to leave the resistance legacy to the ruling conservative-liberal coalition. Kurt Schumacher, the party's leader until his death in 1952, had personally suffered severely at the hands of the Nazis, and he greatly resented the Occupation powers' and Bonn's tendency to ignore or dismiss the Socialist resistance. "We Socialists would have been resisters," he said, "even if the Americans and the British had

---

22 Emrich and Nötzold, "Der 20. Juli," 5.
23 Schramm, *Der deutsche Widerstand*, 73.
24 Hasso von Manteuffel, "Bekenntnis eines freimütigen Deutschen," Bundesarchiv-Militärarchiv, BW9/2118, 127.
25 Statement quoted in Erich Mende, *Die neue Freiheit 1945–1961* (Munich, 1984), 321.

become Fascists."[26] The SPD's failure to parlay what its leaders believed was socialism's moral superiority into effective political power in the early years of the Federal Republic only exacerbated the Socialists' bitterness, their sense that the true resistance legacy was being betrayed by Bonn's new rulers. One aspect of the resistance heritage that seemed especially violated in Adenauer's Germany was the commitment to a moderate socialization of the economy that many of the anti-Hitler forces – even in the conservative camp – had harbored. Another was the concept of Greater Germany – a strong and unified Germany standing astride the European continent. Although no one in Adenauer's government spoke of a permanent division of Germany, the SPD saw the chancellor's focus on the Federal Republic's integration within the West and rearmament within NATO as tantamount to an acceptance of German disunity for the foreseeable future.

Mention of Germany's division introduces the problem of the Cold War, and Cold War politics had a significant influence on the interpretation of the resistance legacy in the Federal Republic during the 1950s. Of course the Cold War perpetuated the tendency in Bonn to exclude the Communist and Socialist anti-Nazi opposition from acceptance into the resistance canon. The emerging theory of totalitarianism, which stressed the similarities between communism and National Socialism, allowed the ongoing opposition to Russian-imposed communism in East Germany to be equated with the earlier resistance against Hitler. Thus the uprising in East Berlin on June 17, 1953, was widely interpreted in the Federal Republic as a latter-day July 20, 1944.[27] From 1954 through the early 1960s, commemorative speeches honoring the Twentieth of July legacy placed these two events on a common footing: They were described as noble, albeit abortive, efforts to overthrow a tyranny.[28] But while West German commemoration speakers generally encouraged the Federal Republic's citizenry to see the 1944 assassination attempt as a historical event, which hardly needed emulation in the West German *Rechtsstaat*, they hoped that their fellow Germans in the Democratic Republic would regard this heritage as an invitation to perpetual

---

26 Ulrich Buczylowski, *Kurt Schumacher und die deutsche Frage. Sicherheitspolitik und strategische Offensivkonzeption von August 1950 bis September 1951* (Stuttgart, 1971), 26.

27 See in particular Hans Rothfels, "Das politische Vermächtnis des deutschen Widerstands," *Vierteljahrshefte für Zeitgeschichte* (hereafter 2 *VfZ*) 2 (1954): 329–43.

28 Emrich and Nötzold, "Der 20. Juli," 5.

resistance. As Ernst Lemmer, minister for Greater German questions, put it in 1962, a year after the building of the Berlin Wall: "Sixteen million of our countrymen are still living under an oppressive fate that the men and women of the Twentieth of July tried to cast off forever."[29]

If the West German leaders employed the resistance legacy in their Cold War jockeying against the rival German state, they also sought to use it in their campaign to get the Federal Republic rearmed within the context of the Western alliance system. This issue is too complicated to discuss in detail here, but I would like to outline its high points, for it offers a revealing case study in the uses and abuses of the resistance legacy in the Federal Republic.[30]

In their effort to find a source of moral and political renewal for the military structure they were contemplating in the early 1950s, West German military planners sought to draw on the military resistance against Hitler. Connections between this planning operation and the resistance movement can be seen in the personnel structure of Bonn's military-planning agencies. Adenauer's first security adviser, Count Gerhard von Schwerin, had ties to the resistance, and Schwerin in turn hired three men who had been connected to the military conspiracy: Count Johann Adolf von Kielmansegg, Achim Oster, and Axel von dem Bussche-Streithorst. About one-third of the men who met at the Himmerod Cloister in October 1950 to discuss German security policy had been connected in one way or another with the anti-Hitler opposition. When Schwerin's agency was replaced a month later by the so-called Dienststelle Blank, the new security adviser, Theodor Blank, retained from Schwerin's staff only those three men connected with the resistance. The point here was to use the association with the resistance legacy as a way of breaking down hostility to the rearmament project, both at home and abroad. It was hoped that the presence of the resistance figures might reassure people that the new army would operate on a higher ethical plane than had the Wehrmacht, that it would never again become a tool of tyranny.

29 Ibid., 5–6.
30 For a full discussion of this issue, see David Clay Large, "'A Gift to the German Future?' The Anti-Nazi Resistance Movement and West German Rearmament," *German Studies Review* 7 (1984): 499–529. See also Donald Abenheim, *Reforging the Iron Cross: The Search for Tradition in the West German Armed Forces* (Princeton, 1988), 136–47; and Wolfgang von Groote, "Bundeswehr und 20. Juli," *VfZ* 14 (1966): 285–99.

This strategy may indeed have reassured some worried citizens, but it also ignited a storm of controversy. The veterans' associations objected that the employment of former resisters represented a "defamation" of the Wehrmacht and of those former soldiers who had "done their duty to the bitter end." They also charged that the incorporation of the resistance legacy, which had of course involved breaking the soldiers' oath to Hitler and insurrection during time of war, would endanger the new army's coherence, discipline, and soldierly spirit. The head of the Bavarian branch of the largest veterans' association, the Verein deutscher Soldaten (VdS), insisted that no "honorable" German officer would serve in an army that included "traitors" from the military resistance movement.[31]

Since the government believed it would have to rely primarily on Wehrmacht veterans to staff West Germany's new army, this grumbling among the former soldiers was a primary concern. It led to efforts by Blank and others in the Adenauer administration to defuse this controversy by assuring that former resisters would get no special treatment and that the vaunted German traditions of obedience (though not "cadaver obedience") and technical expertise would also receive their due. In the course of this discussion the Blank agency itself became sharply split between those who believed that the Twentieth of July legacy offered valuable lessons for the military and those who thought it was a pernicious influence.

But whatever Blank and his colleagues might have wanted, the Bundestag, which heretofore had not played a significant role in rearmament planning, now determined that the resistance legacy should have an important influence on the mentality of the new military. The parliament insisted on the creation of a screening organization (the so-called Personalgutachterausschuss) to vet candidates for top officer positions in the Bundeswehr. This agency, also at parliament's insistence, contained several figures who had been connected to the anti-Nazi opposition. Not surprisingly, the screening board made attitudes toward the military resistance one of the criteria for selecting the new officers. In interviews with the board, all candidates were obliged to discuss their views on the assassination attempt against Hitler, and their recognition that the conspirators had "acted in good conscience" became a sine qua non for acceptance. Such a procedure, of course, was open to the same abuse as the

31 *Frankfurter Allgemeine Zeitung*, October 1, 1951.

postwar de-Nazification hearings – people generally said what they thought their inquisitors wanted to hear, regardless of what they might have genuinely believed. The screening process could and did inspire a similar cynical humor, such as the following joke that made the rounds of the veterans' circles: Screening committee to candidate: "How do you feel about the Twentieth of July?" Candidate: "Oh, I suppose I could just as well come on the nineteenth."[32]

Once the Bundeswehr was established, in late 1955, its leaders were faced with the knotty problem of somehow incorporating this troublesome legacy into the new army's ideological profile – thereby claiming it as a moral inheritance for the nation's "citizens in uniform" – without undermining those principles of obedience and discipline upon which every military organization must be based. On the one hand the Bundeswehr leadership began paying official tribute to the resistance movement, just as Bonn's political leaders did. Gen. Adolf Heusinger, the first general inspector, declared in 1959: "The act of the Twentieth of July 1944 was a shining light in Germany's darkest hour."[33] His successor, General Foertsch, stated: "The men of July 20 were in the true German military tradition. They understood obedience, loyalty, and duty as they should be understood and as we too wish to understand them: as obligations whose meaning rests finally on moral and religious ties."[34] In order further to document this admiration for the heritage of the resistance, the Bundeswehr named five of its posts after prominent July 20 martyrs: Julius Leber, Henning von Tresckow, Erwin Rommel, Claus von Stauffenberg, and Alfred Delp. In addition to these formal gestures, the Bundeswehr leadership published educational tracts for the troops instructing them to respect the Twentieth of July as an example of commitment "to the highest moral values" and as a moment from the past which made the new democratic present more "credible."[35]

At the same time, however, the soldiers were also sternly cautioned against regarding the resistance as a "model" for their own behavior. Like the German citizenry in general, they were reminded that the resistance had occurred under a "tyranny" and that there was no legitimacy for such oppositional activity in a *Rechtsstaat*. They

32 Large, "Gift," 522.
33 Quoted in Terence Prittie, *Germans against Hitler* (Boston, 1964), 284.
34 Quoted in ibid.
35 Golo Mann, in *Schriftenreihe innere Führung*, no. 26.

were also reminded that the Twentieth of July activists had belonged to a small elite whose background, education, and careers had prompted them to take the stand that they did.[36] Clearly the average soldier could not be expected, let alone encouraged, to take upon himself such awesome moral responsibility. For the Bundeswehr, this struggle over defining a proper place for the resistance legacy in its own hierarchy of traditions and values was obviously fraught with contradiction. On the one hand, the Twentieth of July legacy was offered as proof of the Wehrmacht's essential decency and honor; on the other, it was reduced to an act of an unrepresentative minority.

But it should not surprise us that the Bundeswehr had difficulty reconciling the need for order and discipline with the right or duty of soldiers to disobey orders that contravened alleged "timeless" standards of human decency. Two hundred years ago Edmund Burke observed: "The speculative line of demarcation where obedience ought to end and resistance must begin is faint, obscure, and not easily definable."[37] In February 1988, Israeli defense minister Yitzak Rabin attacked liberal legislators in the Knesset who insisted that soldiers in the occupied territories had the right to disobey orders they considered illegal. Israeli radio quoted him as saying: "There is nothing more dangerous for Israel than soldiers deciding what is bad and what is good, which orders to accept and which to reject. It's a call to anarchy, for the Lebanonization of Israel."

Of course the military was not the only institution in the Federal Republic that had to grapple with its role in the Third Reich and with its relationship to the resistance legacy. The universities, unions, business associations, and churches all had to engage in *Vergangenheitsbewältigung* – reckoning with the past. For want of space, I will confine myself here to a few brief remarks on the ways in which the churches confronted the resistance legacy and their place within it.

Both Catholic and Protestant church organizations had a mixed record of compliance with and opposition to Nazism, and in the Federal Republic they continued to assess the meaning of their behavior during the Third Reich in widely varying ways. In general the Catholics were less self-critical than the Protestants, and their bishops did not hesitate to claim a position of spiritual leadership

---

36 Siegfried Grimm, *"Der Bundesrepublik treu zu dienen..."* (Düsseldorf, 1970), 179.
37 Edmond Burke, *Reflections on the Revolution in France* (Indianapolis, 1955), 34.

based on the role of anti-Nazi clerics like Cardinal Faulhaber, Bishop von Galen of Münster, Father Lichtenberg, and Father Delp, the last two of whom died at the hands of the Nazis. Delp, a South German conservative who despised Prussians and Slavs and who saw Hitler as a National Bolshevik, evolved plans for a post-Nazi neo-Carolingian Western Europe based on Franco-German cooperation that anticipated in many respects the postwar project of Konrad Adenauer.[38]

The postwar Evangelical Church of Germany (EKD) engaged in an intense, sometimes self-lacerating, dissection of Protestantism's role in the Third Reich. At its foundation in 1945, the newly unified EKD made the following statement: "A falsely understood Lutheranism allowed us to believe that we had only one duty to the state – namely to obey official authority and to admonish Christians to such obedience, as long as the state did not call upon us openly to sin."[39] Also in that year Protestant representatives issued the so-called Stuttgart Confession, in which they castigated themselves for not resisting sooner and more systematically.[40] Silence in the face of injustice, they noted, was itself injustice. For some Protestants, especially those from the Confessing Church, which had actively resisted the Nazis, the main lesson to be drawn from the Third Reich was the need for all Christians to be more politically vigilant, to take a strong and public stand on political issues from the Christian point of view. Thus Protestant church figures like Gustav Heinemann and Martin Niemöller campaigned actively against Adenauer's rearmament policy, insisting it was both impolitic and immoral.[41] Other church leaders, however, clung to the old Lutheran position that political decisions of this sort belonged entirely in the hands of the secular leadership. But the Heinemann–Niemöller perspective had a lasting impact on the Protestant church, especially on the Evangelical academies, which, since the early days of the Federal Republic, have played a leading role in the public discussion of such

---

38 Terence Prittie, "The Opposition of the Church of Rome," in Hans–Adolf Jacobsen, ed., *July 20, 1944: The German Opposition to Hitler as Viewed by Foreign Historians* (Bonn, 1969), 100.

39 Quoted in Alfred Grosser, *Deutschlandbilanz* (Munich, 1972), 360.

40 On this see Johanna Vogel, *Kirche und Wiederbewaffnung. Die Haltung der Evangelischen Kirche in Deutschland in den Auseinandersetzungen um die Wiederbewaffnung der Bundesrepublik 1949–1956* (Göttingen, 1978), 20.

41 Dieter Koch, *Heinemann und die Deutschlandfrage* (Munich, 1972).

issues as reunification, nuclear arms and nuclear power, and the environment.[42]

Let me conclude my discussion by returning to the secular realm and offering a few observations about the fate of the resistance legacy in the 1960s and in more recent years. From the mid-1960s through the 1970s, as CDU domination in Bonn gave way to the Grand Coalition and then to the SPD–FDP partnership, official commemoration speeches on the resistance movement shifted emphasis from this legacy's possible Cold War applications to its relevance to challenges such as student unrest, the extraparliamentary opposition, the gains of the Nationaldemokratische Partei Deutschlands (NPD), and above all terrorism. The anti-Hitler resisters' commitment to the restoration of a *Rechtsstaat* was recalled in light of threats to the rule of law from the extreme Left and Right. Another new accent in the commemoration speeches was a willingness to expand the resistance legacy beyond the Twentieth of July conspiracy – to include the leftist resistance and the opposition of workers, youth groups, women, and concentration camp inmates.[43]

This broadening of the resistance legacy reflected a similar tendency in historical scholarship, which, from the mid-1960s on, focused increasingly on resistance groups outside the Twentieth of July movement, particularly those on the Left, as well as on unorganized forms of opposition to Nazi policy that occurred in daily life.[44] At the same time, scholars subjected the Twentieth of July movement to harsher scrutiny. In their influential dissections of the conservative resistance, Hermann Graml and Hans Mommsen argued that these Hitler opponents harbored many of the aspirations of the very people they hoped to overthrow and that their views did not provide an alternative that would be in keeping with the circumstances of modern industrial society.[45] Somewhat later, the influential sociologist and FDP politician Ralf Dahrendorf offered a similar assessment.[46]

42 Schramm, *Der deutsche Widerstand*, 62–5.
43 Emrich and Nötzold, "Der 20. Juli," 6–11.
44 For a good collection of the new historiography on the resistance, see Jürgen Schmädeke and Peter Steinbach, eds., *Der Widerstand gegen den Nationalsozialismus* (Munich, 1986). See also Hans Mommsen, "Die Geschichte des deutschen Widerstands im Lichte der neueren Forschung," *Aus Politik und Zeitgeschichte*, 50 (1986): 3–18.
45 Hermann Graml, "Die aussenpolitischen Vorstellungen des deutschen Widerstandes," and Hans Mommsen, "Gosellschaftsbild und Verfassungspläne des deutschen Widerstandes," in W. Schmitthenner and H. Buchheim, eds., *Der deutsche Widerstand gegen Hitler. Vier Studien* (Cologne, 1966).
46 Ralf Dahrendorf, *Society and Democracy in Germany* (Garden City, N.Y., 1967).

In 1968, in the midst of student unrest and the beginning of the urban terrorist campaigns waged by the Baader–Meinhof gang and the RAF (Rote Armee Fraktion), the West German parliament passed a series of emergency laws granting the government broader powers to deal with political violence. As a counterweight to this expansion of executive power, the parliament also included a new clause in the Basic Law which said: "When other avenues are not open, all Germans have the right to resist attempts to impose unconstitutional authority."[47]

Here, then, was the "right to resist" finally enshrined in the constitutional order, but the questions of exactly what it meant and how far it went were subject to much acrimonious debate. The old argument against trying to make resistance to illegal government a right of law surfaced in the phrase of legal philosopher Arthur Kaufmann: "One cannot normify the unnormative."[48] For groups on the Left, the constitutional right to resist, and indeed the historical resistance legacy, were held to be applicable to their opposition to all sorts of government policies and to the entire "Americanized, plastic consumer society" of modern West Germany. What one saw in the late 1960s and early 1970s was a dramatic inflation in the concept of resistance, so that it included the whole countercultural style – from torching department stores or storming nuclear reactors to wearing dead-rat necklaces and black leather jackets with "No Future" painted across them.

This development prompted one commentator, Count Peter von Kielmansegg, to protest against the misuse and debasing of the ideal of resistance by people who claimed a moral stature they did not deserve. "We Germans, who have had the opportunity to learn what resistance against a tyranny means, ought to be the last people to allow themselves this confusion."[49] Socialist politician Herbert Wehner made a similar argument when in the late 1970s he chastised the unions for invoking the right of resistance against the government's budgetary policy. Both men clearly saw a need for the German people to retain a sense of what resistance against Hitler's tyranny had really been about.

But if one could justly worry about the increasing reduction of the resistance ideal to a kind of conceptual hodgepodge, without rigor or

47 Article 20, Section 4, of the Basic Law.
48 A. Kaufmann and L. E. Backmann, eds., *Widerstandsrecht* (Darmstadt, 1972), x.
49 Peter Graf von Kielmannsegg, "Frieden geht nicht vor Demokratie," *Die Zeit*, October 7, 1983.

historical validity, the opposite danger was also present. In 1977 the Kuratorium 20. Juli invited – and then uninvited – Herbert Wehner to speak at that year's commemoration of the military resistance in the Bendlerstrasse. Stauffenberg's son had argued that Wehner, whose resistance to Hitler had been exercised from his Moscow exile, would not be an appropriate speaker.[50] (On the other hand, Stauffenberg had no objection to inviting Hans Karl Filbinger, a prominent CDU politician and a former Reichskriegsmarine judge who, in the last days of World War II, had sentenced several young sailors to death for desertion.) The symbolism of the Twentieth of July, he seemed to be saying, did not belong to the entire people but only to a particular political group.

The controversy over this incident showed that Germans still were not in agreement over what their resistance against Hitler really meant and to whom it belonged. And the fight continued into the 1980s, when it featured in the so-called *Historikerstreit* and the debate over how to portray the Third Reich and the resistance legacy in Bonn's projected Museum of German History.[51] Thus it was thoroughly appropriate that President Weizsäcker, in his famous speech to the German people on May 8, 1985, insisted that it was important to honor the memory of all of those Germans who had sacrificed their lives resisting Hitler, without exception.

Yet it is somewhat doubtful that Weizsäcker's appeal had much resonance among the German population at large. In a public opinion poll taken just the year before, only 30 percent of the respondents designated "Der deutsche Widerstand" as an achievement in which the German people should take pride; this figure placed the resistance behind "The Bravery of German Soldiers," "Reconstruction after the War," "Our Social Security System," and "Automobiles from the Federal Republic."[52]

Yet whatever its meaning for the man in the street, the resistance legacy continued to figure prominently in the rhetoric of German politics, especially as the two German states began their headlong rush toward national unity in 1989–90. In its first (and undoubtedly

50 Erich Kosthorst, "Didaktische Probleme der Widerstandsforschung," *Geschichte in Wissenschaft und Unterricht* 9 (1979): 554.
51 On the debate over the new museum, see Charles S. Maier, "A Usable Past? Museums, Memory, and Identity," in Maier, *The Unmasterable Past* (Cambridge, Mass., 1988), 121–59.
52 Allensbach poll (September/October 1984), reprinted in Harro Honolka, *Schwarzrotgrün. Die Bundesrepublik auf der Suche nach ihrer Identität* (Munich, 1987), 209.

its last) official commemoration of the Twentieth of July putsch (July 20, 1990), the East German parliament issued a statement recognizing the resisters' legacy as an "admonition to resist dictatorships in every form and to maintain peace in Germany and Europe forever."[53] At the annual commemoration in the Bendlerstrasse on the same date, West Berlin mayor Walter Momper insisted that the resistance legacy was more relevant than ever, since enthusiasm for unity might breed a dangerous revival of chauvinism. "Beware of the beginnings!", he warned.[54] One could only hope that this time someone was listening.

---

53 "Verpflichtung für den Frieden," *Frankfurter Allgemeine Zeitung*, July 21, 1990.
54 "Gedanken an den 20. Juli 1944," ibid.

Selected Bibliography

The following list of books is a selected bibliography of the enormous literature on the various forms of resistance to National Socialism in Germany. It attempts to highlight a number of aspects of resistance scholarship. The path-breaking work of the late 1940s and early 1950s met with significant disfavor in German public opinion, and it involved professional risk and required personal courage on the part of those scholars who pursued it. Recent research has often applied new methodologies and pursued new emphases, but in a significant sense it has built upon the foundations laid by the early scholars. This selected bibliography also includes recent work on the resistance, much of it pursuing these new emphases. Finally, the bibliography highlights translations into English of works originally in German and works written for an English-reading audience.

The first section lists helpful and often indispensable bibliographies of resistance literature. The second section lists the resistance literature itself.

BIBLIOGRAPHIES OF RESISTANCE LITERATURE

Altgeld, Wolfgang. "Zur Geschichte der Widerstandsforschung. Überblick und Auswahlbibliographie." In Rudolf Lill and Heinrich Oberreuther, eds., *20. Juli. Portrait des Widerstandes*, 377–91. Düsseldorf, 1984.

Aretin, Karl Otmar. "Bericht über den deutschen Widerstand. Literaturbericht." *Geschichte in Wissenschaft und Unterricht* 25 (1974): 507–12, 565–76.

Büchel, Regine. *Der deutsche Widerstand im Spiegel von Fachliteratur und Publizistik seit 1945.* Munich, 1975.

Cartarius, Ulrich, ed. *Bibliographie "Widerstand." Mit einer Einleitung von Karl Otmar Frhr. von Aretin.* Munich, 1984.

Hochmuth, Ursel. *Faschismus und Widerstand – Ein Literaturverzeichnis.* Frankfurt, 1973.

Mann, Richard. "Widerstand gegen den Nationalsozialismus." *Neue Politische Literatur* 22 (1977): 425–42.

Mommsen, Hans. "Begriff und Problematik des deutschen Widerstandes gegen Hitler in der zeitgeschichtlichen Forschung." In *Widerstandsbewegungen in Deutschland und Polen während des Zweiten Weltkrieges*, 2d ed., 16–23. Braunschweig. 1983.

"Die Geschichte des deutschen Widerstands im Lichte der neueren Forschung." *Aus Politik und Zeitgeschichte*, supplement to *Das Parlament*, 50 (1986): 3–18.

Müller, Klaus-Jürgen, ed. *Der deutsche Widerstand, 1933–1945*. Paderborn, 1986.

Plum, Günther. "Widerstand und Resistenz." In Martin Broszat and Horst Möller, eds., *Das Dritte Reich. Herrschaftsstruktur und Geschichte. Vorträge aus dem Institut für Zeitgeschichte*, 248–73. Munich, 1983.

Nicosia, Francis R., and Lawrence D. Stokes. *Germans against Nazism: Noncompliance, Opposition and Resistance in the Third Reich. Essays in Honor of Peter Hoffmann*. New York, 1990.

Ueberschär, Gerd R. "Gegner des Nationalsozialismus 1933–1945. Volksopposition, individuelle Gewissensentscheidung und Rivalitätskampf konkurrierender Führungseliten als Aspekte der Literatur über Emigration und Widerstand im Dritten Reich zwischen dem 35. und 40. Jahrestag des 20. Juli 1944." *Militärgeschichtliche Mitteilungen* 36 (1984): 141–96.

RESISTANCE LITERATURE

Abshagen, Karl Heinz. *Canaris: Patriot und Weltbürger*. Stuttgart, 1954. Translated into English by A. H. Brodrick as *Canaris*. London, 1956.

Adler, H. G. "Selbstverwaltung und Widerstand in den Konzentrationslagern der SS." *Vierteljahrshefte für Zeitgeschichte* 8 (1960): 221–36.

Albrecht, Richard, and Otto R. Romberg, eds. *Widerstand und Exil, 1933–1945*. Frankfurt, 1986.

Arendt, Hannah. *Eichmann in Jerusalem*. Munich, 1964.

Balfour, Michael. *Withstanding Hitler in Germany, 1933–45*. London, 1988.

Balfour, Michael, and Julian Frisby. *Helmuth von Moltke: A Leader against Hitler*. London, 1972.

Ben-Israel, Hedva. "Im Widerstreit der Ziele: Die britische Reaktion auf den deutschen Widerstand." In Schmädeke and Steinbach, eds., *Der Widerstand gegen den Nationalsozialismus*. 732–50.

Besier, Gerhard, et al., eds. *Bekenntnis, Widerstand, Martyrtum*. Göttingen, 1986.

Blasius, Rainer A. *Für Grossdeutschland – gegen den grossen Krieg. Ernst von Weizsäcker in den Krisen um die Tschechoslovakei und Polen*. Cologne, 1981.

Bleistein, Roman. *Dossier, Kreisauer Kreis. Dokumente aus dem Widerstand gegen den Nationalsozialismus aus dem Nachlass von Lothar König, S.J.* Frankfurt, 1987.

Bracher, Karl-Dietrich. "Anfänge der deutschen Widerstandsbewegung." In Bracher, *Deutschland zwischen Demokratie und Diktatur* (Bern, 1964), 251–72.

Braubach, Max. *Der Weg zum 20. Juli 1944*. Cologne, 1953.

Bräutigam, Walter. *John Rittmeister – Leben und Sterben*. Ebenhausen, 1987.

Buchmann, Erika, ed. *Die Frauen von Ravensbrück*. Berlin, 1961.

Buchstab, Günther, Brigitte Kaff, and Hans-Otto Kleinmann. *Verfolgung und Widerstand, 1933–1945. Christliche Demokraten gegen Hitler*. Düsseldorf, 1986.

Büdde, E., and Peter Lütsches. *Die Wahrheit über den 20. Juli*. Düsseldorf, 1953.

Deutsch, Harold C. *The Conspiracy against Hitler in the Twilight War*. Minneapolis, 1968.

Hitler and His Generals: The Hidden Crisis, January–June 1938. Minneapolis, 1974.

Dilks, David N., ed. *The Diaries of Sir Alexander Cadogan, O.M.* London, 1971.

Donate, Claus. "Deutscher Widerstand gegen den Nationalsozialismus aus der Sicht der Bundeswehr." Ph.D. diss., University of Freiburg, 1976.

Donohoe, James. *Hitler's Conservative Opponents in Bavaria, 1930–1945: A Considera-tion of Catholic, Monarchist, and Separatist Anti-Nazi Activities.* Leiden, 1961.

Elling, Hanna. *Frauen im deutschen Widerstand 1933–1945.* Frankfurt, 1981.

Emrich, Ulrike, and Jürgen Nötzold. "Der 20. Juli in der öffentliche Gedenkreden der Bundesrepublik und in der Darstellung der DDR." *Aus Politik und Zeitges-chichte*, supplement to *Das Parlament* 26 (1984): 3–12.

Europäische Publikation, e.V. *Die Vollmacht des Gewissens.* 2 vols. Munich, 1956, 1965.

Finker, Kurt. *Stauffenberg und der 20. Juli 1944.* Berlin, 1967.

Ford, Franklin. "The Twentieth of July in the German Resistance." *American Historical Review* 51 (1946): 609–26.

Franz, Helmut. *Kurt Gerstein: Aussenseiter des Widerstandes der Kirche gegen Hitler.* Zürich, 1964.

Gaertringen, Friedrich Freiherr Hiller von, and Klaus Peter Reiss. *Die Hassell-Tagebücher 1938–1944. Ulrich von Hassell, Aufzeichnungen vom Andern Deutsch-land.* Berlin, 1988.

Gallin, Mary Alice. *Ethical and Religious Factors in the German Resistance to Hitler.* Washington, D.C., 1955.

Gerstenmaier, Eugen. "Der Kreisauer Kreis." In Zimmermann and Jacobsen, eds., *20. Juli 1944*, 5th ed., 39–42. Bonn, 1960.

"Der Kreisauer Kreis." *Vierteljahrshefte für Zeitgeschichte* 15 (1967): 221–46.

Gollwitzer, Helmut, Käthe Kuhn, and Reinhold Schneider, eds. *Du hast mich heimgesucht bei Nacht. Abschiedsbriefe und Aufzeichnungen des Widerstandes 1933–1945.* 3rd ed. Munich, 1955.

Graml, Hermann. "Der Fall Oster." *Vierteljahrshefte für Zeitgeschichte* 14 (1966): 26–39.

Graml, Hermann, ed. *Widerstand im Dritten Reich. Probleme, Ereignisse, Gestalten.* Frankfurt, 1984.

Herlemann, Beatrix. *Auf verlorenem Posten. Kommunistischer Widerstand im Zweiten Weltkrieg: Die Knöchel Organisation.* Bonn, 1986.

Hill, Leonidas. "The Wilhelmstrasse in the Nazi Era." *Political Science Quarterly* 82 (1967): 546–70.

"Towards a New History of German Resistance to Hitler." *Central European History* 14 (1981): 369–99.

Hill, Leonidas, ed. *Die Weizsäcker-Papiere.* 2 vols. Frankfurt, 1974, 1982.

Hinsley, Francis Harvey. *British Intelligence in the Second World War.* 5 vols. New York, 1979–90.

Hoch, Anton. "Das Attentat auf Hitler im Münchner Bürgerbräukeller 1939." *Vierteljahrshefte für Zeitgeschichte* 17 (1969): 383–413.

Hoffmann, Peter, *Widerstand gegen Hitler. Probleme des Umsturzes.* Munich, 1979; 2d rev. ed. 1984.

Widerstand, Staatsstreich, Attentat. Der Kampf der Opposition gegen Hitler. 4th ed. Munich, 1985. First edition translated into English by R. H. Barry as *The History of the German Resistance, 1933–1945.* Cambridge, Mass., 1977.

German Resistance to Hitler. Cambridge, Mass., 1988.

Jacobmeyer, Wolfgang. *Widerstandsbewegungen in Deutschland und in Polen während des Zweiten Weltkrieges.* Braunschweig, 1983.

Jacobsen, Hans-Adolf, ed. *July 20, 1944. The German Opposition to Hitler as Viewed by Foreign Historians: An Anthology.* Bonn, 1969.

"Spiegelbild einer Verschwörung." Die Opposition gegen Hitler und der Staatsstreich vom 10. Juli 1944 in der SD-Berichterstattung. Stuttgart, 1984.

Jahnke, Karl-Heinz. *Jugend im Widerstand 1933–1945.* Frankfurt, 1985.

Kershaw, Ian. *Popular Opinion and Political Dissent in the Third Reich: Bavaria, 1933–1945.* Oxford, 1983.

Kettenacker, Lothar. "Die britische Haltung zum deutschen Widerstand während des Zweiten Weltkrieges." In Kettenacker, ed., *Das "Andere Deutschland,"* 49–76.

Kettenacker, Lothar, ed. *Das "Andere Deutschland" im Zweiten Weltkrieg.* Stuttgart, 1977.

Klemperer, Klemens von. *Die "Verbindung zu der grossen Welt."* Aussenbeziehungen des deutschen Widerstands 1938–1945. Berlin, 1991.

Klemperer, Klemens von, ed. *A Noble Combat: The Letters of Shiela Grant Duff and Adam von Trott zu Solz 1932–1939.* Oxford, 1988.

Klessmann, Christoph, and Falk Pingel, eds. *Gegner des Nationalsozialismus. Wissenschaftler und Widerstandskämpfer auf der Suche nach historischer Wirklichkeit.* Frankfurt, 1980.

Kosthorst, Erich. *Die deutsche Opposition gegen Hitler zwischen Polen- und Frankreichfeldzug.* Bonn, 1957.

Kramarz, Joachim. *Stauffenberg, 15. November 1907–20. Juli 1944. Das Leben eines Offiziers.* Frankfurt, 1965. Translated into English by R. H. Barry as *Stauffenberg: The Architect of the Famous July 20th Conspiracy to Assassinate Hitler.* New York, 1967.

Krausharr, Luise, et al., eds. *Deutsche Widerstandskämpfer 1933–1945.* 2 vols. Berlin, 1970.

Langbein, Hermann. *– nicht wie die Schafe zur Schlachtbank. Widerstand in den nationalsozialistischen Konzentrationslagern 1938–1945.* Frankfurt, 1980.

Large, David Clay. "'A Gift to the German Future?' The Anti-Nazi Resistance Movement and West German Rearmament." *German Studies Review* 7 (1984): 499–529.

Leber, Annedore, Willy Brandt, and Karl-Dietrich Bracher, eds. *Das Gewissen steht auf. 64 Lebensbilder aus dem deutschen Widerstand 1933–1945.* Berlin, 1954. Second edition ed. Karl-Dietrich Bracher. Berlin, 1957. (Many later editions.) Translated into English by Rosemary O'Neill as *Conscience in Revolt: Sixty-four Stories of Resistance in Germany, 1933–45.* London, 1957.

Das Gewissen entscheidet. Bereiche des deutschen Widerstandes von 1933–1945 in Lebensbildern. Berlin, 1957.

Lindgren, Henrik. "Adam von Trotts Reisen nach Schweden 1942–1944. Ein Beitrag zur Frage der Auslandsverbindungen des deutschen Widerstandes." *Vierteljahrshefte für Zeitgeschichte.* 18 (1970): 274–91.

Löwenthal, Richard, and Patrick von zur Mühlen, eds. *Widerstand und Verweigerung in Deutschland 1933 bis 1945.* Berlin, 1982.

Ludlow, Peter W. "The Unwinding of Appeasement." In Kettenacker, ed., *Das "Andere" Deutschland,* 9–48.

Lukaschek, Hans. "Widerstand im Dritten Reich." *Erziehung und Beruf* 9 (1959): 95.

Malone, Henry Ozelle. "Adam von Trott zu Solz: The Road to Conspiracy against Hitler." Ph.D. diss., University of Texas, Austin, 1980.

Manvell, Roger, and Heinrich Fraenkel. *The Men Who Tried to Kill Hitler*. New York, 1966.

Mason, Tim. "Workers' Opposition in Nazi Germany." *History Workshop Journal* 11 (1980): 120–37.

Merson, Allan. *Communist Resistance in Nazi Germany*. London, 1985.

Militärgeschichtliches Forschungsamt, ed. *Aufstand des Gewissens. Der militärische Widerstand gegen Hitler und das NS-Regime, 1933–1945*. Herford, 1984.

Moltke, Helmuth James von. *A German of the Resistance: The Last Letters of Count Helmuth James von Moltke*, ed. Lionel Curtis. London, 1946.

Letters to Freya 1939–1945. New York, 1990.

Mommsen, Hans. "Gesellschaftsbild und Verfassungspläne des deutschen Widerstandes." In Walter Schmitthenner and Hans Buchheim, eds., *Der deutsche Widerstand gegen Hitler*, 73–167. Translated into English by Peter and Betty Ross as "Social Views and Constitutional Plans of the Resistance," in Schmitthenner and Buchheim, eds., *The German Resistance to Hitler*, 55–147.

"Die Geschichte des deutschen Widerstands im Lichte der neueren Forschung." *Aus Politik und Zeitgeschichte*, supplement to *Das Parlament*, 50 (1986): 3–18.

Müller, Christian. *Oberst i.G. Stauffenberg. Eine Biographie*. Düsseldorf, 1970.

Müller, Klaus-Jürgen, ed. *Der deutsche Widerstand, 1933–1945*. Paderborn, 1986.

Nicosia, Francis R., and Lawrence D. Stokes. *Germans against Nazism: Noncompliance, Opposition and Resistance in the Third Reich. Essays in Honor of Peter Hoffmann*. New York, 1990.

Nitzsche, Gerhard. *Die Saekow-Jacob-Bästlein Gruppe*. Berlin, 1957.

Pachter, Henry. "The Legend of the 20th of July, 1944." *Social Research* 29 (1962): 109–15.

Pechel, Rudolf. *Deutscher Widerstand*. Erlenbach, 1947.

Peter, Karl Heinrich, ed. *Spiegelbild einer Verschwörung. Die Kaltenbrunner-Berichte an Bormann und Hitler über das Attentat vom 20. Juli 1944. Geheime Dokumente aus dem ehemaligen Reichssicherheitshauptamt*. Stuttgart, 1961.

Peukert, Detlev. *Ruhrarbeiter gegen den Faschismus. Dokumentation über den Widerstand im Ruhrgebiet 1933–1945*. Frankfurt, 1976.

Die Edelweisspiraten. Protestbewegung jugendlicher Arbeiter im Dritten Reich. Eine Dokumentation. Cologne, 1980.

Die KPD im Widerstand. Verfolgung und Untergrundarbeit an Rhein und Ruhr, 1933–1945. Wuppertal, 1980.

Volksgenossen und Gemeinschaftsfremde. Anpassung, Ausmerze und Aufbegehren unter dem Nationalsozialismus. Cologne, 1982.

Peukert, Detlev, and Jürgen Reulecke, eds. *Die Reihen fast geschlossen. Beiträge zur Geschichte des Alltags unterm Nationalsozialismus*. Wuppertal, 1981.

Prittie, Terence. *Germans against Hitler*. London, 1964.

Ritter, Gerhard. *Carl Goerdeler und die deutsche Widerstandsbewegung*. Stuttgart, 1954. Translated into English by R. T. Clark as *The German Resistance: Carl Goerdeler's Struggle against Tyranny*. London, 1958.

Romoser, George, K. "The Crisis of Political Direction in the German Resistance to Nazism." Ph.D. diss., University of Chicago, 1958.

"The Politics of Uncertainty: The German Resistance Movement." *Social Research* 31 (1964): 73–93.

Roon, Ger van. *Neuordnung im Widerstand. Der Kreisauer Kreis innerhalb der deutschen Widerstandsbewegung.* Munich, 1967. Translated into English by Peter Ludlow as *German Resistance to Hitler: Count von Moltke and the Kreisau Circle.* London, 1971.

Widerstand im Dritten Reich. Ein Überblick. Munich, 1977.

Rothfels, Hans. *The German Opposition to Hitler.* Hinsdale, Ill., 1948. Translated into German as *Die deutsche Opposition gegen Hitler. Eine Würdigung.* Krefeld, 1949.

"Die politische Vermächtnis des deutschen Widerstands." *Vierteljahrshefte für Zeitgeschichte* 2 (1954): 329–43.

Scheurig, Bodo. *Freies Deutschland. Das Nationalkomite und der Bund deutscher Offiziere in der Sowjetunion 1943–1945.* Munich, 1960. Translated into English by Herbert Arnold as *Free Germany: The National Committee and the League of German Officers.* Middletown, Conn., 1969.

Schlabrendorff, Fabian von. *Offiziere gegen Hitler,* ed. Gero v. S. Gaervernitz. Zurich, 1946. Translated into English by Hilda Simon as *The Secret War against Hitler.* London, 1965.

Schmädeke, Jürgen, and Peter Steinbach, eds. *Der Widerstand gegen den Nationalsozialismus. Die deutsche Gesellschaft und der Widerstand gegen Hitler.* Munich, 1986.

Schmitthenner, Walter, and Hans Buchheim, eds. *Der deutsche Widerstand gegen Hitler. Vier historisch-kritische Studien von Hermann Graml, Hans Mommsen, Hans-Joachim Reichardt und Ernst Wolf.* Cologne, 1966. Translated into English by Peter and Betty Ross as *The German Resistance to Hitler.* Berkeley and Los Angeles, 1970.

Schnorbach, Hermann. *Lehrer und Schule unterm Hakenkreuz. Dokumente des Widerstands von 1930 bis 1945.* Königstein, 1983.

Scholl, Inge. *Die weisse Rose. Der Widerstand der Münchner Studenten.* Frankfurt, 1955. Translated into English by Arthur R. Schultz as *The White Rose: Munich, 1942–1943.* Middletown, Conn., 1983.

Schramm, Torsten-Dietrich. *Der deutsche Widerstand gegen den Nationalsozialismus. Seine Bedeutung für die Bundesrepublik in der Wirkung auf Institutionen und Schulbücher.* Berlin, 1980.

Schramm, Wilhelm Ritter von. *Conspiracy among Generals.* London, 1956.

Beck und Goerdeler. Gemeinschaftsdokumente für den Frieden 1941–1944. Munich, 1965.

Sykes, Christopher. *Troubled Loyalty: A Biography of Adam von Trott zu Solz.* London, 1968.

Syrkin, Marie. *Blessed Is the Match: The Story of Jewish Resistance.* Philadelphia, 1948.

Szepansky, Gerda. *Frauen leisten Widerstand: 1933–1945. Lebensgeschichten nach Interviews und Dokumenten.* Frankfurt, 1983.

von Groote, Wolfgang. "Bundeswehr und 20. Juli." *Vierteljahrshefte für Zeitgetschichte* 14 (1966): 285–99.

Weisenborn, Günther. *Der lautlose Aufstand. Bericht über die Widerstandsbewegung des deutschen Volkes 1933–1945.* Hamburg, 1953.

Winterhager, Wilhelm Ersnt. *Der Kreisauer Kreis. Porträt einer Widerstandsgruppe.* Mainz, 1985.

Young, Arthur Primrose. *The "X"-Documents: The Secret History of Foreign Office Contacts with the German Resistance, 1937/39*, ed. Sidney Astor. London, 1974.

Zahn, Gordon C. *Er folge seinem Gewissen. Das einsame Zeugnis des Franz Jägerstätter*. Graz, 1978.

Zeller, Eberhard. "Claus und Berthold Stauffenberg." *Vierteljahrshefte für Zeitgeschichte* 12 (1964): 223–49.

—— *Geist der Freiheit. Der 20. Juli*. Munich, 1965. Translated into English by R. P. Heller and D. R. Masters as *The Flame of Freedom: The German Struggle against Hitler*. London, 1967.

Zimmermann, Erich, and Hans-Adolf Jacobsen, eds. *20. Juli 1944*. 5th ed. Bonn, 1960. Translated into English by A. and L. Yahraes as *Germans against Hitler: July 20, 1944*. Bonn, 1969.

Zorn, Gerda, and Gertrud Meyer. *Frauen gegen Hitler. Berichte aus dem Widerstand 1933–1945*. Frankfurt, 1974.

Index